THE STAR OF BETHLEHEM

DAVID COLLINS

AMBERLEY

First published 2012

Amberley Publishing
The Hill, Stroud
Gloucestershire, GL5 4EP

www.amberley-books.com

British Library Cataloguing in Publication Data.
A catalogue record for this book is available from the British Library.

ISBN 978 1 4456 0675 0

Typeset in 10pt on 12pt Sabon.
Typesetting and Origination by Amberley Publishing.
Printed in the UK.

CONTENTS

ACKNOWLEDGMENTS

The various illustrations displayed throughout this book would not have been possible without the invaluable assistance of my friends and colleagues who are fellow members of the Irish Astronomical Association: Andy McCrea, Richard Archer, Barry Loane, and Terry Moseley. I am also indebted to Nic Leitch for his contribution towards the supporting diagrams and Colin Watson, who very kindly provided a number of sketches.

INTRODUCTION

When Jesus was walking in Capernaum, a town situated on the northern shores of the Sea of Galilee, he met a man sitting outside the customs house. He said to him 'follow me' and the man arose, and followed, becoming a disciple. This was Matthew, and it is only within the Gospel that bears his name, as part of the New Testament, that a reference is made to a star leading the wise men to the infant Jesus. Whether the Gospel was actually written by the apostle Matthew, or a later Christian, remains uncertain however and this is a matter that will be discussed in more detail within the first chapter.

The author's reference to the star of Bethlehem remains a great astronomical mystery which has intrigued theologians, historians and astronomers throughout the ages, and continues to do so. It may be true to say that no one seems to have come up with a completely satisfactory solution to a problem which has fascinated mankind for almost 2,000 years.

In recent times there has been a definite shift in the consensus of opinion towards the idea that its inclusion in the story of the nativity was simply contrived in order to lend support to the assumed divinity of Christ. Many Christians now believe that the star, and the whole infancy narrative for that matter, were introduced to give weight to the significance of the birth and regard the whole story as too elaborate, viewing it in the same way that they would a fantasy or fairytale. Some, however, still cling to the idea that the appearances of the star represented a miracle and therefore cannot be explained rationally or scientifically and any attempt to explain it is therefore to limit its importance. They accept that every word in the infancy narrative of Matthew reflects a true and accurate account, without any desire to question an apparently incredible sequence of events. A further school of thought considers that an astronomical occurrence did exist in some form or other but that it has been exploited in Matthew, its significance being exaggerated out of all proportion.

The purpose of this book is to attempt to explain the star of Bethlehem. It is very much a search for the truth, so all possibilities have to be considered and weighed up. Therefore we cannot dismiss the possibility that it was simply an invented story or, conversely, a 'miracle'. Like any good detective story all the available evidence has to be collected, assessed and considered. No preconditioned assumptions have been made in its composition and I would like to think that I have approached the subject in an objective manner, not being influenced by religious bias, which is obviously the case in certain other works that have been written on the topic and which are based upon the assumption that the story is true and so do not present, in any real detail, any evidence which suggests otherwise.

In the past, numerous theories have been proposed to explain an actual physical phenomenon, most of which are logical and plausible, others absurd. Whilst the description in Matthew is ambiguous, as will be seen later there are astronomical objects which could possibly satisfy the brief references that are made to the star and these are supported by contemporary evidence. In order to establish what exactly the star was, if such an object ever did exist, we first of all have to use the clues provided within the New Testament so as to ascertain when Jesus was born. Having calculated a period for this as accurately as possible it is then a matter of determining what exceptional celestial objects were or may have been visible around that time. Additional factors have to be considered and these include the conditions that existed within Judea, the role of King Herod, the nature of the wise men or Magi and other events of that time.

Perhaps, however, the real answer lies in understanding the mind of the author; through his writings – and if we can then grasp an insight into his background, his knowledge and beliefs – we might just be able to identify how the star became interwoven within his story of the nativity. In other words, we have to try and step into his shoes. It then becomes feasible to conjecture from where the references to the star originated. Consequently the early chapters of this book attempt to deal with the background to the writings in Matthew and the beliefs and conditions existing in Palestine before and after the birth of Jesus. The later chapters (from 6 to 12) are concerned with astronomical events which occurred within the general time-frame of the birth of Jesus.

Use has been made of various sources of evidence, some contemporary and some from before and after the event. These include the use of images on ancient coins, mainly Roman, and perhaps surprisingly, Ancient British. Ultimately the main source of evidence is, of course, provided by the references within the Bible itself, and for this purpose the Authorised Version has been used, this having been translated from the original Greek.

PART I
THE BACKGROUND
TO THE NARRATIVE

1
MATTHEW & THE EARLY GOSPELS

The general opinion is that the book of Matthew was not written by the apostle of that name and it is accepted by most biblical scholars that the real author remains anonymous. This also applies to the authors of the Gospels of Mark, Luke and John. It is likely that none of the Gospels were written by eye witnesses to the events that they describe and none of the authors would ever have had the privilege of meeting Jesus. There is a general consensus that Matthew was completed sometime around the period AD 80 to 85 and was based upon a number of earlier sources including the Gospel of Mark, those derived from other miscellaneous writings including those known as 'Q', and oral tradition.

The Synoptic Gospels

The Gospels of Matthew, Mark and Luke are known as the Synoptic Gospels in that they have many parallel or stereoscopic passages, being very similar, if not identical, in wording. The word 'synoptic' actually means 'to see together'. One of the reasons for this is that the authors of Matthew and Luke both used material from the Gospel of Mark as a source in compiling their testaments, editing and changing details in the process. Frequently they would rearrange the order of events and change words for what are clearly the same stories. It is generally accepted that Mark's Gospel is the most historically reliable in the description of Jesus' life and ministry, having probably been completed around AD 65. However, it makes no reference to the events surrounding the birth of Christ.

The apparent reliance upon Mark, by both Matthew and Luke, cannot be underestimated. From a study of the 1,071 verses within the book of Matthew it has been found that 387 are in common with Mark and Luke; 130 with Mark alone; 184 with Luke alone and the remainder – only 370, being considered unique.

Another reason for the similarities between Matthew and Luke are that both appear to have used sayings from a possible earlier source known as 'Q'. It is called 'Q' after the German word *quille*, meaning source, following pioneering research by German scholars. It is based upon a hypothetical pre-Christian document, as so far no copy has been found. Nevertheless it is sometimes referred to as the Gospel of Q and it has been estimated to have been written between AD 40 and 50. It was almost certainly based upon oral tradition and has been described as the missing link between the Jewish world of Jesus and the early Christian Church. It appears to have been mainly a collection of sayings, not dealing extensively with incidents within the life of Jesus, and unfortunately, like the Gospel of Mark, it would seem not to have made any reference to the birth of Christ or the events surrounding it. Although unlikely, it is always possible that a document containing the Q writings may still be unearthed.

An Earlier Matthew?

Both the Gospels of Matthew and Luke incorporated material from a number of other unknown independent sources, but mainly oral tradition. These reflected accounts passed on by reminiscences and it is not surprising that there is no reliable information as to their origin. In 1924 Burnett Hillman Streater, a British biblical scholar, suggested in *The Four Gospels: A Study of Origins* that a separate hypothetical source was used by the author of Matthew, having no parallel in Mark or Luke, which he named 'M'. In 1953 Pierson Parker, a former professor of the New Testament at the General Theological Seminary, put forward the theory of a 'proto-Matthew'. This proposed that an earlier version of Matthew had been used as a primary source for both Mark and Matthew, in addition to the Q source which was also used by Matthew.

There are various other theories as to who exactly wrote the Gospel of Matthew. It has been suggested that the author was an early Christian, perhaps named Matthew, who put together a collection of Messianic prophecies in the Hebrew Bible. At some later stage these were assembled together with further supplementary material to create our present Gospel. It could be that the completed version also took a number of years to compile.

Whilst it is generally accepted that Matthew was completed around the period AD 80 to 85, it should be mentioned that there is a minority opinion that suggests a date going back to around AD 70 and perhaps even earlier. This would therefore raise the possibility, albeit remote, that it might after all have been written by the apostle Matthew as such a date could conceivably be within his own lifetime. The early Christian church certainly assumed that the author was the apostle. Around the year AD 100 the theologian Papias of Hierapolis, an early Christian bishop, attributed the Gospel to him and this was never seriously challenged by the church. The historian Augustine of Hippo in fact considered it to be the earliest Gospel to be written, and it is for this reason that it appears first in the New Testament. It is also the only Gospel to be mentioned by Ignatius, a Bishop of Antioch, in his Letter to the Ephesians, which can be dated to around AD 110. Consequently there continues to be a small core of opinion that conforms to this early Christian tradition, accepting that Mark borrowed from Matthew, known as Matthean priority, believing also that Matthew was first written in Aramaic, which is ancient Hebrew.

Although most in the present-day Catholic Church consider that Matthew was, in all likelihood, written after Mark, many do continue to believe that the book of Matthew was written by the apostle. This is supported by Henry Wansbrough, who, writing for the Catholic Truth Society, states that, 'It is hard to believe that anyone would recount his own call by Jesus in the words of another. This apostle would also have been of a great age when it came to the detailed work of composing this finely honed work, for it must have been written well after Mark.'

Some argue that there are indications in Matthew's Gospel of 'modesty' on the part of the author, which might suggest that it was written by the apostle. Whilst both Mark and Luke refer to the pair of disciples 'Matthew and Thomas', his Gospel refers instead to 'Thomas and Matthew'. Then we have Mark and Luke telling us, in so many words, that Matthew gave a banquet for Jesus, whereas Matthew 9:10 also tells us about the banquet, but does not mention that he, himself, was the host.

In the mid-1990s it was suggested by Thiede and D'Ancona in *The Jesus Papyrus* that a date no later than AD 66 could be attributed to the Gospel. This followed careful research by them into small fragments of papyrus manuscript kept at Magdalene College, Oxford, on which were written, in a form of shorthand Greek, verses which they claimed represented part of a complete Gospel. As the fragments had writing on both sides it was clear that they came from codex, or ancient manuscript, rather than a scroll. Their conclusion was largely based upon the type and style of handwriting, known as uncial, on the fragments, being found to be of a form that was in common use in the mid-first century. Unfortunately, because the fragments are so small it was not considered practical to have them carbon dated, although such a technique would have an error factor of plus or minus fifty years. Originally it had been thought that these fragments dated to around AD 200 and many continue to believe that this is the case, viewing Thiede's and D'Ancona's conclusions with considerable skepticism.

Later Versions

Some early fragments from the book of Matthew, also written on papyrus, are held within the Chester Beatty Library in Dublin, and date from the early third century. The earliest surviving complete texts of Matthew are from the fourth century and are known as the Codex Vaticanus, which is housed in the Vatican, and the Codex Sinaitacus, presently kept in the British Museum. Obviously, these represent copies from earlier Greek manuscripts.

By the fourth century, several different translations were in use and their reliability was considered to be somewhat doubtful. Pope Damascus (AD 366–384), in an attempt to prevent further mistakes creeping in, commissioned one of the leading scholars of the day, known as Jerome, to prepare a revised Latin translation, which he completed in 383. The text, known as the Vulgate, became recognised as the standard Gospel text until the Reformation.

The General Consensus

It would seem that a majority accept that the Gospel of Matthew was not written by the apostle Matthew and although it was probably the product of a converted Jew, it was not completed until the time of the second or third generation of Christians.

At some later stage it was ascribed to the apostle. The main reasons for this may be summarised as follows:

1. Whilst original source material or texts of the Gospel may have been in Aramaic, the final version was completed in Greek.

2. There is a heavy reliance upon Mark.

3. The theology and Greek used in the text is very sophisticated.

4. It does not seem to reflect the manner or characteristics of eye-witness accounts.

5. There are hints that it shows knowledge of the four Pauline Epistles.

6. There are suggestions that some considerable time had elapsed since the crucifixion, as the phrase 'to this day' is used on more than one occasion.

7. Although it does not specifically mention the destruction of Jerusalem, in certain instances possible references to historical events and individuals around the year AD 70 may be established, inferring that it was written within a later social context. An example of this can be found in Matthew 22:7, telling us, 'The king was angry, and he sent his troops and destroyed those murderers and burned their city.'

8. There is an awareness of the persecution of Christians by Jews, indicating a date no earlier than AD 80. Consequently we find a strong anti-Jewish sentiment running throughout the Gospel.

Overall the attitude towards Judaism would seem to reflect the strained relationship between Jews and Christians which existed towards the end of the first century.

The Apostle Matthew

So what exactly is known about the apostle Matthew? Early tradition identifies him as Levi Matthew, the name Levi in Hebrew meaning 'gift of Yahweh' or gift of God. His name also indicates that he was a member of the Levites, a tribe which at that time had authority and control over the conduct of worship at the Temple of Jerusalem. Mark 2:14 indicates that his father was known as Alphaeus and Mark 3:18 suggests that he had a brother called James. Later, for theological reasons, the Gospel gave preference to his second name of Matthew.

An Occupation in Capernaum
His occupation was effectively that of a 'publican' or customs official, at a post on the outskirts of the town of Capernaum, on the northwest shore of the Sea of

Galilee, and reference to this can be found in Matthew 9:9, Mark 2:14 and Luke 5:27–28. Capernaum had developed quickly from being a small fishing settlement to an important military port, complete with its own Roman garrison. This was under the command of a centurion who was responsible for overseeing the collection of taxes. This included a levy on fishermen and a customs duty which was charged on goods passing through the busy trade route known as the Via Maris. This route ran between Damascus and the Mediterranean, going through the tetrarchy of Philip and bordering on the Galilean lands of Herod Antipas. It is probable that he held a comfortable position and may have been a tenant or leaseholder of the customs station. It would seem therefore that financially he was well-off, and this is implied by Luke 9:29 mentioning that he 'held a great banquet for Jesus at his home'. It also seems that he was an experience writer.

The Romans were content to contract out the collection of taxes to publicans in return for the payment of a franchise fee. These collectors were therefore seen to be collaborating with their Roman counterparts and, to make matters worse, they frequently extorted higher rates of tax than that required, in order to line their own pockets. Sometimes they would even enlist the use of military force to ensure that their demands were met. It is not surprising therefore that they were despised and rejected by Orthodox Jews who regarded them as being sinners and outcasts. So in consequence we find that Levi Matthew was looked down upon and rejected by such Jews and Jesus himself was criticised for being involved with him (Matthew 9:11).

Capernaum was also a convenient place for pilgrims to gather on their journeys to and from Jerusalem, attending the Passover and other feasts. It attracted the two pairs of brothers Peter and Andrew, who settled there, and James and John, who became frequent visitors, and it has been said that these four effectively represented the inner circle of the disciples. Jesus was a regular guest and appears to have stayed in the town on a number of occasions, teaching in the synagogue and healing the sick.

Meeting Jesus
Matthew's name first appears in the Bible in Matthew 9:9 which states:

> As Jesus was walking, He saw a man named Matthew sitting by the customs house, and He said to him, 'Follow me'. And he got up and followed Him.

Matthew's willingness to sacrifice his lucrative activities in order to follow Jesus reflects his desire to reject money and material wealth, helping to support an important ideal for early Christians to observe. This rejection of money was soon to become a major feature of early Christianity, with the emphasis being that wealth was not for selfishly keeping for oneself, but for sharing. It was, instead, spiritual wealth that mattered. In the Gospel he is openly described as 'Matthew the tax collector' in order to stress that there were no exclusions as to who qualified as a disciple.

His Later Years

The last mention of Matthew in the New Testament is in Acts 1:13 when the apostles meet in an upper room of a house in Jerusalem. As no biography was ever written about Matthew, very little is known about his later life although it is thought that he spent fifteen years preaching in various locations including Persia, Parthia, Greece, Syria and parts of North Africa. A second-century historian, Heracleon (AD 80–145), claims that he did not become a martyr, dying a natural death. A fourth-century bishop of Cyprus called Epiphanius however claims that he was martyred in Hierapolis in Parthia, whereas the *Roman Martyrology* states that he met this fate in Ethiopia. The *Martyrology of Jerome*, on the other hand, suggests that this happened in Tarsuana, to the east of the Persian Gulf. Some believed that his remains were taken to Brittany from Ethiopia and later, in the eleventh century, removed by Robert Guiscard to Salerno in Sicily.

Due to his previous occupation, he has become recognised as the patron saint of bankers and tax officials. Early paintings usually portray him as a scribe, surrounded by writing instruments, and are similar to the imagery of the other apostles. Later depictions however show him with a sword, as it was assumed that this was the implement of his martyrdom.

The Evolution of the Gospels

It seems likely that the early Gospels developed rather erratically, and not in the order that they appear in today's Bible. The earliest books in the New Testament, including Acts and Corinthians, focused primarily upon the death and resurrection of Jesus and then the deeds and words of Jesus' ministry, details of which had been passed down by way of collections of sayings, parables and miracles. Mark's Gospel begins with Jesus meeting John the Baptist and ends with the resurrection, as does the Gospel of John.

It has been argued that details of the birth of Christ have been written almost by way of a later secondary response, being overshadowed by the essential and primary message of salvation, as conveyed through the earlier writings covering the death, resurrection and ministry of Jesus. In the case of Luke it would certainly seem that the writer, who also composed the book of Acts, has incorporated his infancy narrative almost by way of a preface after having completed the account of the ministry of Jesus. There also appears to be no reason why this does not also apply to the infancy narrative within Matthew's Gospel and it is difficult to imagine that it was simply written in chronological order beginning with chapter one, verse one.

Why Were the Birth Narratives Written?

Some of the possible reasons for the birth narratives' inclusion in the Gospels of Matthew and Luke can be summarised as follows:

1. Curiosity – the early Christians subsequently wanted to know more about their Lord and master, his background and family.

2. As a response to contemporary Jewish skepticism about the Messiah, providing an explanation as to his divinity. By moving backwards in time it helped to provide evidence of Jesus' real identity. This was in contrast to the Gospel of Mark which used identification of Jesus as the Messiah during his later lifetime, whereas John utilised a different route by way of pre-existence before creation.

3. It provided a more appropriate introduction to the story of Jesus, at the same time providing the authors of Matthew and Luke with the opportunity to exercise a greater freedom of composition and not having to rely upon the earlier works of Q and Mark.

4. It helped to support the overall message of Christianity.

5. According to Raymond E. Brown, in *The Birth of the Messiah*, it made 'Jesus' origins intelligible against the background of the fulfillment of Old Testament expectations', acting as a vital link between the Old and New Testaments.[1]

Rifts Between Christians and Jews
We also have to take into consideration the developments which were taking place in the relationship between the early Christian Jewish sects and the more orthodox Jews. Rifts were unfolding with Jews becoming increasingly agitated and suspicious about the new religion which seemed to be emerging from within their ranks. To them it was beginning to represent a very serious threat to their underlying beliefs and thoughts. We can certainly pinpoint key events which contributed towards a widening of the divisions between them:

1. In AD 62 James, the brother of Jesus, as leader of the Christians in Jerusalem, was stoned to death along with others on the orders of Anarius the High Priest, the account being well documented by the contemporary Jewish historian Josephus. The executions were clearly intended as a warning, in an attempt to end the conversions to Christianity, which was by that time flourishing. This event is seen by many as a turning point in the unbridgeable divide between the early Christian Church and Jews.

2. Shortly afterwards, in July, AD 64, fire destroyed most of Rome. Nero, in fear that he himself would be held responsible, conveniently attributed the blame to a suitable scapegoat, namely the Christian community in Rome. Persecutions commenced in the spring of AD 65 and continued until Nero's death in AD 68. Such upheaval sparked arguments and disagreements between Christians, causing splits to develop amongst their ranks, culminating in the capture of Peter and Paul and their subsequent execution. The division between Christians and Jews widened further during this period as the Roman authorities were out specifically

to punish Christians, whereas the Jews remained unscathed. Allegiances had to be made to either one side or the other.

3. In AD 70, following years of rebellion, Jerusalem fell to the Romans, with the city and Temple, including its library, being decimated. The Christians, who had not participated in the revolt, were allowed to return to the city but the Jews were banished. The days when Christians and Jews would congregate and intermingle at the Great Temple were over.

4. By about AD 80, Jewish sects had become dominated exclusively by the self-righteous Pharisees. Around that year they proceeded to reformulate the twelfth of the eighteen Benedictines, known as the *Shermoneth Esreh*, which was one of the main synagogue prayers. This now introduced a curse upon heretics, particularly those who believed that Jesus was the Messiah. The Christians were also barred from entering Jewish synagogues. It is therefore not surprising that we find the author of Matthew frequently referring to *their* synagogues, clearly distinguishing between the meeting places of the Christians and those of the Jews, from which they had now been expelled.

The inclusion of the infancy narratives within Matthew and Luke may have been in partial response to such developments, in an attempt to stress the divinity of Jesus by going right back to his birth. Both also had in mind the necessity to strengthen the Christian cause by trying to win over new converts in the light of severe Jewish skepticism and opposition.

Discrepancies Between Matthew and Luke's Accounts

Although the authors of Matthew and Luke appear to have had access to the same source material, they seem to have written independently of one another and without being aware of each other's work. Therefore, any areas of agreement between their separate infancy narratives clearly suggest an earlier common tradition. Brown has identified eleven points of agreement between the two narratives regarding the infancy of Jesus and these are outlined as follows:

1. The parents of Jesus are Joseph and Mary.

2. Joseph is a descendant of David.

3. An angel announces the forthcoming birth of Jesus.

4. Joseph is not the father of the child.

5. The true father is the Holy Spirit.

6. The angel directs that the child is to be called Jesus.

7. The angel states that Jesus is to be a Saviour.

8. Jesus is born after Mary and Joseph start to live together.

9. The birth takes place in Bethlehem.

10. The birth of Jesus takes place during the reign of King Herod.

11. Jesus is brought up in Nazareth.

However, whilst the above common areas of agreement exist, there remain very serious differences between the two narratives. Many theologians have wondered as to how the stories became so diversified, assuming that they both relied upon the same sources. Consequently it has been suggested that each account ,or at least parts thereof, cannot be considered historically correct and that extracts from Old Testament stories have conveniently been reformulated into sections of the narratives. The historic accuracy of the events described in Matthew and Luke must therefore be considered as very questionable. This is reinforced by the fact that no one who accompanied Jesus during his ministry would have been present at his birth and no one appears to have been aware of any unusual events or circumstances surrounding it.

A Lack of Witnesses

Nevertheless, if we are to accept the narratives as having some historical accuracy, we can always turn to Joseph and Mary as well as the Magi and shepherds, or can we? By the time of the commencement of Jesus' ministry, Joseph was most likely already dead, as is suggested in Mark 6:3, which makes reference to his immediate family and does not mention him. Mary does not appear to have been closely involved with the disciples of Jesus during his ministry, although Acts 1:14 implies that she may have been associated with them after the crucifixion. We cannot disprove that Mary was a source for Luke but it does seem improbable. As pointed out by Brown, when Luke's introduction to his Gospel refers to traditions in 1:2, 'from those who were from the beginning eye witnesses and ministers of the word', he is clearly referring to the followers and companions of Jesus during his ministry and the apostles as indicated in Acts 1:21 and 22. It also seems very unlikely that Mary was a source for Matthew, which appears to concentrate primarily upon Joseph. As for the Magi, Matthew has them leaving to journey back to their own country, whereas Luke has the shepherds returning to their fields. So both of these sets of apparent witnesses exit the scene quickly, never to be mentioned again anywhere in the New Testament. Consequently there seems to be no corroborating witness to the events as outlined in Matthew and Luke.

Difficulties Reconciled?

Attempts have of course been made to reconcile these difficulties. One of the reasons suggested is that each of the synoptic Gospels was written by very different individuals for different potential converts. Matthew is a converted Jew and whose earliest writing is thought, by many, to have been in Aramaic, and therefore designed for fellow Jews. Luke is also a converted Jew but whose writing was primarily for Gentiles, based upon the reasoning that it was first written in Greek. Whilst the author of Matthew is clearly very Jewish in his thinking he is also very critical of contemporary Judaism, in particular their leaders, scribes and the Pharisees and appears to be well aware of their hostility towards his fellow Christians.

Another reason suggested for the divergences between Luke and Matthew's infancy narratives is that each is covering a different time-frame and in this respect each may have had access to a separate distinct source. Whereas Luke makes reference to the visit of the shepherds, Matthew's account covers the visit of the Magi and the appearances of the star and there would seem to be a considerable period of time between these two events. It is clear that the shepherds visit immediately after the birth of Jesus, whereas the Magi come along perhaps as much as two years later. It is obvious from the account in Matthew that Jesus is an infant whenever the Magi visited Herod, and it is for this reason that the author has Herod deciding to have all the male children less than two years old murdered. Therefore it would seem that Luke concentrates upon events evolving around the actual birth of Christ whereas Matthew deals with a summary, covering a later and wider aspect of time.

Those who believe that the narratives are true, or at least partially true, suggest that the star is not mentioned by Luke because it had not assumed significance until sometime after the birth and it is only included by Matthew in relation to the visit by the Magi, at a later date. Such reasoning lends support to the hypothesis that Matthew's star, if it actually existed, was not as brilliant as one might have presumed, implying that it was perhaps not even a widely observed phenomenon.

A Brief Overview of the Gospels

In the *New Testament in Modern English*, J. B. Philips, a clergyman and Bible translator, describes the writings of Matthew as being 'lucid, calm and tidy, with a certain judiciousness as though he himself had carefully digested his material and is convinced not only of its truth, but of the divine pattern that lies behind the historical facts'. Many references are made to the Old Testament and the author has clearly been influenced by the prophecies therein anticipating the arrival and teachings of Jesus.

Irenaeus, a second-century Bishop of Lyon, stated that 'Matthew published his Gospel amongst the Hebrews in their own tongue'. It seems likely that the author of Matthew was a Greek-speaking Jewish Christian possibly based in Antioch, Syria writing for Jews and as such he would have been fluent in both Aramaic and Greek. Other suggestions for the place of origin have been Caesarea, Alexandria and Capernaum.

Matthew's descriptions of the fulfilment by Jesus of many of the Old Testament prophecies, through the events of his life, are often completed by the words 'and so the prophecy might be fulfilled', or words to that effect. In order to emphasise the point it is clear that he sometimes fashions the scriptures in order to fit the facts within the life of Jesus, or fashions the facts in order to fit the prophecies.

The general consensus is that Luke's Gospel was completed between that of Mark and Matthew, around the year AD 75 and possibly also in Antioch, although Greece or Rome have been conjectured. It was written in Greek and because the wording is the most fluent of the four Gospels, it is likely that this was his native tongue. A second-century tradition identified the author as Luke, a physician and companion of Paul, on the grounds that the writer, who also wrote Acts, used the word 'we' in sections of that book and it was assumed that he was referring to Paul and himself. Such identification however is now considered questionable on the grounds that the Book of Acts contains certain inaccuracies concerning the career of Paul as well as variances from Paul's line of thought as reflected in the Epistles.

Mark's Gospel was written originally either in Aramaic or Greek but with a certain roughness which is far removed from the polished style of Luke. It is the earliest Gospel and best estimates suggest a year around AD 65 for its composition. There is no certainty as to the precise location where it was written. While there is a strong case for Antioch, the balance of opinion favours Rome on the grounds that it was clearly intended for Gentiles already familiar with, and in anticipation of, persecution for their faith. The Gospel can be effectively split into two parts dealing firstly with the miraculous deeds of Jesus, and later with the emphasis shifting towards his teachings. In between there is the account of an incident at Caesarea Philippi when Peter, on behalf of the disciples, expresses their conviction that their master is the true Messiah. For many theologians this, rather than the birth narratives of Matthew and Luke, is regarded as the first recognition of Jesus as the Messiah by earthly humans.

The Other Gospels

John

Let us now turn our attention to the other Gospels. John did not make use of the Synoptic Gospels and is very different from them in its style and content, dealing instead with spiritual themes and Christ's relationship with God. It may have been written as a responsive supplement or possibly a corrective to them, and it was because of this that it was one of the last to be accepted into the New Testament canon. It seems likely that the original manuscript was written in Greek at Ephesus around the year 100. A small fragment of the Gospel, written on papyrus, was recovered from an island in the Upper Nile and can be dated to around the year 125.

The Apocryphal Gospels

Apart from the mysterious Q there are many other Gospels which did not make it into the New Testament. These are known as the Apocryphal Gospels as opposed to the four canonised Gospels of Matthew, Mark, Luke and John. They presently number about forty and most of them were written in the second and third centuries of Christianity. Some have only recently been discovered and a number only exist in fragmentary form. Through time some have been destroyed and are only known through quotations. There is no doubt that there are further Gospels awaiting discovery.

Perhaps the best known of the Apocryphal Gospels are those of Thomas and Peter. Thomas is really a collection of sayings attributable to Jesus. During an excavation in the Egyptian city of Nag Hammadi in 1945, a complete manuscript written in Coptic was found. It was said to be the work of Didymus Judas Thomas who also claimed to be the twin brother of Jesus! It is accepted that Jesus did have four brothers, the eldest of whom was James, the others being Joses, Juda, and Simon and at least two sisters (Mark 6:3). However, the very idea of Jesus having a twin is just beyond the comprehension of most people and is universally rejected. The Gospel of Peter, fragments of which were found in 1886, provides an account of the death and resurrection of Jesus.

Other References to the Star

The Protoevangelium of James

Included in the Apocryphal Gospels are two that make reference to the star of Bethlehem. The Protoevangelium of James is an early Gospel which was written after Matthew's account. The relevant passages in relation to the star occur when King Herod speaks to the Magi:

> And he questioned the Magi and said to them, 'What sign did you see concerning the new born King?' And the Magi said, 'We saw how an indescribably great star shone amongst these stars and dimmed them, so they no longer shone, and so we knew that a King was born for Israel. And we have come to worship him.' And Herod said, 'Go and seek and when you have found him, tell me, that I may also come to worship him.' And the Magi went forth. And behold, the star which they had seen in the east went before them, until they came to a cave. And it stood over the head of the child.

These passages are very similar to what we find in Matthew, although there are two differences. Firstly, reference is made to a cave instead of a house, and secondly, and more importantly from our point of view, the description of the star implies that it was extremely bright.

Traditionally it was thought that this book was written by James, the eldest of Jesus' brothers, but this now seems doubtful and it was probably written sometime in the early second century. It is likely that the author was not Jewish, and the objective of the writing was the glorification of Mary in opposition to certain Jewish mockery concerning the birth of Jesus. Consequently it seems likely that the author has attempted to deliberately exaggerate the events surrounding the birth of Christ, particularly with his description of the star.

The Letter to the Ephesians

Written by Ignatius, the Letter to the Ephesians dates to around AD 110 when he was held in captivity and the reference to the star is made in chapter nineteen:

> A star shone in heaven beyond all stars; its light beyond description and its newness caused astonishment; all the other stars, with the Sun and the Moon gathered in chorus around the star, but it far exceeded them all in its light.

Further Accounts

There are various further accounts of the star of Bethlehem in later non-Gospel writings, details of which I will not go into other than to say that as time progressed the descriptions of the star appear to become more and more played up, to the point of becoming ridiculous. Generally this is a response by the writers to over-emphasise the divinity of Jesus in order to attract converts. Consequently the relatively simple account within Matthew of the star, which historically is the earliest, has to be considered as the most reliable.

The Relevant Verses

At this stage, it may be considered appropriate to reproduce the verses contained within chapter two of the book of Matthew, as extracted from the authorised version:

1. Now, when Jesus was born in Bethlehem of Judea in the days of Herod the king, behold, there came wise men from the east to Jerusalem,
2. Saying, Where is he that is born King of the Jews? For we have seen his star in the east, and are come to worship him.
3. When Herod the king had heard these things, he was troubled, and all Jerusalem with him.
4. And when he had gathered all the chief priests and scribes of the people together, he demanded of them where Christ should be born.
5. And they said unto him, In Bethlehem of Judea: for thus it is written by the prophet,
6. And thou Bethlehem, in the land of Juda, are not the least among the princes of Juda: for out of you shall come a Governor, that shall rule my people Israel.
7. Then Herod, when he had privately called the wise men, inquired of them diligently what time the star appeared.
8. And he sent them to Bethlehem, and said, Go and search diligently for the young child; and when you have found him, bring me word again, that I may come and worship him also.

9. When they had heard the king, they departed; and, lo, the star, which they saw in the east, went before them, till it came and stood over where the young child was.
10. When they saw the star, they rejoiced with exceedingly great joy.
11. And when they were come into the house, they saw the young child with Mary his mother, and fell down, and worshipped him: and when they had opened their treasures, they presented unto him gifts; gold, and frankincense and myrrh.
12. And being warned by God in a dream that they should not return to Herod, they departed into their own country by an alternative route.
13. And when they were departed, behold, the angel of the Lord appeared to Joseph in a dream, saying, Arise, and take the young child and his mother, and flee into Egypt, and remain there until I bring you word: for Herod will seek the young child to destroy him.
14. When he arose, he took the young child and his mother by night, and departed into Egypt:
15. And was there until the death of Herod: that it might be fulfilled which was spoken of the Lord by the prophet, saying, Out of Egypt have I called my son.
16. Then Herod, when he saw that he was mocked of the wise men, was exceedingly wroth, and sent forth, and slew all the male children that were in Bethlehem, and in all the coasts thereof, from two years old and under, according to the time which he had diligently inquired of the wise men.
17. Then was fulfilled that which was spoken by Jeremy the prophet, saying,
18. In Rama there was a voice heard, lamentation, and weeping, and great mourning, Rachel weeping for her children, and would not be comforted, because they are not.
19. But when Herod was dead, behold, an angel of the Lord appeared in a dream to Joseph in Egypt,
20. Saying, arise, and take the young child and his mother, and go into the Land of Israel: for they are dead which sought the young child's life.
21. And so he arose, and took the young child and his mother, and came into the land of Israel.
22. But when he heard that Archelaus did reign in Judea in the room of his father Herod, he was afraid to go thither: notwithstanding, being warned by God in a dream, he turned aside into the parts of Galilee:
23. And he came and dwelt in a city called Nazareth: that it might be fulfilled which was spoken by the prophets, He shall be called a Nazarene.

Luke's reference to the birth is covered within the first part of chapter two of that Gospel, and the verses therein are also reproduced as follows:

1. And it came to pass in those days, that there went out a decree from Caesar Augustus, that all the world should be taxed.
2. And this taxing was first made when Quirinius was the governor of Syria.
3. And all went to be taxed, every one to his own city.

4. And Joseph also went up from Galilee, out of the city of Nazareth, unto the City of David, which is called Bethlehem; because he was of the house and lineage of David:

5. To be taxed with Mary his espoused wife, being great with child.

6. And so it was, that, while they were there, the days were accomplished that she should be delivered.

7. And she brought forth her first born son, and wrapped him in swaddling clothes, and laid him in a manger; because there was no room for them in the inn.

8. And there were in the same country shepherds abiding in the field, keeping watch over their flock by night.

9. And, lo, the angel of the Lord came upon them, and the glory of the Lord shone round about them: and they were sore afraid.

10. And the angel said unto them, Fear not: for, behold, I bring you good tidings of great joy, which shall be to all people.

11. For unto you is born this day in the city of David a Saviour, which is Christ the Lord.

12. And this shall be a sign unto you; you shall find the babe wrapped in swaddling clothes, lying in a manger.

13. And suddenly there was with the angel a multitude of the heavenly host praising God, and saying,

14. Glory to God in the highest, and on earth peace, good will toward men.

15. And it came to pass, as the angels were gone away from them into Heaven, the shepherds said one to another, Let us now go even unto Bethlehem, and see this thing which is come to pass, which the Lord has made known unto us.

16. And they came with haste, and found Mary, and Joseph, and the babe lying in a manger.

17. And when they had seen it, they made known abroad the saying which which was told them concerning this child.

18. And all they that heard it wondered at those things which were told them by the shepherds.

19. But Mary kept all these things, and pondered them in her heart.

20. And the shepherds returned, glorifying and praising God for all the things that they had heard and seen, as it was told unto them.

2
GOSPEL TRUTH?

Was the star of Bethlehem simply invented or contrived by the author of Matthew? Many present-day Christians believe that this is actually the case and that it may have been introduced into the infancy narrative through the use of Midrash, that is by the application of a modernised reinterpretation of certain extracts of Old Testament scripture. The term originated from ancient Jewish translations of Old Testament narratives in an attempt to popularise and expand upon them, but above all to make them understandable. For our purpose however, it could also be regarded as incorporating the process whereby important and influential Old Testament parables and events are applied to and absorbed into the infancy narratives, where they are disguised and played out. For both Matthew and Luke such narratives presented them with an opportunity to introduce Jesus, whilst at the same time providing a transition from the Old Testament to the New through drawing heavily upon those ancient works.

The Genealogy of Jesus?

Before the infancy narrative is introduced in Matthew we are presented with a detailed chronological genealogy of Joseph, the husband of Mary the mother of Jesus. Luke also provides a genealogy, although this comes after his birth narrative, not before. They are, however, contradictory and also controversial.

Matthew starts off his listing with Abraham, covering a lineage totalling forty-one to Joseph. Luke on the other hand, goes back all the way to Adam and covers seventy generations, with fifty-five from Abraham through to Joseph. Both attempt to trace the line through Joseph, rather than Mary, even though he is *not* the real father of Jesus.

Whereas Matthew and Luke each go back a considerable distance and both include King David, Matthew traces the linage through Solomon, the son of David and his royal, and legally recognised successors, whereas Luke traces a different route, through the brother of Solomon, known as Nathan. The subsequent names and the numbers used by each are therefore completely at variance. To make matters worse it ends up that each do not even agree with one another on the father of Joseph!

How can this be? A common explanation is that Matthew is tracing the genealogy through Joseph whereas Luke is tracing this through Mary. However, you hardly need to be a rocket scientist to realise that this is not right because Matthew 1:15 and 1:16 tell us that Matthan was the father of Jacob, who, in turn, was the father of Joseph, whilst Luke 3:24 tells that 'He [Jesus] was the son, so it was thought, of Joseph, the son of Heli [or Eli] the son of Matthat'. So it is quite clear that both are using the genealogy of Joseph.

Now, various attempts have been made to explain this away and many different permutations have been postulated. One possible explanation, put forward by the Quartz Hill School of Theology, in America, is that Luke uses a lineage through the father of Joseph whereas Matthew has used Joseph's maternal grandfather. In other words Matthew traces Joseph back through *his mother* but without mentioning her and instead jumps directly to her father.

This all sounds like wishful thinking and it has been suggested that a much more likely explanation is that it is all simply an elaborate fiction. In other words, it is artificial. This is supported by the fact that the time span covered from Abraham through to the birth of Jesus comes to a period of about 1,750 years, which is considered far too great to contain a mere forty-two generations. It would also appear that different sources have been used by each author in a desperate attempt to legitimise and boost their claim that Jesus was the Messiah.

The author of Matthew also leaves people out of his genealogy. No less than three individuals are omitted from the Gospel, namely Ahaziah, Joash and Amajiah. These appear to have been disregarded in order to provide a harmonising theme, or framework, utilising the 'magic number' of fourteen, as provided in Matthew 1:17:

> So all the generations from Abraham to David *are* fourteen generations; and from David until the carrying away into Babylon *are* fourteen generations; and from the carrying away into Babylon unto Christ *are* fourteen generations.[2]

Matthew's genealogy also includes four women, Tamur, Rahab, Ruth and Bethsheba, which may provide some support for the theory that, somewhere down the line, it is the genealogy of a woman.

At least both Matthew and Luke agree that Joseph, and therefore Jesus indirectly, were descended from David, as well as Abraham. It was essential to include David in order to comply with Jewish expectations of a Messiah descended from that dynasty. It also satisfied two important prophecies – that of Balaam and Micah, of which more shortly. The author had to provide this vital unification with the past, forging the missing link between the Old Testament and the New Testament through the utilisation of Joseph. His royal ancestry is later recognised and confirmed in the infancy narrative, when the Angel of the Lord, appearing in a dream to Joseph, addresses him as a 'son of David'. It was imperative therefore that Joseph accepted Jesus as though he were his own son.

The descriptions in the genealogy of Joseph do not provide us with a great deal of confidence when we are later introduced to the infancy narrative of Matthew. Clearly historical accuracy was of relatively minor consequence to the author, as his primary purpose was to promote the theme of the spiritual divinity of Jesus.

The Prophecy of Balaam

Some have argued that the introduction of the star into the story was in order to satisfy an Old Testament prophecy, in this particular instance that as recorded in

Numbers 24:17 which is known as Balaam's prophecy:

> I shall see him but not now
> I shall behold him but not near
> There shall come a star out of Jacob
> And a sceptre shall rise out of Israel
> And shall smite the corners of Moab
> And destroy all the children of Sheth

These passages were based upon one of seven prophecies made by Balaam, a Babylonian soothsayer. It is difficult to date but it probably goes back to about the seventh century BC. So, what does it all mean? Moab was an area close to Jericho and its borders were being threatened by Israeli settlers. The King of Moab, known as Balak, summoned Balaam to him in the hope that he would foretell that doom and disaster would befall the Israelites, thus preventing further incursions into his country. However Balaam, who believed in the God of the Israelites, known as Yahweh, foretold in his oracles the destruction of Moab's population and also those living in the borderlands of Canaan.

Many present Christian scholars do believe that Old Testament narratives have been reformulated in such a way to produce a New Testament tale in order to satisfy the above prophecy. However, one argument against this is that the author of Matthew was obviously well acquainted with the writings in the Old Testament, and may have realised or interpreted that the prophecy had already been satisfied many centuries earlier, when the victorious King David came to power having defeated the King of Moab. The star and the sceptre represented David ruling over the newly combined Kingdom of Judea and Israel.

Nevertheless it seems that in the period immediately preceding Christ's birth the interpretation of the prophecy *would* in fact have been applied to the Messiah as the anointed King of Israel. This is verified by references to it by the Qumran community, a Jewish sect which actually anticipated the Messiah, and whose writings were found within the Dead Sea Scrolls. To them the star from Jacob represented an 'Interpreter of the law', or high priest of the 'end times', whilst the sceptre represented the 'Prince of the whole congregation' or the Davidic Messiah. It would also explain why, in the second century AD, Simon Bar Kosibah, a Jewish revolutionary leader was hailed by Rabbi Aquiba as the Messiah and became known as Bar Cochba, meaning 'son of the star'. So is it possible that in the first century AD the interpretation of Balaam's prophecy had given rise to the belief that an actual physical star would rise symbolising the emergence of the Messiah?

The story of Balaam involves a soothsayer or an occult visionary who could interpret dreams. However, he has also been described as a Magus, or a magician, and Numbers 23:7 refers to him as having come 'from the mountains of the east', with Numbers 22:22 mentioning that he was also accompanied by two servants.

He proceeded to dash the hopes of King Balak by foretelling through his oracles the future of Israel. Balaam later returned to his own country.

Such a story sounds very familiar with Herod being visited by wise men or Magi from the East. Both Herod and Balak were also attempting to take advantage of the Magi's ability to predict future events, but both were foiled. In the end both Balaam and the Magi appear to make a quick exit, returning to their place of origin.

The Prophecy of Micah

The author would also have been aware of a further Old Testament prophecy, namely that as outlined in Micah 5:2:

> But thou, Bethlehem Ephratah, though thou be little among the thousands of Judah, yet out of you shall he come forth unto me that is to be the ruler in Israel, whose goings forth have been found from old, from everlasting.

This created an expectation that the Messiah would be born in Bethlehem. However it is possible that the prophet Micah did not necessarily mean that he would actually be *born* there, but rather that he would simply be born out of the royal House of David, as it was David who, centuries earlier, had been born in that town. Nevertheless, the author, in Matthew 2:5 and 2:6, appears to have utilised the prophecy in such a way in order to record that Christ *was* born in Bethlehem, as well as emerging from within the House of David. There is little doubt that he is specifically referring to Micah 5:2. This also helps to explain why he goes to great lengths, at the beginning of his Gospel, to trace the genealogy of Joseph right back to David, as well as to Moses and Abraham.

The Pillar of Light

Although the Balaam story does not fit in with the description of a star *leading* the Magi, there is a reference to a light which lit up the night and *went before* the Israelites, leading them as mentioned in Exodus 13:21:

> And the Lord went before them by day in a pillar of cloud, to lead them the way; and by night in a pillar of fire, to give them light; to go by day and night.

References to this pillar of light or fire can also be found in Exodus 40:38, Nehemiah 9:19, and Psalms 78:14 and 105:39. In this particular context it is referring to the Israelites in the desert fleeing from the pursuing armies of Pharaoh. It does not take a great deal of imagination to suspect that Matthew has used this description when he refers to the star as having 'went before' the Magi, leading them to find the child Jesus. As Brown points out, it could be conceived that Matthew was now applying this divine light to the Gentiles, in the form of the star of Bethlehem.

The Birth of Moses

Another aspect of the account in Matthew of the nativity is that part of it closely resembles the birth narratives of Moses in the Old Testament. It has been suggested that Matthew has deliberately incorporated those accounts of Moses, albeit in a disguised and reshaped form, to support the claim that Jesus was the Messiah. The striking similarities of the stories have been recognised by Brown and he has prepared a comparison of events which are summarised as follows:

Old Testament	New Testament
Exodus 2:15 The Pharaoh sought to do away with Moses so Moses went away.	Matthew 2:13–14 Herod was going to search for the child to destroy him, so Joseph took the child and his mother and went away.
Exodus 1:22 The Pharaoh commanded that every male born to the Hebrews be cast into the Nile.	Matthew 2:16 Herod sent to Bethlehem and massacred all the boys of two years of age and under.
Exodus 2:33 The King of Egypt died.	Matthew 2:19 Herod died.
Exodus 4:19 The Lord said to Moses in Midian ... 'return to Egypt, for all those who were seeking your life are dead'.	Matthew 2:19–20 The Angel of the Lord said to Joseph in Egypt, '.... Go back to the land of Israel, for those who were seeking the child's life are dead'.
Exodus 4:20 Moses took his wife and his children and returned to Egypt.	Matthew 2:21 Joseph took the child and his mother and went back to the land of Israel.

In non-biblical tradition the parallels between the infancies of Jesus and Moses are even more stark. There also seems little doubt that such non-biblical stories about the birth of Moses were in circulation when the infancy narratives were being written for they are mentioned by both Philo in his *Life of Moses* and Josephus in *Antiquities*. Such details included reference to the Pharaoh receiving a warning from a 'sacred scribe' about the birth of a Hebrew who would pose a threat to his kingdom. Different stories mention that the Pharaoh in a dream was warned of the birth but which had to be interpreted by Magi or magicians. Brown suggests that Matthew may have substituted the Magi and star tale for an earlier pre-Matthian story which referred instead to Herod having a dream that had to be interpreted, this being carried out in order to give his birth narrative more independence. However, he does point out that whereas in the Moses legend the Magi assisted the Pharaoh, in Matthew's version they are favourable to Jesus and did not trust the wicked king.

Josephus' story of Moses also mentions that the Pharaoh was alarmed on hearing of the imminent birth of the Hebrew leader and that the Egyptians were filled with dread. Likewise Herod, in the infancy narrative on hearing of the birth of Jesus, 'was startled, and so was all Jerusalem with him'. Josephus also refers to God appearing in a dream to Moses' father, Amram, whose wife was about to give birth, reassuring him that the child would escape his enemies and later would 'deliver the Hebrew race from their bondage in Egypt'. This is very similar to the position of Joseph with Jesus' birth, being warned in a dream to leave Israel and flee to Egypt, Matthew 1:21 going on to state that Jesus 'will save his people from their sins'.

Joseph was clearly capable of interpreting his own dreams and it has been suggested that the inclusion of this ability was based upon Joseph the patriarch, who in Genesis was described as a 'man of dreams'. Likewise the patriarch Joseph went to Egypt as did Joseph and his family, albeit for different reasons.

In subsequent legends, which are not mentioned in the Old Testament, the birth of Moses is said to have been accompanied by a great light like that of a star or the Sun and the Moon. The birth of Abraham was said to have been accompanied by a star that was seen to rise and eat up other stars, indicating that the child would grow up to conquer the Earth. Astrologers informed the evil King Nimrod of this and recommended him to kill all the male children.

Luke's Shepherds

In contrast to Matthew, Luke has shepherds visiting Jesus. Although in those times shepherds were considered to be amongst the lowest elements of society and were not to be trusted, it may be that the author of Luke chose them symbolically because of the links between Bethlehem as the City of David, and David the shepherd. However, another possibility is that the author of Luke recognised shepherds in the region between Jerusalem and Migdal Edar near Bethlehem, also known as the 'Tower of the Flock', as being sacred as they provided the animals in that area for the temple sacrifice.

By having the shepherds travel to Bethlehem, Luke also satisfied the prophecy in Micah, but this time more broadly, in chapters four and five, which makes reference to a future victory of Jerusalem or Zion being achieved through a leader from Bethlehem. It also told of a subsequent influx of peoples and nations to Jerusalem which could have inspired the author of Luke to write about the movement of the whole world as a response to the census of Augustus, this being the reason why he has Joseph and Mary travelling to Bethlehem. So it would seem that Luke's infancy narratives may, like Matthew, have Old Testament themes underlying them.

Bethlehem

Serious doubts have also been raised as to whether Jesus was actually born in Bethlehem. So serious that C. Burger, in his book entitled *Jesus*, writes, 'The overwhelming evidence ... has made the thesis that Bethlehem was not the historical birthplace of Jesus the common opinion of New Testament scholarship.' Although both Luke and Matthew agree on its location as the place of birth, each has Joseph and Mary residing there under very different circumstances. Luke has Bethlehem as a temporary location for them as a result of the census being carried out there with Nazareth as their homeland, whereas Matthew implies a more permanent residence, having Jesus aged about one or two years old and staying with his parents in a house. It has been argued that both Luke and Matthew chose Bethlehem because Jesus was regarded as having been descended from David, representing the Davidic Messiah, and therefore it had been expected that he should be born in the historic town of David. This is reaffirmed by Matthew 2:4–6 and John 7:41–42. Some have also claimed that Bethlehem was simply chosen by the authors by way of a response to Jewish ridicule towards a Messiah who seemed to have come from Nazareth in Galilee, an area which would have been viewed by them as being completely inappropriate.[3]

From studies of the New Testament it does seem more likely that Jesus' home town was Nazareth. Whereas both Matthew 2:22–23 and Luke 2:51 agree that Jesus proceeded to grow up in Nazareth, it is them and them only that make specific reference to Bethlehem as the place of Jesus' birth. Nowhere in the rest of the New Testament does anyone seem to be familiar with a birth having taken place in Bethlehem. Mark, as the most likely contender, does not indicate any prior knowledge of Jesus having been born there, with Mark 6:2–3 implying that his neighbours did not regard his family as strangers and were astonished at his apparently sudden rise to fame, seemingly unaware of anything previous which might have been considered exceptional regarding their situation within Nazareth. In addition John 7:41–42 certainly makes it clear that it was not known that Jesus came from Bethlehem, thus casting doubts upon some that he was the Messiah. Whilst most of those who dismiss Bethlehem as the place of birth suggest Nazareth as the most likely alternative, some also suggest Capernaum as this was where most of Jesus' ministerial activity is seen to take place.

If Jesus was not born in Bethlehem this then begs the question, how then can we have a star of Bethlehem? It would suggest that the whole story of the nativity is indeed Midrash and that it has no historical substance whatsoever.

There are nevertheless a number of objections in favour of Jesus having been born in Bethlehem. Both Matthew and Luke agree that whilst Jesus was born in Bethlehem, he was reared in Nazareth (Matthew 2:1, Luke 2:4–6). So it is quite plausible that it may have been assumed that he was born in Nazareth as he had simply spent most of his life there. Few, if any, would have known, or been expected to know, whether or not his family had been in Bethlehem around thirty years earlier.

We also have to consider the probability that the birth narratives were written long after Jesus had been accepted as the Messiah by the early Christians, so there was really no necessity to introduce, by way of invention, a birth in Bethlehem. Both could simply have settled for a mature Messiah to suddenly emerge or be introduced into their respective Gospels in the same fashion that Mark has Jesus appearing for the first time for baptism. Alternatively they could have adopted the approach that John takes, by way of introducing a 'hidden' Messiah, with no one knowing where he came from (John 7:27).

Origen, a third-century Christian historian, in *Contra Celsum* suggested that Jewish scholars attempted to reduce expectations that Bethlehem would be the birthplace of the Messiah, implying that they acknowledged Christian beliefs on this point, and it is interesting to note that subsequent Jewish objections concerning Jesus as the Messiah did not include a denial that Bethlehem was his place of birth.[4]

However, many leading Christian writers agree that Matthew fashioned Old Testament narratives and Jewish legend in such a way to support the story of Jesus' birth. Brown accepts that Matthew's Gospel contains material which comprised an editing of Old Testament texts and also of 'more episodic narratives', rearranging and retelling them in his own language in order to be in harmony with his own idealistic and theological vision.

The Star

One of the main arguments put forward against the above theory, in relation to the star, is that Matthew does not at any stage use the phrase, 'and so the prophecy might be fulfilled'. This therefore suggests that the writer has not included the story of the star as a response to Balaam's prophecy and in a way this actually lends support to the theory that it could have been based upon a real event.

Other critics argue that the inclusion of the star in the birth narrative was made simply to give it added significance. To counteract this we again have to go back to the author's judicious understanding of the Old Testament. As a converted Jew he would have been aware that the Old Testament discouraged the use of astrology to explain events, and associated such practice with non-believers or heathens. To illustrate this point Jeremiah 10:2 states, 'Thus said the Lord, learn not the way of the heathen, and be not dismayed at the signs of heaven; for the heathen are dismayed at them.' It has been postulated therefore that it would have been unlikely for the author of Matthew to incorporate a statement of a star in his narrative unless he had some firm belief in its truth and actual existence.

An Association with Divinity

One argument for the story of the star having been invented, or at least exaggerated, is that for centuries it was relatively commonplace for a great king or emperor to be associated at some stage with a stellar event, whether it be when they were born, came to power, or when they died. They wanted to be associated with divinity and this was a particularly common feature with Roman emperors, as shall be seen later. It also applied to the rulers of Judea. Coins originating from a period when Herod became king, in 37 BC, whilst not mentioning his name or featuring his portrait (which is a great pity, as I am sure that we would all have liked to have viewed the face of one of the New Testament's great villains), illustrates his royal helmet capped by a star just above it. Consequently the author of Matthew may have felt obliged, when writing the infancy narrative, to include some reference to a celestial event in order to justify Christ's divinity. Also, without the star the whole story ran the danger of not being taken seriously by his intended audience. There was no choice in the matter, so, if the star did not exist, then one would have to be introduced.

Against this theory we have to consider the fact that the description in Matthew of the star does not appear to be exaggerated or played up, unlike later versions. The star is not described as being particularly bright. We also have to bear in mind the honesty and diligence of the author. Therefore it is necessary to contemplate the possibility that a real celestial event did occur which coincided with the birth of Jesus.

Written After a Long Passage of Time

Another problem to be considered is that the author of Matthew was writing his Gospel almost a century after the actual birth of Jesus. The story of the star, if there was one, may have been portrayed to him either by word of mouth or through an earlier written source, as obviously he would not have experienced the celestial event for himself. He would have to rely upon past accounts and decide as to whether to accept them as the truth. The recording of an event which may have occurred so many years before must obviously cast doubt upon its credibility. Could original eye witness accounts, if they existed, be considered reliable or had they become corrupted over time to the extent that they had developed into something resembling myth, legend or folklore?

Conclusion

The advantage that we have over the above doubts is that generally speaking a celestial event is normally witnessed by large numbers of the population, particularly if it occurs in space, being well beyond the upper atmosphere of the Earth. Such events may be witnessed on a global scale and not merely restricted to particular regions or countries. Therefore it is possible to correlate the description of the star in Matthew with contemporary written records which exist from other countries and this will be dealt with in subsequent chapters.

The fact however remains that many New Testament scholars are sceptical as to whether the star of Bethlehem represented a genuine celestial object. For instance, Brown states, 'A star that rose in the east, appeared over Jerusalem, turned south to Bethlehem, and then came to rest over a house would have constituted a celestial phenomenon unparalleled in astronomical history, yet it received no notice in the records of the times.' So on the face of it there would seem to be no astronomical event with which we are familiar that could explain such strange occurrences. However, as shall be seen later there is a celestial visitor which does, to a large extent, satisfy the description in Matthew and which can be verified by contemporary records.

Could the star of Bethlehem have been a miracle? Certainly some Christians think so, mostly on the grounds of faith, accepting that the star was a special sign announcing the birth of the Messiah, representing a divine manifestation. They consider that as it was the will of God, it did not require explanation; God does not have to account for his actions. Put another way they would accept that anything is possible and that, rather than being scientific, it is unscientific to completely dismiss miracles. Consequently numerous biblical accounts are to be found which appear to be miraculous or supernatural and very difficult to comprehend, but this should not stop us from attempting to understand and explain them.

3
HEROD

Most of our knowledge about Herod the Great comes from the work of Flavius Josephus, a Jewish historian from the first century AD, who concentrated on writing long and detailed descriptions of events in Palestine. Born in AD 37, in the affluent upper city of Jerusalem, he was originally known as Joseph ben Matthias. His father was a priestly aristocrat known as Mattityahu and his mother was descended from the Maccabean kings of Israel. Josephus himself had a very eventful life. As a youth he became a priest, and was to excel in the study of Jewish law. At the age of twenty-nine, he became a commander in the Jewish army, being later involved in the defence of the hill fortress of Jotapata against the Romans. Following a controversial surrender, he became an historian to the Emperors Vespasian and Titus and consequently was branded a traitor.

Josephus has attracted criticism from historians on the grounds that some of his commentaries appear to overstate certain incidents and events. He was obviously well trained in rhetoric, many of his works being full of dramatic flourishes and elaborations so as not to appear boring to the reader. However, whilst he has clearly exaggerated events within his own life in his autobiography, most historians agree that overall he is a reliable and accurate source. His work has greatly assisted archaeologists in their excavations, particularly at Caesarea, Jerusalem, Masada and Herodium, and they have found his descriptions of the physical layout of these places to be very precise.

His works cover a period extending from about 200 BC through to AD 75, and include Judean history and culture, the war with the Romans and details of his own career. We are very fortunate that his works have survived. One of the reasons suggested for this is that he is one of only three known first-century historians, outside the writers of the New Testament, to actually mention Christ, the early Christian church therefore finding it in their best interests to have his works preserved.[5] He makes only a brief reference to Christ when he refers to the trial in AD 62 of his brother James, telling us that he was 'the brother of Jesus, who was called the Christ'. There is a more detailed second reference to Christ, although historians and theologians are reasonably certain that it represents the work of later Christian scribes who deliberately inserted it during the process of copying the translation, in order to provide further evidence for the historical existence of Jesus.[6] He also makes reference to John the Baptist and Pilate.

Herod's Rise to Power

Herod was the second son of Antipater the Idumaen, who was the founder of the Herodian dynasty. His mother, Cydros, was an Arabian princess from Petra in Nabataea, which is now part of Jordan. Although not Jewish at birth he was brought up in Palestine and so acquired many of the ways and traditions of the Jewish community. His family had close connections with the elite in Rome and in 47 BC his father was made Procurator over Judea and he then appointed the twenty-five-year-old Herod as the governor of Galilee. In 43 BC Antipater was poisoned and Herod had the suspected assassin, a tax collector, executed. His brother Antigonus was then installed as the new ruler. In 41 BC Herod was made tetrarch by Mark Antony, who was at that time effectively a joint-ruler of the Roman Empire together with Octavian and Lepidus under the terms of the Second Triumvirate.

Antigonus' reign proved unpopular and in 37 BC he was captured, imprisoned and later executed. Herod was then appointed King of Judea by Antony. To strengthen his position and gain legitimacy from the Jews, Herod divorced his first wife, Doris, and married a teenage princess, Mariamme, from the former Hasmarean dynasty. They were actually the true titular rulers of Judea and as such Mariamme probably had a stronger claim to the throne than Herod himself.

Following Antony's defeat at the Battle of Actium in 31 BC, Herod found himself in the awkward and precarious position of having to pay homage to Antony's rival, Octavian, in an attempt to have his royal throne reaffirmed. This he achieved with Octavian, soon to be known as Augustus, content to allow Herod to continue to rule over Judea. Over the coming years both in fact developed a considerable degree of mutual respect for one another.

Accountability to Rome

Ever since Jerusalem was taken by Pompey in 63 BC, Judea was effectively controlled by Rome through a series of puppet, or client kings, and Herod, although on good terms with Augustus, remained no exception. He was accountable to Rome's authority and only governed with its approval. Nevertheless the Romans generally took a back seat in the day-to-day running of the country, their attitude being one of tolerance and this was reflected in Jewish exemption from Roman religion, which included emperor worship. The Romans deified their emperors and the combination of secular and spiritual power strengthened their grip over their subjects. At the same time, however, they were pragmatic, realising that the Jews were not prepared, under any circumstances, to worship idols. The kings of Judea were also permitted to issue coinage in their own name, although there were restrictions imposed. Between the years 37 BC and AD 67 no coins containing Aramaic or Hebrew inscriptions were allowed to be minted or circulated within the country. The coinage therefore normally contained Greek inscriptions and sometimes showed the head of Caesar. In fact the only coins issued by Herod were bronze and therefore of low value. In addition the kings of Judea still had an obligation to collect and pay tribute, or tax, to Rome, known as *fiscus Judaicus*.

Building Projects

Geographically, Judea was well positioned, being in the middle of several major trade routes, which included the transportation of precious merchandises such as incense from Yemen, Arabia and the Mediterranean. Its fertile land produced a variety of valuable commodities including olives, dates and grapes. The lucrative trade generated large revenue and this enabled Herod to carry out building programmes on a truly massive scale, and he is recognised today by archaeologists as one of the most prolific builders of the ancient world. He built cities, fortresses, and palaces including the port of Caesarea, huge fortifications around Jerusalem, including three towers at its entrance and fortresses at Masada, Herodium and Antonia. A massive palace was also built at Herodium which was placed upon an artificially flattened hilltop.

The palace at Herodium, which was surrounded by watch towers, acted as a sanctuary, an administrative centre and a mausoleum. At its base an additional palace was built, being about the size of a small town and this became later known as 'Lower Herodium'. Water was transported from Solomon's Pools and special soil used to enable elaborate gardens to flourish. Caesarea, with its man-made port, became the trading and administrative capital of Judea; however it also incorporated many Roman features, having an amphitheatre or hippodrome for chariot races, bath houses and a temple dedicated to Augustus. However, to the Jews it became a symbol of paganism, in total contravention of their ideologies.

The Great Temple

In an attempt to subdue Jewish resentment and contempt towards him, Herod undertook perhaps the most extravagant of all his projects – the reconstruction of the Great Temple of Jerusalem. This huge development involved thousands of men working solidly for about twenty-six years in its construction, comprising a gigantic platform protected by retaining walls, upon which was the Temple Mount. No expense was spared on the Temple itself, using vast quantities of gold and marble. It is probably best described by Josephus in his manuscript entitled *Jewish War*:

> Viewed from without, the sanctuary had everything that could amaze either mind or eyes. Overlaid all round with stout plates of gold, the first rays of the sun it reflected presented so fierce a blaze of fire that those who endeavoured to look at it were forced to turn away as if they had looked straight at the sun. To strangers as they approached it seemed in the distance like a mountain covered with snow; for any part not covered with gold was dazzling white.

A Symbol of Rome

At the great gate to the main entrance to the Temple, Herod placed a huge golden Roman eagle which aroused bitterness and resentment amongst the Jews, who viewed it as sacrilege. It was later destroyed by a group of students led by two Jewish teachers, Judas and Matthias. Herod had them captured and taken to Jericho where they and forty of their students were burned to death.

Herod also had executed forty-six members of the Sanhedrin, a governing body of the Jews, which comprised priests and scribes, and had his own High Priest appointed. Herod's ruthlessness can be partly explained by his desire to Hellenise or Romanise the Jewish people, meaning that he wanted them to adopt Greek, as well as Roman culture. Towards this end he was prepared to persecute and murder any rabbi who he regarded as not only being a threat to his authority, but also against this policy of Hellenisation. Due to Herod's interference the Temple hierarchy would become very corrupt and the Sadducees, who represented a religious group of the wealthy, came to dominate the Temple, attracting the opposition of the majority of the Jews, known as the Pharisees, and the more extreme minority group, the Zealots. Ultimately it would contribute towards growing nationalistic fervour amongst the Jewish people, eventually boiling over in complete revolt in AD 6. Moreover Herod had effectively fuelled the right conditions for the emergence of a Messianic figure.

His Family

During his life Herod had no less than ten wives who gave birth to fourteen children. As the years progressed he became increasingly paranoid and insecure, obsessed by a fear of losing power and would stop at nothing in order to achieve this. In 29 BC in a mad fit of jealousy he had Mariamme, who was the only wife he ever really loved, strangled. He had his brother-in-law, Aristobulus, whom he had made the High Priest, drowned, and later executed three of his sons, Aristobulus, Alexander and Antipater, in order to consolidate his position. Augustus, weary of Herod's behaviour, is reported to have said that 'it is better to be Herod's dog than one of his children'. He had become a tyrant and one of the most ruthless despots of all time, using a form of secret police in order to root out anyone suspected of plotting against him.

The Death of Herod

Towards the end of his reign Herod suffered from bouts of mental instability, becoming increasingly demented. In the final months of his life he seems to have developed a disease known as Fournier's gangrene, a very serious condition which is described by Josephus in *Jewish Antiquities* 17: 16. 5; it does not make particularly pleasant reading:

> But now Herod's distemper greatly increased upon him after a severe manner, and this by God's judgement upon him for his sins: for a fire glowed in him slowly, which did not so much appear to the touch outwardly, as it augmented his pains inwardly; for it brought upon him a vehement appetite to eating, which he could not avoid to supply with one sort of food or other. His entrails were also exulcerated, and the chief violence of his pain lay on his colon; an aqueous and transparent liquor also had settled itself about his feet, and a like matter afflicted

him at the bottom of his belly. Nay, further, his privy-member was putrefied, and produced worms; and when he sat upright he had a difficulty of breathing, which was very loathsome, on account of the stench of his breath and the quickness of its returns; he had also convulsions in all parts of his body, which increased his strength to an insufferable degree. It was said by those who pretended to divine, and who were endued with wisdom to foretell such things, that God inflicted this punishment on the king on account of his great impiety; yet was he still in hopes of recovering, though his afflictions seemed greater than any one could bear.

It may of course be that Josephus greatly exaggerated the condition of Herod as in all probability he, like most Jews, despised his memory. Tom Mueller, in an article titled *King Herod Revealed*, certainly takes this view writing that 'the symptoms Josephus mentions were part of a shock repertoire of rank and randy ailments, widely considered signs of God's wrath, that had already been used for centuries by Greek and Roman historians to drop the curtain on evil rulers'.

In an attempt to cure himself he travelled with his physicians to Callirrhoe, close to the Dead Sea, to bathe in the warm springs there, but without any success. He returned to Jericho where he slipped into a state of severe depression. Although close to death he still managed to devise a cruel plan, gathering leading Jews from various parts of the country and locking them inside the hippodrome with the instruction that they were to be executed upon his death. One of the reasons for this was his fear of being mocked and ridiculed by the Jewish community whenever he died, and by carrying out such an act he would ensure that the whole country would instead be in a state of mourning, Josephus recording that Herod had said, 'so shall all Judea and every household weep for me, whether they wish it or not'. He then attempted suicide but this was foiled by Achiah, his cousin. Although his plan was abandoned, thanks largely to his sister Salome and her husband Alexus, it illustrates the viciousness and callousness of Herod, right up until his bitter end. Even so, fearing that his imprisoned son, Antipater, would take over his position, he had him murdered. In Jericho, four days after having a new will drawn up, Herod died aged sixty-nine. Josephus writes:

> When he had done those things, he died, the fifth day after he had caused Antipater to be slain; having reigned, since he procured Antigonus to be slain, thirty-four years; but since he had been declared king by the Romans, thirty-seven. (*Antiquities*, 17: 8. I)

He had a very lavish funeral, described in some detail by Josephus:

> There was a bier all of gold, embroidered with precious stones, and a purple bed of various contexture, with the dead body upon it, covered with purple; and a diadem was put upon his head, and a crown of gold above it, and a sceptre in his right hand, and near to the bier were Herod's sons, and a multitude of his kindred, next to which came his guards, and the regiment of Thracias, the Germans, also

and Gauls, all accounted as if they were going to war; but the rest of the army went foremost, armed, and following their captains and officers in a regular manner; after when five hundred of his domestic servants and freed men followed, with sweet spices in their hands: and the body was carried two hundred furlongs [25 miles], to Herodium, where he had given order to be buried.

Josephus' account of the procession suggests that, despite all, some of his subjects still felt considerable respect for him. This may be due to the fact that during his reign Judea had enjoyed a long period of relative peace and prosperity.

Following excavations, begun in 1972, it was announced in May 2007 by Professor Ehud Netzer of the Hebrew University of Jerusalem, that a team of archaeologists had discovered the remnants of the grave and tomb of Herod. This was based upon the discovery of shattered pieces of a limestone sarcophagus which were believed to have been originally part of his tomb. No remains were identified in the container but its location and elaborate appearance indicated that it was almost certainly that of Herod. It was assumed to have been desecrated not long after his demise, probably having been smashed into pieces during the Jewish rebellion of AD 66–72, Herodium having been seized by the rebels during the revolt but handed over to the Romans following the fall of Jerusalem in AD 70, and it was they who proceeded to destroy the town in the following year.

When Did Herod Die?

Thanks largely to the writings of Josephus we are able to determine, with reasonable accuracy, the date of Herod's death. This provides us with a valuable clue as to when Jesus was born, as, obviously, if we know this, it contributes towards giving us the latest possible date of his birth, as both Matthew and Luke agree that Jesus was born during the reign of Herod. Josephus (*Antiquities*, 17: 6. 4) writes:

> Herod ... burnt the other Mathias, who had raised the sedition, with his companions, alive. And that very night there was an eclipse of the Moon.

Fortunately for us, this is the only lunar eclipse that is mentioned by Josephus. He then goes on to mention that the feast of the Passover occurred not long afterwards, coinciding with a period of demonstrations against the new king, Archelaus, one of Herod's sons, and also by Jews distressed that Mathias had not been properly mourned. So it seems clear that Herod died sometime between a lunar eclipse and the feast of the Passover.

The date of the Passover varies each year and can fall into either of the months of March or April. In calculating this date the Jewish lunar year is used and this normally commences in September, being determined by Rosh Hashanah, the Jewish equivalent of New Year's day. The Passover commences on the fourteenth day of the seventh month, known as Nisan, and this represents one day prior to the appearance of a full Moon (since there are almost fifteen days from the commencement of a lunar month to a full Moon). This means that it is possible to ascertain the date of the Passover for any given year in the past.

Comparison of Lunar Eclipses and Passover Dates Between 5 BC and AD 1					
Year (Gregorian)	Date of lunar eclipse visible (from Jerusalem)	Type	Maximum altitude in degrees	Date of Passover	Interval in days between eclipse and Passover
5 BC	23 March	Total	51	21 March	-
5 BC	15 September	Total	50	-	207
4 BC	13 March	Partial 36.5%	36.4	10 April	28
1 BC	9 January	Total	67.5	6 April	88
1 BC	29 December	Partial 57%	1.1*	-	88
AD 1	-			27 March	-

* almost certainly not visible as its altitude at maximum was too low, so it would effectively have been below the horizon for almost all of its duration

As Josephus tells us that the feast of the Passover occurred shortly after the eclipse, it would seem reasonable to assume that he is referring to the events in 4 BC and that Herod died sometime between 13 March and 10 April of that year. This assessment is reinforced by the argument that, had Herod died after a normal full Moon, that is a non-eclipsed full Moon, then there would be no mention by Josephus of the death having been preceded by a lunar eclipse, otherwise it would be an ambiguous statement. As a consequence, the year 4 BC has been widely accepted by historians and biblical scholars as representing the year of Herod's death.

Supporting Evidence for 5 or 4 BC

There is further evidence for early 5 or late 4 BC as relating to Herod's death based upon research carried out by Timothy D. Barnes. In an article titled *The Date of Herod's Death*, he identified and used the dates of certain key historical events to support his reasoning that Herod died in December 5 BC.

The Reigns of the Surviving Sons
We know that Herod was succeeded by his three surviving sons, Archelaus, Herod Antipas and Philip. Archelaus was deposed as King of Judea and died in the year AD 6, in exile in Gaul after reigning for ten years. Herod Antipas as Tetrarch of Galilee reigned for forty-three years but lost his rule during the second year of the Emperor, Gaius Caligula, which equates to AD 38/39. Philip, as Tetrarch of Basham, reigned

for thirty-seven years, ending in the twentieth year of Tiberius, which is AD 33/34. This may now be summarised as follows:

	Archelaus	Herod Antipas	Philip
Year of cessation of reign	AD 6	AD 38/39	AD 33/34
Length of reign (years)	10	43	37
Commencement of reign (1–2)	4 BC	5/4 BC	4/3 BC

From this we can calculate that Herod must have died around the year 4 BC.

Gaius Caesar
The above dates are further supported by the fact that when Archelaus and Herod Antipas presented their individual claims to the Judean throne before Augustus, his heir, Gaius Caesar, was in attendance for the first time at the imperial consilium and that was around 5 or 4 BC. As Gaius departed Rome to quell a Parthian revolt towards the end of 2 BC it seems improbable that he could have attended a consilium in 1 BC.

Julias
Philip as Tetrarch renamed a city Julias after Julia, the only daughter of Augustus, in 2 BC, so he must have succeeded his father prior to that year. In addition, as she was exiled to the island of Pandateria in that same year for adultery and alleged treason, it would hardly have been an appropriate name to use afterwards.

Varus, the Governor of Syria
According to Josephus, just after the death of Herod the governor of Syria was Varus and this can be dated to between 6 and 4 BC. This has also been confirmed from coins of that time.

Barnes conclusion was that Herod died on the seventh day of the Jewish month of Kislev in 5 BC, this day being reserved as a Jewish holiday commemorating the death of Herod. It equates to 6 December 5 BC in our calendar which is not too far away from 13 March 4 BC.

A Later Death?

The determination of the year 4 BC is however complicated by earlier references of Josephus to the reign of Herod. He explains that Herod died thirty-seven years after he had been made king by the Romans which is believed to have been either 41 or 40 BC, therefore giving us 4 or 3 BC, so no real problem there. However he also states that Herod, after having seized Jerusalem, commenced his reign after Antigonus was executed and that he reigned for thirty-four years following this. Antigonus had been taken to Antioch where he was imprisoned but it was not until the following year that he was put to death, which is 36 BC. Apparently the Jews would not accept Herod as king until Antigonus was dead so therefore taking 36

BC as the start of the reign minus thirty-four years implies 2 BC as the year of his death. Now it is possible that Josephus may have used the Jewish 'inclusive' method of measurement whereby both the start and end years would have been included as whole years, rather than fractional years, so this could account for an additional year. This would bring us to 3 BC in the calculation – but still a year out.

The inclusive theory was challenged by a biblical scholar, Ormond Edwards, in *A New Testament Chronology of the Gospels* (1972). Having studied *Antiquities*, carefully noting the length of reigns of earlier kings of Judea, he came to the conclusion that Josephus was actually very accurate in his calculations and did not use the inclusive system of measurement. If this is the case it takes our calculation of the date of Herod's death forward to 2 BC, approaching the date of a lunar eclipse in 1 BC.

Edwards, and also the theologian Florian Riess, argue that there were too many events taking place in the account of Josephus, between the date of the eclipse, on 13 March and the Passover, on 10 April 4 BC, to have been completed within such a short time interval, this subsequently becoming known as the 'impossible month'. As he calculated that all the events involving Herod would have taken about eighty-six days, the eighty-eight-day period in 1 BC provided a sufficient window of time. Both Edwards and Riess therefore concluded that Herod died about three years later, sometime between 10 January and 8 April 1 BC and they have attracted considerable support from some historians. One of these was Ernest L. Martin, who in his book *The Birth of Christ Recalculated*, and more recently in *The Star that Astonished the World*, scrutinised the results of Barnes' research. To support his reasoning that Herod died in 1 BC, he reassessed the main points raised by Barnes as outlined above.

Martin suggested that Herod's eldest son, Antipater, may have been made a co-regent with him sometime in the year 4 BC whenever he was made heir to the throne. This co-regency period would only have been brief however as Antipater departed for Rome and, as we have seen, was later executed by his father. He claimed that the three surviving sons, Archelaus, Herod Antipas and Philip came to power in 1 BC upon Herod's death, and later awarded themselves additional years of sovereignty for political motives, 'antedating' the length of their individual reigns backwards in time to 4 BC, coinciding with the commencement of this so called co-regency, or whenever the sons Aristobulus and Alexander were put to death. In support of this theory it is claimed that the earliest coins for any one of the three surviving sons are found to be dated regnal year 5. He also proposed that Josephus may not have been aware of this antedating.

Martin assumed that Gaius may have made an early return to Rome from his campaigns in the east, as peace was quickly restored with the Parthian king. Consequently this may have given him the opportunity to consult with Archelaus and Herod Antipas when they presented their claims to the throne of Judea.

The renaming of a city to Julias could have been wrongly attributed to Julia by Josephus and may instead have been named after Julius Caesar. Apparently a number of Roman towns or cities were constructed throughout the empire and named Colonia Julia or simply Julia. Likewise Fortress Antonia was named after Mark Antony by Herod. Josephus also incorrectly thought that another city called Julia was named after the wife of Augustus although her name was actually Livia.

Martin suggests that Varus may have secured a second term as governor about the year 1 BC as there remains some uncertainty as to who occupied the post at that time. This is supported by reference to an inscription, discovered in 1764 and located about 1.5 miles from the ancient villa of Varus, near Tivoli, which refers to a man who had been twice governor of Syria.

It has to be said, however, that Martin's arguments are not convincing and there is considerable doubt as to whether Antipater ever became a co-regent in the first place. His antedating theory consequently does not attract a great deal of support and is not helped by the fact that coins of the second and third centuries indicate the founding of a city known as Paneas by Philip in the year 3 BC. Also it seems most unlikely that Gaius would ever have returned to Rome as quickly as is indicated. As for the inscription regarding Varus no-one is quite sure as to whom it is referring, although it has been speculated that it is more likely to be Piso. It all sounds like a case of wishful thinking on the part of the author and the manipulation, or twisting, of historical facts in order to accommodate a later time period for the death of Herod and the birth of Jesus.

An Earlier Death?

There may be a case for the period between the 15 September 5 BC eclipse, and the Passover on 10 April 4 BC for the date of Herod's demise, a long period of 207 days. One of the reasons for this is the argument put forward by Edwards, Riess and Martin suggesting that there were too many events that could have been squeezed into the much shorter period between 13 March and 10 April 4 BC. Also the eclipse of the Moon on 15 September 5 BC was total as opposed to a relatively insignificant partial in 4 BC and its time of occurrence was more favourable, with totality lasting from about 9.30 p.m. to 11.15 p.m. local time. Anyone who has ever viewed an eclipse of the Moon will appreciate that the spectacle of a partial comes nowhere near to that of a total eclipse. With a partial eclipse there is little colour visible in the shadow of the Earth on the Moon. A total eclipse on the other hand can produce vivid shades of brown, orange or red depending upon prevailing conditions within the Earth's atmosphere. The eclipse of 4 BC was only about 36 per cent partial and occurred when most people were asleep, only becoming visible around midnight and finishing around four o'clock in the morning.

A Bad Omen

Unfortunately Josephus does not let us know as to whether the eclipse was total or partial, but then as the saying goes, beggars can not be choosers. But why did he mention the eclipse in the first place? It is in fact the only time that he ever refers to an eclipse and it may simply be put down to the fact that it coincided exactly with the executions of Matthias and his compatriots. However it seems that any eclipse at that time was considered as an unhealthy omen. In this particular instance it was recognised as a sign of Herod's impending doom, but probably with hindsight; in other words after the event, and it is in this context that it is recorded. The fact that it may have been only partial, and not particularly conspicuous, would therefore have been irrelevant.

The Massacre of the Innocents

There is a further time parameter to be taken into consideration when attempting to determine the latest possible date of Jesus' birth. This equates to the age of Christ whenever Herod allegedly ordered the massacre of the innocents, as this is the last mention in the Bible of the living Herod. After the visit by the Magi, Herod would have been extremely anxious and concerned, and when they failed to report back to him with details of Jesus' location, he became enraged, issuing instructions that the children/boys from two years and younger in Bethlehem and the surrounding district should be slain. To remind ourselves of the text in Matthew 2:16:

> Then Herod, when he saw that he was mocked of the wise men, was exceedingly wroth, and sent forth, and slew all the children that were in Bethlehem, and in all the coasts thereof, from two years old and under, according to the time which he had diligently enquired of the wise men.

The actual number of infants of two years and under may not have been that many as Bethlehem was only a small town in those days and its population may not have exceeded 1,000. The number of boys of such age may well have been less than ten. This compares to later Christian writers who claimed that thousands were slaughtered. Josephus makes no reference to this event which has led many to the conclusion that it never happened in the first place. Against this argument we have to bear in mind that in the light of Herod's other 'activities' it may have seemed relatively insignificant and probably not worthy of mention. In any case the accounts of Josephus regarding Herod's reign do appear to contain a number of omissions, contradictions and irregularities and he does not mention anything in relation to the birth of Christ. This may be due to the possibility that he did not want to be associated with the new religion of Christianity as he was actually writing for the Emperor Titus and did not want to run the risk of persecution. It seems more likely though, that Josephus simply did not know about any such massacre. As the Jewish mistress of Titus, Berenice, was descended from the Hasmoneans, who had been the enemies of Herod in the past, it stands to reason that it would have been in his interests to record all of Herod's dark deeds that were known to him and therefore had he been aware of the massacre he would have recorded it.

A Non-Event

It seems quite feasible that the massacre did not happen and that the author of Matthew, writing perhaps about ninety years or so after the event was supposed to have occurred, may possibly have had access to an oral tradition that over the years may have gradually become distorted. The origin of the story could have its roots in Herod's executions of his sons Aristobulus and Alexander in 6 BC and Antipater in 5/4 BC. Word-of-mouth descriptions could easily have been distorted and deliberately exaggerated over time, particularly when one considers the resentment and hatred that the Jewish community had for Herod, and his cruelty would have become legendary. Therefore the story may subtly have changed over the decades, with the author perhaps using some literary freedom of what had earlier been darkly whispered in the bazaars or market places of Judea.

The Age of the Child

When the author has Herod using the term 'boys of two years and under', the immediate assumption is that this equates backwards in time to when the star first appeared. Herod would have, quite naturally, associated the date of the reported first appearance of the star with that of Christ's birth. It has been suggested however, that he may not have been certain as to whether this coincided exactly with the birth as the Magi may not have been able to specify this. Therefore when he ordered the massacre he decided to leave nothing to chance and made the order that boys of two and under should be disposed of. This appears to tie in well with Matthew 2:8 when Herod makes reference to 'the young child' when instructing the Magi to search and find the boy. It may therefore be that Jesus was younger than two years old when the order was made. Also, using the 'inclusive' method of measuring that we came across earlier, it could be that the reference to the two years of age could possibly mean just over one year old, as a Jewish child of thirteen months would have been regarded as having attained the age of two. Thirteen months therefore could have represented the maximum age implied in the order.

If we conclude that Jesus was about one to two years old when the Magi failed to return to Herod and that Herod died in late 5 BC or early 4 BC, then the latest possible date of Christ's birth must be either late 7 BC or early 6 BC. This assumes however that Herod died very soon after the Magi failed to return and the massacre of the innocents, which is pre-supposing rather a lot. Matthew does provide further information regarding the time period between Christ's birth and Herod's death when he refers in Ch. 2:13 to Joseph's dream, where he is told by an angel to flee to Egypt and to stay there until told to return.

The Flight into Egypt

Exactly how long would Joseph and his family have stayed in Egypt? For this answer we have to refer to the writing of the third-century Apologist Origen who wrote that they remained in Egypt for about two years and returned to Israel during the first reign of Archelaus, one of the sons of Herod. This is supported by Eusebius and by traditional stories, passed down over generations. It is however disputed by some and in the *De Vita Christi*, a Franciscan manuscript covering the life of Christ and dating to around the year 1300, it is stated that they remained there for seven years. To further complicate things, Matthew also implies, in Ch. 2:22 that there may have been hesitation on the part of Joseph to return to Judea on hearing that Archelaus had become the new ruler, so that we cannot simply assume that they came back shortly after the death of Herod.

A Matthean Time-Frame for Christ's Birth

We can now attempt to determine a time-frame for Christ's birth based upon the writings within Matthew and using the following assumptions:

1. Jesus is between one and two years old prior to the flight to Egypt.

2. He remains there for about two years; therefore he is around three or four when he is brought back into Judea.

3. Herod dies and Archelaus takes the throne, early 4 BC or late 5 BC.

Therefore, from the interpretation of the texts within Matthew, Christ would appear to have been born sometime around 8 BC, with the Magi visiting Herod in 7 BC, although it is safer to give or take one or two years to allow for the fact that we have used 'round' years in this simple calculation, and also for the underlying uncertainties regarding the periods in 1 and 2 above. This then suggests that Christ was born sometime between 10 and 6 BC, with the subsequent Magi visit around 9 to 5 BC.

The above assumes, of course, that the account in Matthew has some historical legitimacy. As just seen however, it is unlikely that the massacre of the innocents actually ever happened. This consequently raises severe doubts regarding the flight into Egypt, as this was supposedly a direct response to the warning of such an event. Nevertheless it is presumed that the author is still intimating that there is some time interval between the birth of Jesus and the death of Herod, the duration of which remains uncertain. However there are also a number of other biblical clues to be examined and these are dealt with in the following chapter.

4
WHEN WAS JESUS BORN?

It is possible to investigate further implied clues within the New Testament which may or may not help us to confirm the year of Christ's birth, as indicated by Matthew's Gospel and outlined in the previous chapter. This in turn will provide us with a reliable time-frame within which we can begin our search for the elusive star.

The Census

Luke 2:1–5 refers to a census carried out on behalf of the Emperor Augustus which coincided with the birth of Christ. If we assume that this reference has some historical accuracy then, if we can identify the date of the census to which Luke is referring, it would seem that we will have an immediate answer as to when Christ was born.

There are severe problems however. It has been argued that Luke's inclusion of the census in his birth narrative was introduced merely as a device in order to present a reason as to why Joseph and Mary should travel to Bethlehem. This was in order to satisfy the prophecy in Micah which seemed to indicate that the Messiah would be born in the ancestral town of David. It has been suggested that the author of Luke did not take sufficient care to corroborate the dates of the census and that of Christ's birth. Over the centuries attempts have been made to reconcile the difficulties posed by Luke's reference to the census and efforts made to identify such an event which fits in within the time-frame of the birth as indicated by Matthew.

Augustus ordered three censuses during his reign as Emperor (27 BC–AD 14), each of which is supported by contemporary records – that of 28 BC, 8 BC and AD 14. The first, of 28 BC, was carried out when he was still known as Octavian. Some historians have argued that the purpose of these censuses were for the registration only of Roman citizens, and as Joseph was definitely not a Roman citizen, none of them could be the census to which Luke is referring. There were also censuses carried out for non-citizens of Rome for taxation purposes and there are various records of provincial censuses carried out under Augustus, probably the most well documented being that of AD 6. However there appears to be no record of such a census in Judea around the time that we believe Christ was born.

It is possible that the census to which Luke refers may have related to a form of oath of allegiance or obedience to Augustus rather than a census for taxation, and it is interesting to note that the original Greek translation of Luke does not mention or imply that it was for taxation purposes. In *Antiquities*, Josephus refers to some form of act of allegiance to Augustus, stating that 'when all the people of the Jews gave assurance of their goodwill to Caesar, and to the king's government, these very men [Pharisees] did not swear [the oath], being about six thousand!' From the context in which it is written, it would seem that this census took place about one year prior to the death of Herod, which would imply late 6 BC or early 5 BC.

Quirinius

A major problem arises from Luke 2:2 which states that Quirinius was governor of Syria. However, Quirinius did not become established as governor of Syria until AD 6 although it is possible that he was governor on a temporary basis between 3 and 2 BC, but even this is still after the death of Herod. It seems possible that the confusion regarding Quirinius as governor of Syria has arisen from a misinterpretation of the original Greek Hellenistic text of Luke and in particular the translation of the word for first, '*protos*' in Luke 2:2. A biblical scholar, E.V. Hulse, had indicated that translation of this word may have been incorrectly interpreted as 'first' when it really means 'former' or 'prior'. If this is the case then the text should read, 'This census took place before the one when Quirinius was governor of Syria.' The author of Luke was clearly well aware of the AD 6 census as he again mentions it in Acts 5:37 stating that it happened '…in the thirty-seventh year of Caesar's victory over Antony at Actium', which equates to AD 6.

The Census of 8 BC

So exactly which census is Luke referring to? Is it the census of 8 BC, originally thought to have been only for Roman citizens, or is it the oath of allegiance to Augustus? It now seems quite possible that the census of 8 BC did not after all exclude Roman citizens and that Jews were to be included. The reference in Luke 2:1 implies that the whole world was called to be registered by the decree, suggesting that it was not necessarily designed only for Roman citizens. Whilst the term 'whole world' is obviously an exaggeration it probably refers to the known Roman world, in which case it incorporated all the countries which had been conquered by Rome.

The Jewish state had to pay tribute to Rome ever since Jerusalem fell to Pompey in 63 BC. Although the sovereignty of Herod as a client king was respected by Augustus, he was still answerable to Rome. Consequently any taxation decree by Rome had to be honoured by Herod, even though it was distasteful, and it was he who would ultimately be responsible for carrying it out. As a result it would be administered under Jewish custom, meaning that subjects would have to present themselves at their traditional place of family origin, whether convenient or not. It is for this reason that Luke has Joseph and Mary travelling to Bethlehem.

The census of 8 BC may therefore have been effectively a registration for taxation purposes. It is possible that there could have been a delay of a year or so between the actual decree and the completion of the census, possibly as a result of poor communications. Augustus would also have allowed a certain length of time for the decree to be carried out, so although it was made in 8 BC, it may not have been completed until 6 BC. To support this theory historical records tell us that

Quirinius was an emperor's legate, that is a form of administrator for financial matters, around 5/6 BC under Sentius Saturninus who was the governor of Syria. Also the early Christian historian Tertullian attributed the census under Quirinius instead to Sentius Saturninus; in *Adversus Marcion*, 4:19.10, he tells us:

> There is historical proof that at this very time a census had been taken in Judea by Sentius Saturninus, which might have satisfied their inquiry respecting the family and the descent of Christ.

The author of Luke may simply have been misinformed as to who exactly was in charge in Syria at that time. It is clear however that he had shortcomings as an historian. His works, which included Acts, undoubtedly lacked a certain amount of historical precision. Brown mentions an example which can be found in Acts 5:36 where Gamaliel in the mid-AD 30s makes reference to a past revolt by Theudas which did not in fact take place until the AD 40s. He then has Gamaliel refer to a revolt by Judas the Galilean (in AD 6) as though it came after Theudas' revolt.

Completion of the 8 BC census may therefore have been as late as 6 BC and this would have been followed shortly afterwards by the oath of allegiance to Caesar either in the same year or possibly in the year following. Either way, for our purpose, it is not too critical which census the author of Luke is referring to as both probably took place within about two years of one another and we have identified an approximate period – namely between 8 and 6 BC.

A Census in 3 or 2 BC ?

There has been a suggestion that there may have been a census or oath of allegiance to Augustus during the period 3 to 2 BC. This was the view taken by Martin, who as we saw in the previous chapter attempted to make a case for the death of Herod in 1 BC. He referred to the Christian historian, Paulus Orosius (375–420), who made reference to a census or an oath of allegiance to Caesar in the year 2 BC, in his *Seven Books of History Against the Pagans*. In book 6: 21.6 he wrote:

> In the year 752 after the founding of the city of Rome [equating to 2 BC] ... Caesar ordered that the first census to be taken in each and every province and that every man be recorded. God deemed it right to be seen as, and became a man. Christ was therefore born at this time and at his birth was immediately recorded on the Roman census.

Martin implies that a combined census and oath of allegiance to Augustus may have been carried out in connection with the bestowal of the title *pater patriac*, meaning 'father of his country', by the senate on 5 February 2 BC. This was related to Augustus becoming sixty years of age, being marked with many celebrations. He also claimed that Saturninus was the governor of Judea between 4 and 2 BC, whilst

Quirinius was procurator and as such responsible for the census. This then made everything tie up neatly both with the Gospel of Luke and the writings of Tertullian.

Consideration has to be given however to the fact that Orosius was a Christian historian and therefore may have been inclined to distort or twist historical figures and events for his own purpose, in this instance of making it appear that the census mentioned in Luke took place in 2 BC. Such accounts have to be viewed as less reliable than those of Josephus who was writing over 300 years earlier and in a relatively unbiased fashion. This obvious bending or re-shaping of historical facts to make them fit in with the narratives within the Gospels is, unfortunately, something which has continued until this present day.

Other Clues?

Is there any further information to be extracted from the Bible which may provide other hints as to the year in which Christ was born? Going further on through the Gospels there is found a reference to the age of Jesus following his baptism by John the Baptist in Luke 3:23:

> And Jesus himself began to be about thirty years of age, being [as was supposed] the son of Joseph ...

How was the original author able to determine this? It may have been from reports passed down concerning the actual physical appearance of Christ but it seems more likely that it was based upon the fact that at this age the Levites qualified for ministerial service and the original author may simply have assumed that Christ was also around that age. If this is the case then Christ would have to have been at least thirty, or twenty-nine if we use the inclusion method, meaning that he would have been in his thirtieth year. It should, however, be mentioned that Jesus himself was not a Levite, and instead would have been regarded as originating from the tribe of Judah.

The Year of Baptism

Earlier, Luke 3:1–2 gives us an indication as to the year that Jesus was baptised, by John, prior to beginning his ministry:

> Now in the fifteenth year of the reign of Tiberius Caesar, Pontius Pilate being governor of Judea, and Herod being tetrarch of Galilee, and his brother Philip tetrarch of Ituraea and of the region of Trachonitis, and Lysanias the tetrarch of Abilene, Annas and Calaphas being the high priests, the word of God came unto John the son of Zacharias in the wilderness ...

This is very useful as it is known that Tiberius became Emperor on 19 August AD 14 following the death of Augustus. Therefore, depending upon whether the

Julian or regnal year calendar was used by Luke, the fifteenth year of Tiberius was
1 January to 31 December AD 29, or between 19 August AD 28 and 18 August AD
29. Just to complicate things, Tiberius became a joint ruler of Judea with Augustus
in the year AD 11; however as Luke specifically only refers to Tiberius it is widely
assumed that he is referring to the period after Augustus' death.

The Start of the Ministry

How soon after being baptised did Christ begin his ministry? Perhaps the information
available on John the Baptist may help to provide this. The general opinion amongst
theologians is that, on the basis of the synoptic Gospels and particularly Luke 3:1 and
2, John was executed upon the orders of Herod Antipas around the year AD 29–30.
This, of course, is not Herod the Great but his son, born in 20 BC, who ruled the
tetrarch of Galilee and Petra from 4 BC to AD 39 when Emperor Caligula banished
him due to his ambitions to become king. The Gospel of Mark now provides us with
an indicative clue in 6:14 in which Herod Antipas refers to Jesus:

> And King Herod heard of Him; [that is Jesus, for his name was spread abroad]
> and he said, That John the Baptist was risen from the dead, and therefore mighty
> works do show forth themselves in him.

This suggests that the ministry of Jesus did not commence or at least that he had
not become well known until after the death of John the Baptist. It is to some extent
contradicted by Matthew 11:2ff, Luke 7:18ff and John 4:1 and 2, which clearly
indicate that John was still alive when Jesus was active. Therefore the assumption
that Christ's ministry began around AD 28 or 29 seems reasonable.

Zerubbabel's Temple

Another clue is supplied by John 2:20, which refers to the first Passover during
the ministry of Jesus, and tells us that this happened in the forty-sixth year of
the reconstruction of Zerubbabel's Temple, also known as the Inner Temple, in
Jerusalem. It is thought that this began around 20 or 19 BC. This would therefore
imply that the ministry began earlier, around the year AD 26. Close, but not a
perfect fit. But it would fit if we accepted the earlier year for the commencement of
the reign of Tiberius, namely AD 11, instead of AD 14.

The Year of the Crucifixion

The year of the start of the ministry can be confirmed by what is known about
the year of crucifixion. All the Gospels agree that the crucifixion happened on a
Friday with John specifying that it was the day of preparation for the Passover. As
mentioned earlier in Chapter 3 this would suggest 14 Nisan. Within the accepted

time-frame this occurred on a Friday in the years AD 30 on 7 April and AD 33 on 3 April. Whilst John suggests that the ministry of Jesus lasted over three years the other three Gospels indicate that the ministry only lasted a year and a few months, these periods being calculated by reference to the number of Jewish feasts and fasts mentioned in each Gospel. If we assume that Matthew, Mark and Luke are correct (as they have a majority of three against one) and that the ministry lasted for over one year, then it would imply that Christ was crucified on Friday 7 April AD 30 with baptism and commencement of ministry happening in either AD 28 or 29.

A Problem with the Age of Jesus

If Luke's estimate of Christ's age at baptism is taken as thirty, we are left with Christ having been born in 1 or 2 BC. This is far too late for as we have seen Herod died in either 5 or 4 BC. To complicate matters further, later in John 8:57 we find that the Jews respond to Jesus by saying to him 'you are not yet fifty years old'. This implies that Jesus was in his forties when this statement was made, this assumption also being made by Irenaeus, an early Christian writer. The statement precedes the miracle of the healing of the blind man (a beggar), so it is obviously some time prior to the crucifixion. If we estimate from this that Jesus was, say forty-six, a completely arbitrary age for our purpose, by the time of crucifixion, and that this happened in AD 33, as is implied by John when he refers to Christ's ministry lasting for over three years, then we end up with the birth of Christ as 13 BC, which is well outside all our previous calculations.

Could it be that Luke's reference to Jesus as being 'about thirty' was based upon Christ's physical appearance and that he looked considerably younger than he actually was? If Jesus really was the Messiah it stands to reason that he may not have aged in the same way as other men age, being perfect, unblemished and free of corruption. However we also have to bear in mind that John's writings are not as old as those of the other three Gospels and presumably not as reliable.

It seems likely that Luke's age of Christ of 'about thirty' at baptism is simply an under-estimate and many historians and theologians agree on this point. Therefore we could allow perhaps up to an additional five years onto that age, so if Christ was then about say, thirty-five in the year 28/29, he would have been born around 7 or 6 BC.

An Eclipse of the Sun?

A further indication of the date of the crucifixion may be found in Luke 23:44–45:

> And it was about the sixth hour, and there was a darkness over all the earth until the ninth hour.
> And the Sun was darkened. And the veil of the temple was rent in the midst.

Could this indicate a total eclipse of the Sun or perhaps a severe thunderstorm? Some modern versions of the Bible do actually use the word 'eclipsed'. To support their interpretation the Apocryphal Gospel of Peter refers to the same event, stating, 'Many went about with lamps supposing it was night and fell down.' So was there was a total eclipse of the Sun around the year AD 30 visible from Jerusalem? Well, nearly! According to NASA calculations, which are extremely accurate, there was such an eclipse on 24 November AD 29 that was almost total from Jerusalem, commencing in the morning at 7.40 a.m. with a maximum coverage of the Sun of 97 per cent at about 9.00 a.m. and finishing at around 10.30 a.m. However, this was still only partial, but there would nevertheless have been an appreciable reduction in light, and a considerable darkening of the sky may have been discerned, particularly if it had been cloudy. The eclipse was actually total not very far away to the north of the Sea of Galilee, the line of totality being shown on the map below. It would have lasted only for about two minutes, as opposed to Luke's incredible description that it persisted for three hours! Consequently if Luke is describing an eclipse of the Sun he is obviously greatly exaggerating, probably in an attempt to retain the interest of the reader, whilst at the same time emphasising the gravity of the situation. If the

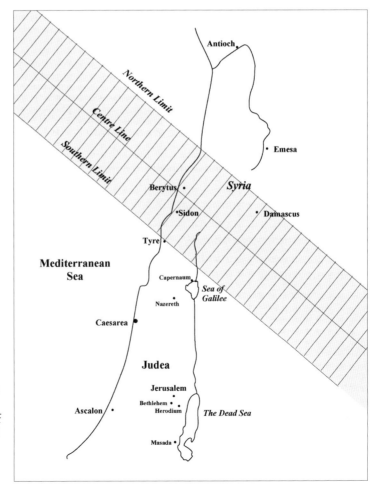

The line of totality of the solar eclipse of 24 November AD 29 which crossed close to the Sea of Galilee. (Prepared and provided courtesy of Nic Leitch)

eclipse did coincide with the crucifixion, which seems very unlikely, then this date, 24 November AD 29, may be substituted for 7 April AD 30 as mentioned above, the difference being only in the region of three and a half months.

The Year of the Birth

A summary is now made of the calculations of Christ's date of birth based upon the information gathered so far in respect of the writings within Luke and John:

	Luke	John
Year of crucifixion	AD 29/30 (April 7 AD 30?) aged 31/32	AD 32/33 (April 3?) aged 46
Length of ministry	A year and a few months	3 years and a few months
Year of Baptism	AD 28/29 aged about 30	AD 28/29 aged, say, 42 (no more than 50)
Year of birth	2/1 BC	13 BC

From the above it can be seen that based upon the writings in Luke, the year of Christ's birth is 2/1 BC. However, substituting the age thirty at baptism to, say, thirty-five, which is an arbitrary estimate, the year of birth goes back to 7/6 BC. Using the writings in John we arrive at the year 13 BC, which assumes that Christ was aged about forty-six at the date of crucifixion.

Perhaps revised models should be introduced in an attempt to produce the most realistic scenario. This involves a compromise between Luke's description that Christ was 'about thirty' and also the date that we have taken for that of his baptism. Earlier we assumed that Luke, when referring to the length of Tiberius' reign, meant that relating to the period after the death of Augustus suggesting that Christ's baptism was around the year AD 29/28. This assumption is now changed to take into consideration the fact that Tiberius ruled over Judea jointly with Augustus, commencing from AD 11, rather than in his sole right from AD 14. At the same time it is assumed that Christ at the age of baptism was 'about thirty' as indicated within Luke.

A further consideration is now made to the length of Christ's ministry. It is difficult to accept the implication in the Gospels of Matthew, Mark and Luke that this only lasted for a year and a few months. Considering all the events which happened during Christ's ministry, between his baptism and the crucifixion, it seems unlikely that they all happened within such a short space of time. Therefore the inclination is to accept the indication in John's Gospel that the ministry of Christ actually lasted for over three years. This has been determined by reference to the number of Passovers mentioned in John during the ministry, and these may be summarised as follows:

1. The period from the baptism to the first Passover (John 2:13).

2. The second Passover (John 4:35 & 5:1). There is no reference to this in Matthew, Mark or Luke.

3. The third Passover (John 6:4). Again, there is no mention of this in the other Gospels.

4. The final Passover (John 11:55).

This assumption is reflected in the model below, in the second column. The implication is that Christ was born sometime between 4 and 5 BC. The determination of this year depends, of course, upon our interpretation of Christ's age at baptism.

An alternative model, in the third column below, assumes that the year of baptism was AD 28/29 being based upon the reasoning that the reign of Tiberius commenced in AD 14 rather than AD 11. The age of Christ has been uplifted at that year to be thirty-three, being based upon the average between thirty and the upper age limit of our interpretation of the description 'about thirty', which had been taken as thirty-five. So an older age for Christ has simply been substituted for a later date for his baptism.

Year of crucifixion	AD 29/30 (April 7 AD 30?) aged about 33/34	AD 32/33 (April 3?) aged 36/37
Length of ministry	3 years and a few months	3 years and a few months
Year of baptism	AD 25/26 aged 'about 30'	AD 28/29 aged, say, 33
Year of birth	5/4 BC	5/4 BC

The conclusion is that the revised models indicate that Christ was born sometime around the years 5 to 4 BC, although this is a little later than that indicated in the previous chapter based upon Matthew's Gospel. The main problem, however, is that the precise age of Jesus when he commenced his ministry is unknown and it is possible to arrive at any year from about 13 BC through to around 4 BC depending upon our guess as to how old he was at that particular moment in time.

Early Records

The first known records that make reference to the year of the birth of Jesus date from the late second and early third centuries and were documented by early Christian writers. Irenaeus and Tertullian both designated the birth to the forty-first year of the reign of Augustus and assuming that this began when he became a consul in August 43 BC, then the year implied would be 2 BC. Tertullian also referred to Christ being born twenty-eight years after the death of Cleopatra and fifteen years prior to the death of Augustus. As Cleopatra died in August 30 BC and Augustus in August AD 14, this confirmed a year in the region of 2 BC or perhaps slightly later.

Clement of Alexander pointed to January 2 BC whereas another Christian writer, Africanus, indicated that it was either 3 or 2 BC. All are therefore consistent in suggesting to us a period hovering around the year 2 BC. However, consideration has to be given to the assumption that they were relying primarily upon the information as provided within the Gospel of Luke and not upon historical fact.

The astronomer David Hughes in his book, *The Star of Bethlehem Mystery*, has examined both early and modern opinions as to the birth year of Christ. From a summary he has determined that the early historians tend to favour a date that clusters around the years 3 and 2 BC, whereas more modern writers prefer a date some three years earlier at around 6 BC.

Was Jesus Born in AD 6?

It should be mentioned that there is a minority opinion that considers that Luke's reference to the census under Quirinius indicates that Christ was actually born around AD 6 to 7. In order to make this theory feasible the assumption is made that the reference to the birth having taken place during the reign of King Herod i.e. Herod the Great, as indicated in Matthew is based entirely upon Midrashim in that it represents a reformulation of Old Testament stories and other non biblical narratives, assembled together in such a way to create the whole infancy episode. In other words it is accepted that Matthew's account has little or no historical background.

When Luke in 1:5 begins his introduction to the birth of John the Baptist as having taken place 'in the days of Herod, King of Judea' it is generally assumed that he is referring to Herod the Great. However, this has, in the past, also been attributed to Archelaus, one of his surviving sons, who reigned as King of Judea from 4 BC to AD 6. The grounds for this designation were first suggested by J. D. M. Derrett in *Further Light on the Narrations of the Nativity* in which he pointed out that the name Herod was substituted for the name Archelaus on coins issued during his reign and also in *Commentaries* by Dio Cassius, the Roman historian. This raises the possibility that Luke's reference to the birth of John the Baptist took place close to the end of Archelaus' reign, around AD 6, and that Jesus was subsequently born six months later, after the deposition of Archelaus during the Roman occupation, with Quirinius organising the census in the same year, or the year afterwards.

Another possibility is that Luke, by connecting the births of John the Baptist and Jesus is not reflecting historical fact but theology. It may be that Luke (as well as Mark) regarded John the Baptist as representing a return of Elijah, sent again by God to Earth in order to herald the coming of the Messiah. It has therefore been suggested that whilst John the Baptist was born during the reign of Herod the Great, Jesus was born some considerable time later during the census of Quirinius.

Such theories run up against the problem created by Luke 3:1 and 3:23 which state that Jesus was about thirty years old when he was baptised by John and that this occurred during the fifteenth year of Tiberius' reign, implying, as seen earlier, either AD 25/26 or AD 28/29. It has been proposed that this represents an inaccuracy and it gives rise to a further discrepancy regarding the date of the subsequent fate of John the Baptist. As mentioned earlier, John appears to have been executed not long after having baptised Jesus. This was a result of his public criticism of the marriage of Herod Antipas, the Tetrarch of Galilee and Perea, and Herodias who had divorced his half-brother, also known as Herod. Herod Antipas' repudiation of his first wife, who was an Arabian princess, subsequently led to a war with the Nabataean Arabs. An independent account of these events is provided by Josephus in *Antiquities*, xviii, 5, 1–2, writing that Herod's subsequent defeat by the Arabians was viewed by the Jews as a reprisal by God for his actions against John:

> Some of the Jews thought that the destruction of his army came from God, and that very justly, as a punishment for what they did against John who was called the Baptist.

This defeat took place shortly before the death, in March AD 37, of Tiberius. A natural assumption therefore would be to consider that John was executed within a short period prior to this date, but this then would be in conflict with AD 26 or 29 as suggested earlier by Luke.

If we are to attempt to reconcile these dates we would have to assume that the Arabians must have delayed a considerable period of time before deciding to reap their revenge, and the defeat of Herod Antipas must have been attributed by the Jews to an event which must have happened at least seven or eight years earlier. However as D. E. Nineham suggests in *Saint Mark*, 'as we know nothing of the attendant circumstances, neither of these possibilities can be ruled out'.

Now, it is known that Pontius Pilate was the prefect of Judea from AD 27 to 37 as Josephus tells us that his procuratorship corresponded with the final ten years of the reign of Tiberius (*Antiquities*, xviii, 4). That at least provides us a parameter within which we have to remain. Independent confirmation that Christ was crucified on the orders of Pilate are to be found in the writings of the first-century Roman historian Tacitus, who states that 'Christus, the founder of the name, was put to death by Pontius Pilate, procurator of Judea in the reign of Tiberius'. Consequently if John the Baptist had been put to death say, in AD 35, then Jesus must have been crucified in the following year, during the Passover, assuming that his ministry lasted for just over a year. This would fit in with Luke 3:23 which states that Jesus was about thirty at baptism, since if he was born in AD 6 then he would have been around twenty-nine years old, or thirty if we use the inclusion method.

Such proposals were put forward in the 1960s by Hugh Schonfield, a British biblical scholar specialising in the New Testament and taken up more recently by Michael Baigent in *The Jesus Papers* in an attempt to support his theory that Christ survived crucifixion in AD 36 and proceeded to live on past the year AD 45. Not surprisingly, he claims that the star of Bethlehem was Messianic in nature, and not astronomical, stating the following:

The star is the Messianic symbol of the line of David. The star of Bethlehem can also be termed 'the Messiah of Bethlehem'. This would suggest that we need not look for astronomical supernova or stellar conjunctions to explain the arrival of the Magi in Bethlehem, a stronghold of the line of David. It was a matter of dynasty rather than astronomy

The main flaw in such a theory is that it ignores the writings in Matthew that clearly inform us that Christ was born during the reign of Herod the Great, this being supported by the reference to the return of his family from Egypt after Herod's death, during the reign of Archelaus. Baigent relies instead on Luke who was, as suggested earlier, not a historian and who appears to have simply used the census as an excuse to have Mary and Joseph travelling to Bethlehem so that we find Jesus, as the Messiah, being born in the town as prophesied in Micah. However, it is of course quite possible that Luke was accurate about the census, or enrolment, except for his reference to Quirinius and that he may well have been referring to a previous event, as indicated earlier.

To support his argument Baigent states that the marriage of Herod Antipas and Herodias took place in AD 35 'as far as can be ascertained'. This is presumably based upon Josephus' account which indicates that the war with the Nabataean Arabs took place around AD 36 or 37. However it may well be that there was a considerable delay in time between the marriage and the war due to other political factors, and opinions differ considerably on the actual year of the marriage with some suggesting as early AD 23.

There would seem to be little doubt that Luke in 1:5 is referring to Herod the Great. Josephus and the New Testament do not at any stage refer to Archelaus as Herod and a certain element of common sense would suggest that had the author of Luke meant Archelaus then he would simply have used that name in order to avoid any confusion. Thus when Luke 1:36 refers to the conception of Jesus being six months behind that of John it seems safe to conclude that both were born during the reign of Herod the Great.

The theory that Jesus was born in AD 6 also creates rather too tight a fit when it comes to working out a time scale. If Jesus was in his thirtieth year this would then imply that he was baptised around AD 35/36, so even if the ministry of Jesus did last only a year and a few months, we are presented with the year of AD 37 for the crucifixion. As Pilate ceased to be Prefect in that year then it assumes that this happened just shortly before he left. However, taking the more realistic view that the ministry lasted for over three years, then the crucifixion would have been in AD 39, which does not fit at all, as Pilate would have already packed his bags some two years earlier.

Calendar Problems

It will be clear to the reader that our calendar year does not accurately reflect the number of completed years since the birth of Christ. Our present calendar dates back to AD 525 when a Roman scholar and monk called Dionysius Exigiuus (sometimes known as Dennis the Little), determined the original AD or *Anno Domini*, meaning in the year of our Lord. Originally he had been requested by the leaders of the early Christian church to construct a table of the Easter cycle. This was to update that as prepared by Cyril of Alexander, who died in AD 444, in which he had used the date of death of the Emperor Diocletian, AD 305, as his starting point. Dionysius decided to commence his table from the birth of Christ, finding it inappropriate to have it based upon a pagan emperor who had been responsible for the persecution of Christians. At a stroke he had ended the so called era of Diocletian, at the same time helping to promote Christianity. To calculate the date he measured the reigns of all the Roman emperors and then totalled them. He calculated that the year AD 1 coincided with the Roman year 754, this having been based upon the years since the founding of Rome by Romulus and Remus. Working forward from this he arrived at his current year of AD 525.

Dionysius however made two miscalculations in his determination of his year of AD 525. Firstly, through no fault of his own, he failed to take into consideration the year zero. Such a figure did not exist in those days and it was not until centuries later that it was to be introduced by Arabian mathematicians. Consequently Dionysius in his calculations jumped from 1 BC to AD 1 rather than proceeding from 1 BC to year 0 and then to AD 1, effectively losing one year. The second error he made was in his measurement of the length of time that Augustus reigned as emperor. Basically, he did not take into consideration the fact that Augustus had reigned for four years under his original name of Octavian. Amazingly, this mistake was not discovered until the year 1605 when it was identified by a Polish historian, Laurentius Syslyga.

The effect of both errors meant that Dionysius was out by a total of five years in his determination of the year of Christ's birth. There could, of course, be further errors in his calculations which remain unidentified and which may never be detected. However it is interesting to know that, if we allow for the years that he missed out on, our calendar should read five years later than it actually does. It also means that after taking into consideration the omissions, Dionysius implies a year for Christ's birth of 5 BC.

Christ's Birthday?

Having established a general time-frame for the birth of Christ, is it possible to be more precise and determine the actual time of year that the birth took place? Christians celebrate this on 25 December and this date has been used ever since it was set in the year AD 336 under the auspices of Constantine the Great, the first Christian emperor. However this date was used in order to replace an earlier pagan festival known as *Sol Invictus* which means the unvanquished Sun. This represented a celebration at the completion of the winter solstice, when the Sun started to rise earlier and set later in the sky. The same day was also assumed by Dionysius as that relating to Christ's birth. By substituting Christmas for an old pagan festival, the early Christian church in a sense strengthened its position in that many accepting the celebration would be more inclined to convert to the new religion.

So does the Bible give us any further clues regarding the specific time of year that Jesus was born? One indication comes from Luke 2:8:

> And there were in the same country shepherds abiding in the field, keeping watch over their flocks by night.

It has been suggested that shepherds would not tend their sheep at night during the middle of winter, even if it were in Judea as the conditions there would not have been that dissimilar to our own, with snow a distinct possibility on hillsides. This seems even more likely in the area around Bethlehem which stands about 2,500 feet above sea level. Consequently the sheep may have been kept under shelter during these months. This would be normal practice in preparation for the lambing season which would occur in spring and when the animals would be put out to pasture. Springtime would seem to be the most important time of the year when the shepherds really did have to watch their flocks by night, providing protection against attacks by wild animals and being on hand for the birth of lambs. Although Luke's text does suggest that Jesus may have been born in the spring, between March and May, this theory is not without its critics. They argue that shepherds could have been out at night at any time of the year in order to tend sheep intended for temple sacrifices.

Another clue is provided by John 1:29 and 36, where John the Baptist greets Jesus twice with the words 'The Lamb of God', just prior to baptism. Such a term may be linked to the possibility that Christ was born close to the Passover, whenever unblemished lambs were chosen for sacrifice. On the other hand, of course, he may simply be referring to Christ as the Son of God. Nevertheless Passover time would appear to satisfy the date that Jews anticipated the birth of the Messiah.

A researcher into the star of Bethlehem, Colin Humphries, has suggested another reason why Christ may have been born around Passover. He advises that censuses were not carried out on any one particular day but over a period of time, and as all men were expected to travel to Jerusalem for Passover, Joseph may have decided to effectively 'kill two birds with one stone' and visit Bethlehem for both the census and the Passover, in order to save an extra journey. This would also help to explain why he and Mary had such great difficulty finding a room to stay in, since Bethlehem, being very close to Jerusalem, may have been crowded.

Attempting to calculate a specific date for Christ's birth would seem to raise more questions than it answers, any endeavour at such an exercise being considered far too precarious. However some ancient writers have attempted to determine a specific date, for example Hippolytus (AD 165–235), 2 April; Clement of Alexandria (AD 150–215), 18 November; Epiphanius (AD 315–403), 20 June or 20/21 May. More recent conjectures include that of John Addey, 22 August; G. Mackinley, 20 September; David Hughes, 15 September and Michael Molnar, 17 April. Mark Kidger and Colin Humphries do not give a specific date but suggest sometime in springtime.

5
MYSTERIOUS MAGI

No one knows how many wise men, or Magi, the author of Matthew is referring to when they are mentioned in that Gospel's version of the nativity. The common assumption that there were three has been based simply upon the number of different gifts they bore: gold, frankincense and myrrh. There was obviously more than one as Matthew uses the plural and earlier interpretations as depicted on early Christian artworks have shown varying numbers ranging from only two to as many as eight. Some early Christian writers have mentioned even more, with John Chrysostum, a late-fourth-century Archbishop of Constantinople, suggesting fourteen.

The text recording the visit of the Magi to Jesus shows a remarkable similarity to that recorded in the Old Testament book of Isaiah, which also prophesied the birth of the Messiah. Isaiah 60:1 to 60:6 includes the following:

Arise, shine; for thy light is come, and the glory of the Lord is risen upon you.

... And the Gentiles shall come to thy light, and kings to the brightness of thy rising.

The wealth ... of nations will come to you ... all those from Sheba will come bringing gold and frankincense, and proclaiming the salvation of the Lord.

Did the author of Matthew simply incorporate this prophecy to describe the visit of the Magi? It has been argued that this seems unlikely because he does not refer to them as kings and that this fact helps to reinforce the opinion of some that the whole story is based upon actual events. On the other hand, however, he may have realised that to have described them as kings may have made it so obvious that he was simply contriving a tale in order to satisfy the prophecy. For the time being, however, we will just assume that it is not contrived and that the introduction of the Magi has some historical credibility.

Their Identity

There are many questions that remain to be answered regarding the wise men, or Magi, as mentioned in Matthew. One thing is certain – they definitely were not kings. It was Tertullian who first referred to them as kings around the year AD 207, but it was not until the sixth century that the Christian church formally recognised them as such. Present-day Bibles refer to them as wise men, although the original wording in the Greek text is *Magoi*, which in its English translation has become Magi. In ancient times this word had connotations with the supernatural and sorcery and it has created the modern word magician. It was the Greek historian Herodotus (born 485 BC) who described them as a mysterious religious community who lived as priests amongst the Medes in the sixth century BC close to the shores of the Caspian Sea, which is now part of northern Iran. They later became religious leaders and priests of ancient Persia. Evidence of this can be found by way of fourth-century Christian artwork within the catacombs of Rome which depicts them as wearing pointed caps, cloaks and trousers, which is unquestionably the attire of ancient Persians.

It is also possible that they originated from the ancient city of Babylon, the capital of Babylonia, where over time they had become highly respected, but also feared as they were involved in sacred rituals, incarnations, astrology and the interpretation of dreams. Together with the 'synergon', a group of aristocratic councillors, they became a powerful force and so highly regarded as advisers that they would certainly have had an influential position within the royal court, and this association with royalty could be the reason why they later became described as kings.

In 586 BC Jerusalem was sacked by the Babylonians. The Jews were taken into exile and from that time onwards Babylon became host to a distinctive Jewish colony. Subsequently, whenever the Jews were granted their freedom and came out of captivity, many became merchants and traders utilising the trade routes that stretched from Persia to Jerusalem and elsewhere. Communities of Jews soon developed within all the major caravan towns and cities in the east and because they shared a common language with the Persians, namely Aramaic, many ideas and mythologies would have been exchanged amongst them.

Over time the Jewish prophecies of a saviour king would have become familiar to the Babylonians, and in particular the Magi. Some of the Magi subsequently migrated from Babylon to adjacent countries including Arabia where they became teachers of astronomy and astrology, two subjects which were intertwined and indistinguishable in those days.

Some early Christian writers such as Justin Martyr believed the Magi who visited Jesus travelled from Arabia based upon the reasoning that frankincense and myrrh originated from that region. However, whilst this conclusion seems plausible it does not take into consideration the fact that these commodities were widely traded between neighbouring countries.

Recorded Visitations of Magi

It was not unusual for Magi to travel long distances in order to visit dignitaries in far off countries. For instance, the historians Suetonius, Tacitus and Dio Cassius tell us of impressive processions of Magi, from the east, travelling to Rome led by the Armenian king, Tiridates, in AD 66 in order to pay homage to the Emperor Nero. Interestingly their journey would have taken them through Northern Syria, close to areas associated with early Christianity and where the Gospel of Matthew may possibly have originated. Also, the King of Armenia did not return by the same way he had followed in coming, sailing home by a different route, and this represents a remarkable parallel to the nativity story in Matthew.

In AD 44 Helen, the Queen of Adiabene, which bordered on Parthia, travelled to Jerusalem bringing gifts for people affected by a famine which had devastated the land. Also of great interest, Josephus mentions that Magi, bearing gifts, visited King Herod in 10 BC following the completion of the construction of the Caesarea Maritima.

Zoroastrianism

Underlying the Magi's power was a mysterious religion known as Zoroastrianism, named after its prophet founder Zoroaster. It seems likely that the name Zoroaster originates from the Greek meaning camel handler. Legend has it that he was born in a town called Urmiyah in Persia. We are not sure as to when the religion started, it may be as late as the sixth century BC but it may have begun up to a thousand years earlier. The religion is still in existence today in parts of Iran. Although some of its beliefs, which included the ritual worship of fire, differed from Jewish and early Christian religions, it did have a number of important similarities. These included the belief in a single god known as *Ahura-Mazda*, the resurrection of the body, life after death, the judgement, and most importantly from our perspective, the arrival of a saviour king or Messiah. This is supported by an early Christian manuscript known as the *Arabic Gospel of the Infancy*, which in chapter 7:1 suggests that Zoroaster predicted the birth of Jesus Christ and the journey of the Magi to Bethlehem, stating that 'the Magi arrived from the east in Jerusalem as Zoroaster had predicted'.

The Gifts

Since the Magi would have been aware of the prophecy in Isaiah they would have known to bring with them the gifts of gold and frankincense. Each of the gifts had their own symbolic meaning. Gold, being such a scarce commodity, was the most precious metal in the ancient world and was said to possess magical qualities as its colour never faded and its surface never tarnished. It was considered to have divine properties whilst still being a product of the earth, and as such it symbolised royalty. It may have been mined in Persia but could also have originated from Egypt, Midian, Arabia or possibly Armenia.

Frankincense is a gum or sap extracted from behind the bark of a rare tree from the *Boswellia* family, and when it hardens forms a resin that produces a sweet perfume when heated or set alight. It was so precious that it was literally worth its weight in gold. Because it was used as anointing oil in religious rituals it symbolised the holiness or divinity of Christ. A purified extract of the resin has also been used for thousands of years as a herbal preparation, in order to treat a variety of common ailments, ranging from joint pain to stomach upset.

The gift not mentioned in the prophecy, myrrh, comes from a rare plant known as *commiphura myrrha* and was to be found in southern Arabia. Weight-wise, it was worth about seven times the value of gold, and was prized for its miraculous healing qualities, being used by Persian physicians. It produces a highly fragrant resin and was also used to anoint and embalm the dead and consequently this gift symbolised the future crucifixion and the death of Christ.

Astrologers and Astronomers

There was also a Zoroastrian legend that the Messiah's birth would be announced by the appearance of a star. As astrologers they were ideally placed to interpret the meaning of events in the night sky and in a privileged position to know when and where to travel if and when they felt it appropriate, so when the time came they would be prepared. As astrologers they would have been familiar with the twelve signs of the zodiac and their different meanings. These zodiacal signs were virtually identical to those of today, which are used in horoscopes.

From what we can gather, it seems that it was the Babylonians who were the great astronomers of that time as they kept very detailed records or diaries of events in the night sky. Following excavations, clay tablets – some complete, but most in fragmentary form – have been found, many of which are now housed in the British Museum. They have been dated from about 700 BC to AD 50. Characters were cut in the tablets by using a wedge-shaped tool and this style of writing became known as 'cuneiform script'. They were then oven baked which gave them considerable durability. As they were written in the alphabet of the ancient Sumerians they proved difficult to decipher. However, thanks to the dedication of academics and the fortuitous discovery of some fragments which contained a Greek translation on their opposite sides, they have been successfully translated. The results confirmed that the Babylonians kept detailed records of astronomical events, being described under yearly columns. Many appear to be copies of earlier records, including one known as the Venus Tablet which appears to record astronomical observations of Venus about one thousand years previous. It is probable that they wanted to keep accurate and reliable records of earlier occurrences in order to identify astronomical trends or repetitions of events so that predictions could be made of future movements in the heavens. Their records include accounts of eclipses of the Sun and Moon, occultations, comets and planets.

As for astrology, relatively little information has been obtained from the tablets but this may simply be due to the fact they are so scarce. There are a few which make reference to the astrological effects and predictions of planetary conjunctions known as the Amen texts. However, hardly any mention has been found that makes reference to predicted events outside their own country. Consequently this could imply that the Magi did not come from Babylonia but perhaps neighbouring Persia as suggested earlier. The only problem is that virtually no records have been found of Persian astronomical observations. Given the fact that the Persians had conquered Babylon and Mesopotamia, it would seem most unlikely that they would not have acquired their astronomical and astrological knowledge and beliefs over time.

The Route

Judea was positioned hundreds of miles from Babylon along a well-known trade route. Magi from that country almost certainly would not have travelled on their own as this would have been far too dangerous, and they would probably have joined a caravan, possibly of travelling merchants, for security and protection. Even so such journeys would not have been without dangers – from outlaws and hostile tribes, never mind having to cross parts of an inhospitable desert. However, they probably would not have taken the most direct route, which was straight across the Syrian desert and which would have been about 600 miles. David Hughes has suggested that the Magi would, most likely, have travelled from one oasis to another, taking a more indirect, longer but easier route through the Arabian settlements of Mari, Haleb, Hameth, Kadesh and Damascus, measuring about 800 miles.

Hughes suggests that if instead of travelling from Babylon they came from Persia, then the journey may have been twice as long, the route encompassing the southern part of the Persian Royal Road to Tigranacerta in Armenia, crossing the Euphrates to Antioch and then on to Damascus and finally to Jerusalem. Such a journey may have taken up to a year to complete. This may help to explain why there was such a delay between Christ's birth and the Magi's visit, as indicated in Matthew when Herod ordered the massacre of boys aged two and under and which we earlier interpreted as meaning boys under thirteen months old. The delay of over one year suggests that the Magi did have very far to travel and that Persia, rather than Babylon, was the original starting point.

An Audience with Herod

When the Magi finally arrived in Jerusalem they were summoned to appear before Herod. When they explained that they were on a mission to find the new King of the Jews for they had seen a star in the east, Herod become perturbed. It is clear from Matthew that Herod had not been aware of either the star or its significance. Why was this? There are three possible explanations. Firstly, Herod and his advisers may not simply have had the opportunity to view the star due to prevailing weather conditions. In other words it may have been too cloudy, obscuring its appearance. This seems rather unlikely for if the star or object had been visible for any reasonable length of time eventually weather conditions were bound to have improved, providing clear skies and the chance to witness the occurrence.

The second explanation is that there may have been no-one in the court of Herod who was capable of interpreting the meaning of the star or aware of the true nature of the anticipated Messiah. It is possible that Herod had surrounded himself with advisers who were not professional astrologers and this could be due in some part to the attitude of the Jewish religion towards astrology as the Old Testament had been clearly against its use. It seems that the teaching of astrology by Jews would have been given a low priority in relation to other subjects.

Herod's advisers may simply have been members of the Sanhedrin in which case he would probably have had no astrologers to turn to. It could also be that, although the star was visible, it remained unnoticed due to it being inconspicuous. So perhaps Herod not only lacked qualified astrologers at his court but also astronomers, professional or otherwise.

Another consideration is that Josephus indicates that in the first century BC the Jews did not know what form the Messiah would take or how many there would be. This was confirmed when the Dead Sea Scrolls – discovered in caves near Qumran about twenty miles from Jerusalem – were analysed, suggesting Jewish expectations were not necessarily for a single Messiah, but for a number of Messianic figures.

A third explanation is that Herod did have qualified astrologers or astronomers as his advisers and that they were capable of interpreting the significance of the star. They may have realised that it effectively signalled the birth of a new King of the Jews, and the demise of the old. However Herod at that time was nearing the end of his reign and was of unsound mind, so his reaction to such news was dangerously unpredictable. The fear or paranoia of losing power that he had developed was worsening. His astrologers, fearing for their lives, may have decided that it was safer to keep quiet about the star and its meaning, rather than running the gauntlet by telling him and facing the consequences. They may have been aware of the Old Testament story of Daniel, where in chapter two the Magi of Babylon were summoned before King Nebuchadnezzar in order to explain the meaning of his dreams. When Nebuchadnezzar became unhappy with their interpretations he decided to have them executed, thereby destroying 'the wise men of Babylon'. So it is possible that Herod's astrologers, fearing the worst, may have decided to play safe and say nothing. However, if this had been the case then we might have expected an additional line in Matthew, with Herod questioning his advisers, asking them 'and why was I not told?'

In the East

The term 'in the east' is rather ambiguous – does it mean that the Magi saw the star when they were in the east or that the star itself was positioned in the east, or both? According to David Hughes the original Greek text of Matthew 2:2 says, '*en té anatole*' which means in the east in the singular implying that it is not referring to the location of the Magi. The word *anatole* can be translated as 'rising on high' and for astronomical purposes could be referring to the acronychal rising, whereby a star or planet rises in the east as the Sun, on the opposite side of the sky, sets in the west. The star or planet will then be visible throughout the entire night as it appears to move from east to west in an arc across the sky. When the star or object is exactly opposite in the sky to the Sun they are said to be in opposition.

The word *anatole* however could also imply the 'helical rising' of a star or object. This refers to the earliest appearance of a star at dawn as it emerges above the horizon before disappearing, due to the glare of the rising Sun. Astrologically it was associated with the date of the birth of a child.

Hughes points out that when Herod, having consulted his advisors, asks the Magi, 'and when did the star appear?' the word 'appear' in Greek is *phainesthai*, and in this context, refers to the helical rising of the star, although he accepts that this astronomical event could also be described by the Greek words *epitole* or *phasis*. Therefore, when Herod posed the question he was indirectly asking the Magi, 'And when was the king born?'

Rather a lot depends upon our interpretation of this Greek word *phainesthai*. Various definitions exist and some of these are summarised as follows:

To appear (most common)
To sum up and appear
To show itself
To be in the light
That which stands forth by entering into the light

The word may therefore be interpreted in different ways and whilst it certainly encompasses the term helical rising, it could also be used to describe something which appears other than becoming visible by simply rising above the horizon.

The City of David

When Herod consulted his advisers, after his initial interview with the Magi, they had to remind him, not of the prophecy of Balaam, but that of Micah. As seen earlier, this had indicated that a Messianic figure would emerge from within the House of David and it was interpreted that he would also be born in the ancestral town of Bethlehem.

Following a Star?

At no point does Matthew imply that the Magi followed the star on their journey to Jerusalem, and it may be that, having seen the star or object rising or otherwise, they simply interpreted it as providing a signal for them to travel west to Judea. In fact it is obvious that the star was no longer visible when they arrived in Jerusalem. There is also no indication as to how long they stayed in Jerusalem. It could have been days, weeks or even months. It may of course be that the star reappeared not long after they arrived in Jerusalem. It is also possible that they may have become aware of Herod's mental state and his mood swings, and for this reason it may be reasonable to assume that they would have become anxious to leave Jerusalem at the earliest opportunity.

Fortunately, Herod proceeds to send the Magi on to Bethlehem, with the instruction that once they had found the child to bring him word so that he too may pay him homage. The star or object then seems to have mysteriously reappeared in the sky as they travelled the short distance of about six miles southwards from Jerusalem to Bethlehem. Matthew 2:9 tells us:

When they had heard the king, they departed; and, lo, the star, which they saw in the east, went before them, till it came and stood over where the young child was.

As the journey from Jerusalem may only have taken two to three hours, it seems difficult to believe that the star decided to reappear during this very short interval.

Matthew does not specifically indicate when the star actually reappeared and this may well have happened whilst the Magi were still in Jerusalem.

Not only did the star seem to go before them, it also appears to have stopped and stood over the house where the young child was. Is the author of Matthew simply using artistic license to describe an actual event? Well perhaps to an extent, but as shall be seen later there is an astronomical object which seems to satisfy this rather fantastic description. Filled with joy, the Magi proceeded to enter the house and, finding Mary and the child, they presented Jesus with their gifts of gold, frankincense and myrrh. Then, since they were warned in a dream, they returned to their own country by a different route. They are never mentioned again in the New Testament and appear to have vanished into the mists of time.

Folklore

Through time they have become folklore, with their description becoming elaborated upon over the centuries. It was not long before they were elevated to the status of kings as mentioned earlier. They also acquired names. In eastern tradition the earliest known identifies them as Hormizdah, a King of Persia, Yazdegerd, a King of Saba and Perozadh, a King of Sheba. These names may be attributable to a sixth-century Syrian work known as *The Cave of Treasures*, although it has been suggested that they could have originated as much as two centuries earlier by reference to a Syrian writer known as Ephraem. An Ethiopian Christian work, *The Book of Adam and Eve*, ascribes the names of Hor, King of the Persians; Basanater, King of Saba; and Karsudan, King of the East. In the west they became identified with the more familiar names of Balthazar, Melchior and Gaspar, the earliest reference to these being by way of a translation in Latin from a sixth-century Greek chronicle, known as the *Excerpta Latina Barbari*. Later their physical appearance changed with one Asian, one African and one European. The Venerable Bede, one of the few Saxon scholars whose works have survived, in this instance from the early eighth century, wrote that the Magi mysteriously represented the three parts of the world, namely Asia, Africa and Europe.

Traditionally it was claimed that their remains were discovered in the fourth century and were transported from Persia to Constantinople in AD 490 by the Emperor Zeno. Another legend has it that they were found by St Helena, a Christian relic hunter who was the mother of Constantine the Great. They were later transferred to Milan by St Asacius, where they were housed in the Basilica of the Three Kings. In 1164 their relics were given to the Bishop of Cologne by Emperor Frederick Barbarossa who had plundered Milan during his invasion of Italy. They are presently housed in Cologne Cathedral, which was built in their honour, and are kept within a precious golden casket. Within the cathedral's obituary notice, in its *Calendar of Saints*, is written the following fictional information about them:

> Having undergone many trials and fatigues for the Gospel the three wise men met at Sewa [now Sebaste in Armenia] in AD 54 to celebrate the feast of Christmas.

Thereupon, after the celebration of Mass, they died; St Melchior on 1 January aged 116; St Balthazar on 6 January aged 112; and St Gaspar on 11 January aged 109.

Recent examination of a fragment of a shroud that originally covered their bones has shown that it was made from a very expensive material using silk from China and coloured with a rare dye produced from snails that can be dated to between the second and fourth century AD, its place of origin being present-day Syria. So, unfortunately, they can not represent the relics of our biblical Magi.

The modern impression of the Magi is probably best illustrated through paintings which were influenced by the fresco *The Adoration of the Magi*, by Giotto di Bandone, which has also had its inevitable effect on present-day Christmas cards. They have also found their way onto stage and television productions such as the opera, *Amahl and the Night Visitors*, by the late Carlos Menoti, who was influenced by a painting by Bosch (also known as *The Adoration of the Magi*), and of course school presentations of the nativity. Their story is one of values and moral fulfilment, representing a victory of good over evil. Although their actual existence cannot be verified, it is not difficult to imagine that their account might, in some way, be partly true, given the historical and religious backgrounds of that period in time.

Objectivity

Using an objective approach, however, we have to ask ourselves some difficult questions. Why does Herod assemble and consult the priests and scribes, which would have included the Sanhedrin, when we are aware of the suspicions and opposition that existed between them? Why does Herod not arrange to have the Magi followed in their journey from Jerusalem to Bethlehem? Then, after they have departed, he fails to find where they visited irrespective of the marvellous impression they must have left in such a small town. There is also no historical verification of the slaughter of boys under the age of two. According to Mark 6:14–16, it is clear that Herod Antipas, the son of King Herod, seems to have had no prior knowledge of Jesus: this is despite the efforts supposedly taken against Jesus, as a child, by his father.

Midrash

It has to be said that the introduction of the Magi into the infancy narrative reeks suspiciously of Midrashim, and it seems very doubtful as to whether it incorporates any grains of truth. It is likely that the original inspiration for the story of the Magi is to be found deep in Old Testament themes. Brown suggests that it represents a combination of three different citations. Firstly, the Balaam narrative in Numbers, discussed earlier in Chapter 2, which involves a seer or Magi from the east who prophesied the emergence of a great leader, symbolised by a rising star.

Secondly, the reference to this same rising star may have directed the writer to Isaiah 60:1 which mentioned a rising light in relation to Jerusalem or Zion waiting for a deliverer. This is followed shortly by 60:5–6, which brings in representatives from nations, presumably Gentiles, bringing gold and frankincense to Jerusalem because the light of the Lord has risen upon her.

The third Old Testament narrative to exert an influence comes from Psalms 72:10 stating, 'May the kings of Sheba and Saba bring gifts, may all kings pay him homage.' This may help to explain why the Magi were subsequently transformed into kings by Christians in the sixth century, as they detected the use of this Psalm within Matthew's narrative.

A Reflection of the Times

The introduction of the Magi into the episode may also be viewed as a reflection of the times, in respect of that moment in time when the author began to finalise the Gospel and, as discussed earlier, this was probably around the year AD 85. It reflects the rejection of Jesus as the Messiah by the Jews but his acceptance by the Gentiles. This takes the form of the Magi from the east, the wise men of the Gentiles, who are the first to proclaim him as such. Subsequent writings in the Gospel of Matthew illustrate the hostility by the Jews towards the early Christians, and Matthew 21:42–43 can be interpreted as indicating that whilst the kingdom of God was being given to the followers of Jesus it was being taken away from those who read the scriptures, in other words, the Jews. In particular, the author would have been aware that the Pharisees, the chief priests and elders, had been very hostile and violent towards the followers of Jesus in the years after his crucifixion. Distinctive Christian communities evolved, made up primarily by Gentiles, and it is clear that the author was active within these.

The author's intention is twofold; firstly, by way of a criticism of unconverted Jews who, despite being aware of the scriptures of the Old Testament and the words of the prophets, do not believe, and are not prepared to worship the new born Christ; instead their king, as their representative, contrives to have him eliminated. Secondly, it confirms the acceptance of Jesus by the Gentiles in the form of the wise men from the east. They, and only they, had correctly interpreted the scriptures, recognising the announcement of the Messiah by way of an celestial phenomenon.

Perhaps this is the real explanation as to why the author has Herod and his Jewish advisers apparently unaware of the star and its meaning, as he has designed it to be only recognised by the Magi, representing the true believers. Is it therefore conceivable that the star is merely a literary device used by the author in order to illustrate that non-believers, encompassing Herod and the Jewish nation, are unprepared and unwilling to recognise and accept its light?

1. Jesus meets Matthew at the customs house. (Sketch prepared and provided courtesy of Colin Watson)

Above: 2. The pillar of light shining before the Israelites. (Sketch prepared and provided courtesy of Colin Watson)

Left: 3. Flavius Josephus: a sketch of a Roman bust said to be that of the historian. (Prepared and provided courtesy of Colin Watson)

Right: 4. A model of the Temple of Jerusalem as it would have appeared during the time of Herod the Great. (Courtesy of the Israeli Tourist Board)

Below: 5. The present-day remains of Herodium. (Courtesy of the Israeli Tourist Boar; photo by Yoav Kertese)

6. King Herod questions the Magi. (Sketch prepared and provided courtesy of Colin Watson)

7. The Magi visit Jesus. (Sketch prepared and provided courtesy of Colin Watson)

8. Jesus being baptised. This event, according to the Gospel of Luke, took place in the fifteenth year of the reign of Tiberius, which equates to AD 28/29 or possibly AD 25/26. (Sketch prepared and provided courtesy of Colin Watson)

Above left: 9. A partial eclipse of the Moon, 31 December 2009. (Courtesy of Andy McCrea)

Above right: 10. A total solar eclipse, photographed from Antalya, Turkey, 12 April 2006. (Courtesy of Andy McCrea)

11. The five planets as commonly known to the ancients, as they appeared during a planetary massing (1 May 2002). 1. Mercury, 2. Venus, 3. Saturn, 4. Mars, 5. Jupiter. (Courtesy of Andy McCrea)

Above left: 12. A gold stater of the ancient British King Boudouc, possibly displaying the planets Jupiter and Saturn in conjunction. (*Ancient British Coins,* published by Chris Rudd, Aylsham (2010))

Above right: 13. A gold stater of the ancient British King Eppillus, possibly depicting the planets Jupiter, Saturn and Mars during their massing in 6 BC. (*Ancient British Coins,* published by Chris Rudd, Aylsham (2010))

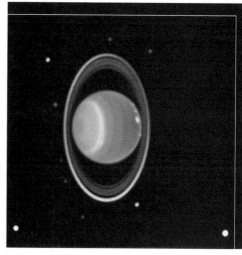

Above left: 14. Venus as imaged by an orbiting probe, *Pioneer*, in 1980. (Courtesy of NASA)

Above right: 15. Uranus. An extraordinary infra-red image taken by the Hubble Space Telescope and processed using a multi-image spectrometer. It shows up its own ring system together with several of its satellites. (Courtesy of NASA)

16. A Hubble Space Telescope image of the powerful and highly unstable variable star Eta Carina and its associated nebulosity. First recorded by Edmund Halley in 1677 from St Helena, its magnitude was subsequently found to fluctuate erratically. At one stage, in 1843, it became almost as bright as Sirius, although since 1870 it has not been visible to the naked eye. Its luminosity, at its height, has been estimated to have reached around 6 million times that of the Sun. (Courtesy of NASA)

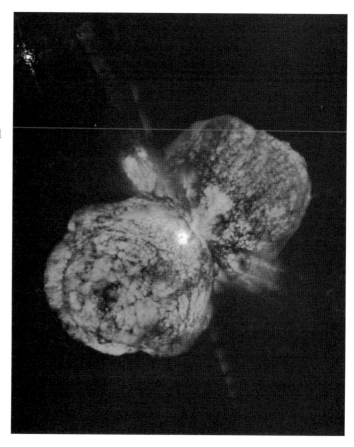

17. The Crab Nebula. The resemblance to the shape of a crab was first noted by the third Earl of Rosse using a 72-inch reflecting telescope in the mid-nineteenth century, from his estate in Birr, County Offaly. (Courtesy of Andy McCrea)

18. A coin of King Eppillus, which had been thought to illustrate a nova in the constellation of Aquila, the eagle. (Photo by Andy McCrea)

PART II
ASTRONOMICAL EVENTS

6
THE DANCE OF THE PLANETS

From the information gathered in previous chapters it is now possible to assemble the various indications and clues that have been established about the mysterious star of Bethlehem, based upon the assumption, for the time being, that there may, conceivably, be some truth in the story. These may be summarised as follows:

1. The star probably first became visible in the east of the sky either at dawn, or at sunset.

2. It probably made two appearances. At some stage it ceased to be visible and later reappeared with the author placing the Magi either in Jerusalem or on their short journey towards Bethlehem.

3. During the Magi's journey from Jerusalem to Bethlehem, the author has the star appearing to go before them and then 'stand over' the house where the young child Jesus was.

4. Shortly after the second sighting of the star, the author has Herod ordering the massacre of boys under two years old, possibly implying an interval of a similar period between the first and second appearances of the star.

5. The appearance of the star had an astrological significance in that it signified the birth of a new king or Messiah.

6. These events occurred sometime between the years 13 and 5 BC.

One theory for the star of Bethlehem, which goes back centuries and which is a popular theme in planetarium shows, is that it represented a triple conjunction of the planets Jupiter and Saturn in the year 7 BC. This involved these two planets appearing to move close to one another in the sky, separate, and then repeat the process two more times. However, before proceeding on this subject it is appropriate first to mention something about the brightness of planets and their nature.

Magnitude

In astronomy, the degree of brightness of a star or planet is determined by its apparent magnitude. The lower the magnitude, the brighter the object and this is measured on a logarithmic scale, in such a way that an object of, say magnitude o is exactly 100 times brighter than an object of magnitude +5. One magnitude is therefore the fifth root of 100 or about 2.512 so we can say that a star or planet of around magnitude +1 is about two and a half times brighter than one of magnitude +2. The limiting magnitude of the human eye under perfect seeing conditions is about +6. The four brightest stars in the sky all have negative magnitudes, with Sirius the brightest at -1.4. Venus, the brightest of the planets, has a maximum magnitude of -4.6, whilst the other planets are as follows: Mercury -1.9, Mars -2.8, Jupiter -2.8, Saturn -0.4, Uranus +5.3 and Neptune +7.7. A full Moon's magnitude is estimated to be around -13 and the Sun about -26.

The Planets

The word planet originates from the Greek words *planes aster*, meaning wandering star, as such objects appeared to wander amongst the twelve constellations of the zodiac. In ancient times there were only five known planets – Mercury, Venus, Mars, Jupiter and Saturn. These were all easily visible with maximum magnitudes varying between -4.6 to -0.4. A sixth planet, Uranus, at a best magnitude of +5.3 is just visible to the naked eye under transparent skies but we have no clear records that it was ever identified as a planet until it was discovered by William Herschel in 1781, with the aid of a telescope. Neptune at magnitude +7.7 would never have been visible and was discovered in 1846 by Johann Galle and Heinrich D'Arrest based upon calculations made by Urbain le Verrier. A ninth planet, Pluto, was discovered by Clyde Tombaugh in 1930 but has recently been relegated to the status of a 'dwarf' planet. Even the world's largest telescopes would only show this small desolate world as a very faint star-like object, although the Hubble Space Telescope has managed to decipher a disc with vague markings upon its surface.

Mercury and Venus are sometimes referred to as inferior planets as they are both closer to the Sun than the Earth. Mercury, the smallest of the planets, is the closest to the Sun and therefore never becomes very conspicuous in the sky. It may be seen in the east before dawn or in the west after sunset and resembles a bright star. Its orbital period around the Sun takes only eighty-eight days.

Venus has sometimes been referred to as the Earth's sister planet on account that it is almost identical in size. It appears as a brilliant shining beacon in the sky and has even been known to cast shadows. It is so bright because it is covered by a dense layer of reflective cloud and is relatively near to the Earth; at its closest it can come to within about 25 million miles, making it the second-nearest natural body to the Earth next to the Moon. Like Mercury it is always seen either in the east before dawn or in the west at sunset. Its orbital period around the Sun takes about 225 days.

Mars, Jupiter and Saturn are regarded as superior planets because their orbits around the Sun are beyond that of the Earth. Mars is a relatively small planet at about 4,200 miles in diameter and has a distinctive orange appearance due to high concentrations of iron oxide in its rocks and soil. For this reason it is known as the red planet, but it is also sometimes referred to as the 'rusty' planet. Its orbital period around the Sun takes 687 days and its brightness fluctuates significantly from about +2.5 to -2.8 depending upon its distance from the Earth on its journey around the Sun. When it is at opposition, that is, at its closest approach to the Earth, an enormous amount of surface detail can be studied using an astronomical telescope. These appear as dark patches, the most well known being the Syrtis Major, a V-shaped feature resembling the shape of India. Because of its reddish hue it is not surprising that the planet became known as Nergal, the Babylonian god of war, as well as being the Roman god of war.

Jupiter is the largest planet in the solar system with a diameter at its equator of about 89,000 miles and for this reason it is normally the second brightest planet as viewed from Earth. Its brightness can vary from about -1.2 to -2.8 depending upon its distance from the Earth. Because it is nearly 500 million miles from the Sun its orbital period takes about twelve years to complete, and this means that Jupiter appears to move slowly across the sky, spending roughly a year in each of the constellations of the zodiac. Through even a small telescope the planet appears to be flattened, or squashed, this being due to its rapid rotation rate of just under ten hours. Its disc is covered with bright and dark belts of red, brown, orange and cream which run parallel to its equator. It also shows spots which frequently appear and disappear. One permanent feature is known as the Great Red Spot, which represents a massive oval-shaped whirling storm that has been observed ever since telescopes first detected it in the seventeenth century. Jupiter is a gaseous planet with its atmosphere comprising mainly hydrogen and helium. It has four large satellites, known as the Galilean Moons as they were first discovered by Galileo in 1610.[7] One or two of these moons would actually be easily visible to the naked eye if it were not for the fact that they appear so close to the planet.

Saturn, at almost 900 million miles from the Sun, has an orbital period of about twenty-nine and a half years so that it appears to move very slowly across the zodiacal constellations. With a magnitude of about o it is much fainter than Jupiter and with the naked eye seems to have a distinctive yellowish appearance. It was Galileo who, also in 1610, first noticed something strange about the appearance of Saturn using a primitive refracting telescope. Initially he thought that the planet had two bright moons, each flanking one side of its disc. It was not until 1656 that the Dutch astronomer Christian Huygens realised that they were actually perfectly formed rings. Through a telescope the planet is transformed into the gem of the solar system. A good astronomical telescope will show up three separate rings, two of which are separated by a gap known as the Cassini Division, which is named after the Italian astronomer who first discovered it in 1675. Although the rings measure around 170,000 miles in diameter, they are paper thin, being only about 50 feet thick and comprising trillions of small bits of icy rubble.

Saturn's brightness actually depends quite a lot on the angle the rings make to our line of sight, as obviously the more they are exposed, or open, the brighter the planet will appear. This angle fluctuates regularly about every fourteen years and depends upon the orbital periods of the Earth and Saturn. When the rings are exactly edge-on to us, as viewed through a telescope, they actually almost disappear. In 7 BC, during the triple conjunction with Jupiter, the angle of the rings has been calculated to have been about 7 degrees.

The disc of Saturn measures 75,000 miles at its equator and displays a number of yellowish bands cross its gaseous globe which is mainly comprised of hydrogen. Like Jupiter, Saturn also bulges at its equator due to its high rotation period which takes slightly over ten hours. It has one large satellite, Titan, also discovered by Huygens, but at about magnitude +8 it is not visible to the naked eye.

Ancient Astronomy

In 7 BC the Babylonians imagined the sky as being shaped like a dome under which all the various celestial bodies moved around. They had divided the part of the sky where the Sun, Moon and planets appeared to wander into twelve sections and these were represented by the zodiacal constellations. These areas of the sky were then broken down into smaller sections so that their observations could be carried out in a very precise and detailed manner.

Particular attention was devoted to the observation of the Sun, Moon and planets. Accurate records were made of eclipses, and the movements of planets were plotted with extreme care. From these observations they realised that planetary motions were irregular with variations in their apparent speed as they moved across the constellations, and these movements were recorded and analysed mathematically, especially when they appeared to stop, go in the opposite direction, stop again and then proceed to move in their normal course. However despite their careful observations and records it seems that the Babylonians did not come to any firm conclusions as to why the planets moved in the manner they did, and no theories were ever formulated by them that explain apparent planetary motion.

Going further afield, the general idea in those days was that the Earth was effectively the centre of the universe with the Sun, Moon, planets and the fixed stars all rotating around it. The Greek, Aristarchus of Samos (310–250 BC), had proposed that the Earth was a planet moving around the Sun but unfortunately was unable to prove his theory and incredibly it was not until 1543 that a Polish monk, Mikolaj Kopernik, better known today as Nicholas Copernicus, published his *De Revolutionibus Orbium Coelestium* (Concerning the Revolutions of the Celestial Bodies) that the true nature of the solar system became known.

Kepler's Laws

The Copernican system, as it became known, took some time to be accepted, particularly by the Catholic Church, and it was not until the early seventeenth century that Johannes Kepler, an astronomer from the German province of Wurttemberg, finally was able to prove its authenticity, using very detailed records of planetary observations previously recorded by the Danish astronomer Tycho Brahe. Not only did he verify the fact that the Earth was a planet that orbited the Sun, just as the other planets did, he also explained other fluctuations in their movements, discovering that their orbits are not circular but elliptical. This led to the development of his Laws of Planetary Motion, which were published between 1609 and 1618. Basically, these laws recognised that planets travel in elliptical orbits around the Sun, rather than in perfect circles. There was also a precise relationship between their orbital periods and their distances from the Sun, so that when a planet is closest to the Sun, known as perihelion, it travels faster than when it is furthest away in its orbit, which is called aphelion. So those planets whose orbits are close to the Sun will travel quicker than those further out; hence we find that Venus, with a mean distance from the Sun of 67 million miles, travels at about 22 miles per second on average in its orbit, whereas Jupiter, whose mean distance from the Sun is about 483 million miles, travels at only 8 miles per second. The Earth, at about 93 million miles from the Sun, travels at about 18.5 miles per second. Details for all the planets are set out in the table below which also gives the maximum and minimum distances of each from the Sun in their elliptical orbits.

Planet	Distance from Sun in millions of miles			Average velocity of orbit in miles per second
	Mean	Maximum	Minimum	
Mercury	36	43	29	29.7
Venus	67	68	67	21.7
Earth	93	94.5	91	18.5
Mars	141.5	154	128	15.0
Jupiter	483	506	459	8.1
Saturn	886	934	835	6.0
Uranus	1783	1862	1696	4.2
Neptune	2793	2813	2763	3.4
Mean yearly motion in degrees per year: Jupiter 30.35 Saturn 12.22				

Although all the planets move around the Sun in elliptical orbits, it can be seen from the above table that all except Mercury and Mars have orbits which are close to being circular, particularly Venus, the Earth and Neptune.

The fact that there is a direct relationship between a planet's orbital period – that is, the time it takes to go around the Sun – and its mean distance from the Sun means it is possible to measure the distance between the Sun and the planets, for if we know their orbital periods and the length from the Earth to the Sun, which can be determined separately, it is then a simple calculation to work out their distances.

The Plane of the Ecliptic

All planets move around in orbits which are approximately within the same plane of one another, and this is the reason why they tend to move within the constellations of the zodiac; in other words, they all follow closely the apparent path of the Sun across the sky, known as the ecliptic. The reason for this is that about 4.5 billion years ago the planets were formed out of a swirling cloud of gas and dust which formed a spiral shape, known as an accretion disc, around the early Sun. Visually it would have resembled something like a fried egg. Over time, gravity caused the dust to coalesce and gradually this accumulated to form the early planets. This gravity-related accretion process is actually still continuing today although now to a much lesser extent. For instance, our Earth continues to receive tens of thousands of tons of material each year by way of dust and material from meteors and falling meteorites. The table below shows the orbital inclination of each planet representing the extent of their deviation from the plane of the ecliptic. This is expressed in degrees and minutes (a minute being one sixtieth of a degree). To obtain a perspective of this, the diameter of the Moon in the sky as viewed from Earth is about half of one degree.

Planet	Orbital inclination
Mercury	7°
Venus	3° 24'
Mars	1° 51'
Jupiter	1° 18'
Saturn	2° 29'
Uranus	0° 48'
Neptune	1° 45'

In a way the variability of each planet's orbital inclination represents an imperfection within the solar system. Imagine if they were exactly in the same plane – we would have planets at conjunction appearing to eclipse, or occult, one another every time they passed each other in the sky, and to the naked eye they would appear as a single bright object!

The Triple Conjunctions of Jupiter and Saturn

Every so often the Earth, Jupiter and Saturn form an approximate line with one another to create a conjunction as viewed from the Earth. Because Jupiter and Saturn's orbits are inclined by 1° 18', and 2° 29' to the Earth's orbital plane or the ecliptic, the minimum separation between them during the conjunction can fluctuate from anything between 0 and 3.8 degrees. When a conjunction occurs the two planets will therefore appear close together and they will both have the same ecliptic longitude in the sky. As Jupiter travels faster in its journey around the Sun the next conjunction will normally happen whenever it proceeds to next lap Saturn, just like an athlete running in the inside lane. To do this it has to travel around an entire circuit of the ecliptic to catch up with Saturn and this is calculated to happen on average about every 19.86 years, as seen from Earth. Clearly a triple conjunction is much rarer and this only happens when the Earth, Jupiter, Saturn and the Sun are all nearly aligned with one another, and only occurs about once every 139 years. For a triple conjunction to occur in the constellation of Pisces, as it did in 7 BC, is rarer still and only happens on average about once every 800 years.

The first diagram below shows the apparent paths that Jupiter and Saturn would have taken in 7 BC through the constellation of Pisces moving anti-clockwise from right to left, a movement which is known as direct motion. For a period however they moved backwards from left to right, known as retrograde motion and on the chart they resemble loops. This is caused by the positions of the Earth and the planets changing in relation to the starry background as the Earth catches up with them and passes them on the inside lane. It is really an effect of perspective and eventually, once the Earth has passed a certain point in its orbit, the planets will appear to continue in their normal direct motion. This is demonstrated in the second diagram below. The true nature of this retrograde motion of the planets could not be explained by astronomers until Copernicus introduced the idea of the heliocentric system, which placed all the planets in orbit around the Sun.

During the triple conjunctions both Jupiter and Saturn were effectively at opposition, that is at their closest points in their orbits to the Earth, and their magnitudes would have been about -2.3 and +0.5 respectively. In early 7 BC the planets approached each other at about 3.5 degrees per month to come to within about 0.98 degrees apart on 27 May. They then proceeded to separate, reaching about 2.9 degrees apart by 27 July. Closing in for the second time, they came to within about 0.98 degrees on 6 October, only to separate to about 1.2 degrees by 1 November. Finally, they closed in towards one another for the third and last time, and by 1 December had come to within about 1.05 degrees of separation. After that date they started to edge away from each other, not to come together again for another twenty years.

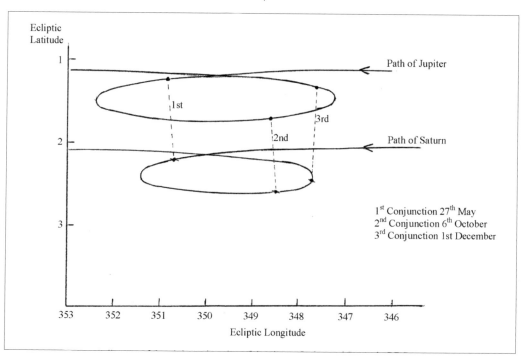

Above: A diagram of the triple conjunction of the planets Jupiter and Saturn in 7 BC. (Prepared by Richard Archer and David Collins)

Right: A diagram of the retrograde motion of an outer planet as seen from the Earth as it moves in orbit around the Sun. (Prepared and provided courtesy of Richard Archer)

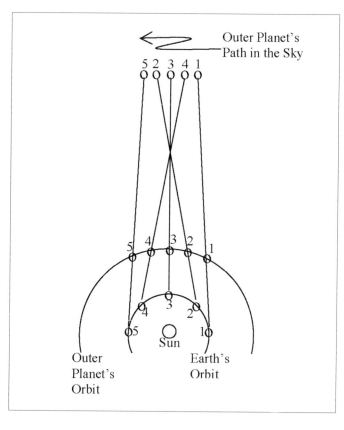

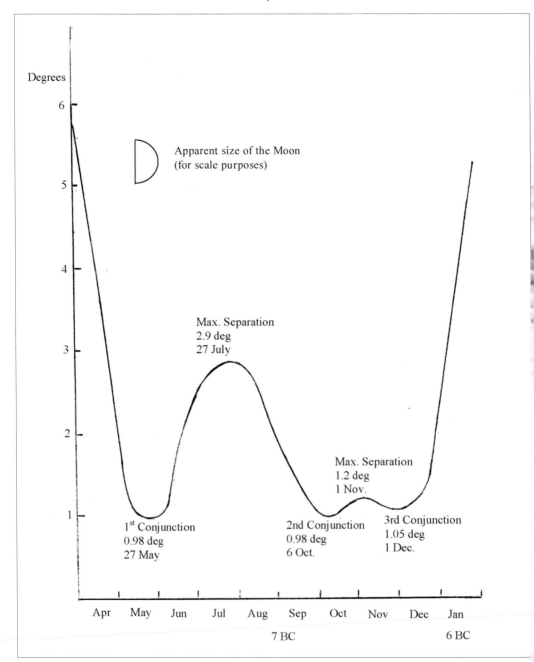

A diagram showing the angular separations of Jupiter and Saturn in 7 BC. (Prepared by Richard Archer and David Collins)

A Planetary Massing

Shortly after the last conjunction Mars proceeded to join the two planets in the sky and by February 6 BC all three were separated by about 8 degrees. On 20 February, the planets were joined by the crescent Moon which passed very close to Jupiter so that two separate pairings were visible comprising Jupiter and the Moon and Mars/Saturn.

Babylonian astronomers attached great importance to the triple conjunction and a clay tablet known as the *Star Almanac of Sippar* was discovered close to Babylon, in present-day Iraq, which records details of this conjunction, having been dated to the year 7 BC. It covers the first seven months of the Babylonian year from March/April to September/October and gives the position of the planets, the Sun and the Moon, recording also a solar eclipse. Another document, known as the *Berlin Table*, is recorded on Egyptian papyrus and is a copy of a table of planetary positions for the years 17 BC to AD 10 and it also records the triple conjunction.

Kepler and the Star of Bethlehem

Traditionally the planetary massing was considered to be very significant and was associated with the birth of Jesus, going far back in time. Kepler became another early proponent of the planetary 'massing' explaining the star of Bethlehem. Having observed for himself a close conjunction of Jupiter and Saturn in December 1603 followed by a planetary massing when Mars joined those planets in September 1604 he became fascinated with the possibility that such an occurrence might also explain the star of Bethlehem. Being a superb mathematician, he was able to calculate that similar massings occurred about every 805 years, so working back he was able to determine that one also took place around 7 BC. He went on to deduce that such massings coincided with other important events in civilisation such as Charlemagne in AD 798, Isaiah 812 BC, Moses 1617 BC, and the Great Flood in 2422 BC.

Kepler was not just a great astronomer, he was also an astrologer, and had referred to the works of Don Isaac Abrabanel, a Portuguese statesman and philosopher, who had in 1497 written *The Wells of Salvation*, which included information concerning the astronomical significance of Jupiter and Saturn and their conjunctions. It also included details of the astrology that the Magi may have used, explaining that Saturn symbolised a godly father figure with Jupiter being his son, and that the constellation of Pisces was associated with Judea. It may well be that this belief had a profound influence on Kepler's reasoning.

Amazingly, on 9 October 1604, a supernova appeared close to the three planets in the constellation of Ophiuchus. This is an extremely rare and unpredictable event and Kepler suggested that this might have been caused by the conjunction itself, not of course having any real idea as to its true nature. Being even more impressed by this new development he now assumed that the star of Bethlehem had to be a nova preceded by the planetary massing around 7 BC.

Ideler's Theory

The triple conjunction theory was followed up in 1825 by the German mathematician and astronomer Dr Christian Ludwig Ideler, who published his *Handbuch der Mathematischen* and *Tecnischen Chronologie*, in which he assumed that the conjunctions in 7 BC met all the criteria as described in Matthew for the star of Bethlehem. He then attempted to determine the exact date for Christ's birth. He suggested that the first conjunction would have drawn the Magi's attention to events in the night sky initiating their journey to Jerusalem, with the third and final conjunction coinciding with the birth. However he made the mistake of thinking that the final conjunction would have had both planets coming together so close in the sky that they would have appeared as one to the naked eye, whereas in fact the separation between the two was considerable.

Modern Support for the Triple Conjunction Theory

The use of the triple conjunction theory to explain the star of Bethlehem has received considerable support in recent years and one of its great advocates is David Hughes. His reasoning is based upon a number of key issues which are summarised below:

1. From the Babylonian tablets it is clear that accurate predictions of the conjunctions, as well as the planetary massing, would have been available to the Magi, giving them ample time to plan and prepare their journey to Jerusalem.

2. The first conjunction, which took place on 27 May 7 BC, was preceded by the helical rising of the planets Jupiter and Saturn in March of that year. The acronychal rising of the planets subsequently took place on 15 September, prior to the second conjunction on 6 October. Either the helical or the acronychal risings would have meant that the two planets appeared to rise in the east, at dawn or sunset, therefore satisfying the descriptions in Matthew.

3. According to Matthew, the star 'went before' the Magi as they journeyed from Jerusalem to Bethlehem and 'stood over' the house where Jesus was. The term 'went before' clearly implies that the star or object physically moved against the starry background guiding the Magi to Bethlehem. Whilst planets do wander or move against the background of stars, it is a relatively slow movement and would only be noticed over days, not hours, and certainly not in the two hours or so that it would take to travel from Jerusalem to Bethlehem. Supporters of the triple conjunction theory explain away this problem by emphasising the fact that when the Magi travelled towards Bethlehem both Jupiter and Saturn would be high up in the southern sky and they would have been travelling in the general direction of those planets. Jupiter and Saturn would have appeared to point the way to Bethlehem or in other words 'go before'. This does seem to be a

reasonable explanation; however we are then presented with the problem of the star appearing to 'stand over' a particular location.

The author, it would seem, must have used considerable license when he describes that the star 'stood over'. This implies that the object stopped moving and hovered over a house! In a discussion on an edition of the *Sky at Night*, on BBC television, both Hughes and Mark Kidger agreed that this was a real 'show stopper!' One way around this is that when the planets are exactly due south, they are also at their highest point in the sky and at their closest position to the zenith, which is the point in the sky exactly above the head of the observer. In mid-September of 7 BC, both Jupiter and Saturn would have been very high up in the southern sky as seen from Jerusalem. The planets would, of course, not have stopped moving across the sky due to the rotation of the Earth, and would not have appeared to stand over any particular dwelling, but over the entire country. Whilst this perhaps is not an entirely satisfactory explanation, it has to be considered the closest possible interpretation of what Matthew is describing if the triple conjunction theory is to be accepted as representing the star of Bethlehem.

4. Astrologically the heliacal rising was significant as it symbolised new birth and the Magi may have witnessed the rising in March, 7 BC of Jupiter and Saturn both close together in the sky. Although little is known of ancient astrology it does seem that the constellation of Pisces was associated with Judea. Traditionally, Jupiter was linked with great rulers and Saturn represented a protector of the Jews. Kepler certainly thought that Pisces was very significant to the Jews astrologically and linked the conjunctions and the planetary massing in the constellation to the emergence of a Messiah king.

Problems with the Theory

The problem with the triple conjunction and planetary massing theory is that it seems to raise more questions than it answers. Going back to the list of biblical indicators and clues which form criteria which have to be satisfied, there are one or two serious shortcomings. Firstly, the conjunction theory does not involve the planets becoming invisible during their long stay in the sky from March of 7 BC onwards. At no time do they disappear and then reappear as is clearly implied by Matthew. One suggestion is that the first appearance could relate to the heliacal rising of the star in March, 7 BC followed by the second or third conjunction representing the second. Alternatively, Matthew could simply be referring to the different positions of the two planets in the sky, at first in the east and later in the south as viewed from Jerusalem or Bethlehem. Such suggestions are not convincing, however, and the simple fact remains that the two planets, Jupiter and Saturn, would always have been visible in the sky.

It has also been suggested that, depending upon our interpretation, Matthew does not necessarily refer to a disappearance and reappearance of the star or object.

However, going back again to Matthew 2:10 it clearly suggests that at some point the star became no longer visible, telling us that the Magi rejoiced at seeing the star for a second time. This is also supported to some extent by the implication that Herod had not been aware of its existence.

Another problem with the triple conjunction theory is that it involves two objects, Jupiter and Saturn, whereas Matthew and even some of the early Christian writers refer to the object as 'star' in the singular. Matthew actually uses the word in the singular on four separate occasions. Supporters of the theory argue that the New Testament word 'star' could be represented by the Greek word *aster*, which can mean any number of stars, and not necessarily a single star. However the same word in Greek does have its equivalent in the plural, *asters*, which means a number of stars and consequently it seems more likely that Matthew would have used this word if he wanted to describe both planets.

One possible answer for the use of the word in the singular is that astrologically only one of the planets represented the star of the Jews and the Messiah. Either of the two planets may have qualified for this distinction depending upon the use of different astrological interpretations. It could also be that Jupiter being about magnitude -2.3 was identified as the singular bright star in the conjunctions as it was about thirteen times visibly brighter than its companion Saturn at magnitude +0.5.

Another argument against the triple conjunction theory also involves the use of the word 'star', for if Matthew is describing a planet why did he not describe it as such especially when there is a Greek word for this as we saw earlier, namely *planes aster* which means a wandering star. An alternative word, *planes*, meaning wanderer, would have also been available. Hughes attempts to solve this problem by suggesting that Matthew may have been more familiar with the Greek word for star, *aster*, from the Greek Old Testament, as it appears there frequently and a word meaning planet is never mentioned.

Hughes points out that in an early manuscript copy of the Apocryphal Gospel, the Protoevangelium of James, there is a reference to the visit of the Magi and the statement, 'and behold they saw stars in the rising and they went before them'. Hughes therefore suggests that this is evidence for there being more than one object in the sky with the word 'rising' referring to the acronychal rising of the planets coinciding with their second conjunction in mid-September, 7 BC. We have to bear in mind, however, that the Apocryphal Gospel of James was written some time after that of Matthew and may therefore be considered as not being as reliable or accurate. Also a later version of that same Gospel makes reference to the Magi, saying, 'We saw how an indescribably great star shone among these stars and dimmed them, so they no longer shone, and so we know that a king was born for Israel.' It seems that the writer has used a great deal of literary freedom in his descriptions and the reliability of his texts must be viewed with great scepticism.

Earlier Jupiter/Saturn Triple Conjunctions

A further problem with the triple conjunction theory is that there were earlier similar events which were every bit as spectacular, if not better, than that in 7 BC. There were six in total between the years 1000 BC and 145 BC, two of which were in the constellation of Pisces in the years 980–979 BC and 861–860 BC. Of these six triple conjunctions, four involved a closer separation in the sky of the planets Jupiter and Saturn than that of the 7 BC conjunctions, which had a minimum separation of about 0.98 degrees. That of 146–145 BC had a minimum separation of only 0.17 degrees, and that of 821–820 BC of 0.37 degrees.

The question this raises is, what was so special about the conjunctions of 7 BC? It could be simply for astrological reasons, as the conjunctions in 7 BC occurred in Pisces which, as has been seen, may have had a special significance for the Jews. Also to be considered is the fact that the expectations of the emergence of a Messiah may not have become heightened until sometime after the Babylonian conquest of Judea and the captivity of the Jews around 586 BC. As the conjunctions of 523–522 BC are considered rather too close to that date it leaves us with that of 146–145 BC, which occurred in the constellation of Cancer. By this time Jewish expectations of a Messiah or saviour king had risen significantly, this being evidenced by writings within the Dead Sea Scrolls. Even with separations of 0.18, 0.25 and 0.17 degrees respectively, the planets would not at any time have been close enough to resemble a single bright object, but nevertheless they would have been a far more spectacular sight in the sky than that of 7 BC. In addition, one or two of the earlier triple conjunctions also involved planetary massings as well as lunar occultations.

It would seem therefore that the triple conjunction of 7 BC may not have been considered that special, even given the fact that it was followed by a planetary massing in February 6 BC and that it occurred in Pisces. Also to be considered is that the planetary separations of 7 BC would have meant that the minimum space between the two planets would still have appeared quite wide, being at a distance apart in the sky equal to that of the diameter of two full moons.

The Planetary Conjunctions and Massings of 126 BC

A spectacular event occurred in the year 126 BC which was far more noteworthy than that of 7 and 146/145 BC. This involved the planet Jupiter having individual conjunctions with Mercury, Venus and Saturn. Each of these had a close separation, being only 0.27, 0.20 and 0.75 degrees apart, but what is more significant is that each conjunction was followed by a planetary massing, the first involving the planets Mercury, Jupiter and Saturn, the second involving Venus, Jupiter and Saturn and the third, Mercury, Venus, Jupiter, Saturn and the Moon!

The political tension within Judea in 7 BC was, of course, far detached from that which had existed in 145 and 126 BC. As we saw earlier, although Judea retained a degree of independence from Rome following its conquest, it had a client king installed who was non-Jewish and as his reign progressed he became more and more pragmatic and ruthless. The Jewish community, living in fear, had built up a repugnance of Herod and his Hellenisation. The conditions had been fuelled for the emergence of a Messianic figure with the potential to lead the Jews away from the forces of evil.

Other Conjunctions

Jupiter and Venus, 3 BC

What about other conjunctions close to our time-frame around the years 12 to 6 BC? An examination was carried out by Roger W. Sinnott, who looked at very close conjunctions between 12 BC and AD 7. As a result his candidate for the star of Bethlehem was that involving Jupiter and Venus, this being influenced by the fact that they are normally the two brightest planets in the sky. He selected their conjunction on 12 August 3 BC in the dawn sky, followed by another on 17 June 2 BC, which was visible in the evening sky. Their minimum separations were 0.20 and 0.05 degrees as viewed from Babylon. The second conjunction was so close that the two planets may have appeared to fuse together as they sank low in the western sky after sunset. This would have been a beautiful theory were it not for the fact that both events occurred after the death of Herod in 5 or 4 BC and therefore cannot qualify as the star described within Matthew.

Jupiter, Regulus and Venus, 3 and 2 BC

Nevertheless, the very close conjunction between Jupiter and Venus in 2 BC has recently been claimed as representing the star of Bethlehem, in association with other celestial events, by an American evangelist, Rick Larson. His theory is that Jupiter, in September of 3 BC, came very close to the bright star Regulus, the 'Regal Star' in the constellation of Leo, performing its dance, or retrograde motion, around it and giving rise to a triple conjunction with that star. Almost nine months after the first close approach to the star, which Larson claims represented the gestation period of Jesus, the close conjunction took place between Jupiter and Venus in June of 2 BC. About six months later Jupiter's movement against the starry background came to a halt prior to it going into retrograde motion, and Larson claims that this occurred on 25 December! Around this date, he suggests, the Magi would have arrived in Bethlehem as Jupiter would have been well placed, high up in the southern sky and appearing to have become motionless against the background stars and seeming to stand over the town of Bethlehem.

Larson deals with the problem he has created for himself in having a date well past that historically accepted for King Herod's death by claiming that the accounts of Josephus of that event were incorrectly copied when being printed onto manuscripts after the year 1544, and never subsequently rectified. He claims that, prior to the Reformation, records suggest a later date for his death in 1 BC. However, as we saw earlier, in the chapter on Herod, the year of either 4 or 5 BC can be corroborated by other contemporary reports referring to the length of the years that his sons reigned and when they ceased to reign, as well as additional supplementary evidence.

The Star Sadalmelik

There are a number of different theories about planetary conjunctions involving a bright star which try to explain the star of Bethlehem. One of these theories was presented recently by Richard Coates in *A&G News and Reviews in Astronomy & Geophysics*, and may be summarised as follows: if we were to go back and identify the names for stars prior to about AD 80, we find that there are some which bear the name *al-sa'd*, which is translated as meaning 'lucky star'. One in particular was known as *al-sa'd-malik* and translated as 'lucky star of the king', or alternatively *al-sa'd al-mulk* meaning 'lucky star of the kingdom'. The westernised name is known as Sadalmelik or Sadalmelek and can be identified as a third-magnitude (2.95) star in the constellation of Aquarius, being designated Alpha Aquarii. This indicates that at some stage in the past it was considered to be the brightest star in that constellation, implying that it may have been somewhat brighter than it is today.

He suggests that this star may have interested astrologers around the time of the birth of Jesus, pointing out that it would rise close to due east in the sky, with its helical rising, 2,000 years ago, taking place in early February each year. Consequently he presents a case that the triple conjunction and planetary massing of 7 and 6 BC, or possibly some other planetary configuration, may have attracted the attention of the Magi to that particular star at the time.

Jupiter and Venus, 1 BC

Another suggestion for the star was a close conjunction that took place between Jupiter and Venus on 21 August 1 BC. At their closest approach they reached to within about 0.107 degrees of one another. Now that is close, but not quite close enough to appear as one object to anyone with normal eyesight, being about the diameter of the Mare Imbrium, which is very easily visible to the naked eye as part of the face of the 'Man in the Moon'. However, the closest approach occurred when both planets were just below the eastern horizon as seen from Judea, and the bright Sun would have risen before them so that they would not have been visible before dawn. At any rate, the date is also well after the death of Herod.

Do Ancient British Coins Show the Conjunctions of 7 BC?

It is a well-known fact that the ancient Celtic tribes of Western Europe had a fascination with anything to do with the night sky, and over time they developed a profound understanding of the movement of the celestial bodies.

Druidism and Julius Caesar

It is perhaps not surprising that in 56 BC Julius Caesar himself proceeded to hold talks with knowledgeable Gauls concerning the measurements made to calculate and confirm the length of the 'northern summer night', and it was not long before he visited Britain. It was the acquisition of such information that contributed towards his subsequent reform of the Roman calendar in AD 46, during his period of dictatorship, as their ancient calendar had gradually drifted out of kilter from its original alignment with the solar year.

Whilst in Britain he became familiar with the activities of the priestly Druids, who exerted considerable influence and guidance on all manner of affairs, and who, at that time, were recognised as being a leading authority in the study of astronomy, astrology and religion. Their teaching schools also attracted students from all over Western Europe. He proceeded to record in his *Commentaries*, written in 53 BC:

> The Druids .... Hold long discussions about the heavenly bodies and their movement, the size of the universe and of the Earth, the physical constitution of the world, and of the power and properties of the gods; and they instruct the young men in all these subjects.

Further evidence of the Druid's power, knowledge and influence can be found from a translation by T. D. Kendrick of Pomponius, a Spanish geographer from the first century AD, who tells us:

> Teachers of wisdom called Druids .... profess to know the size and shape of the world, movements of the heavens and of the stars, and the will of the gods.

The Bodouc Gold Stater
There seems little doubt that the Druids also exerted considerable influence over the images displayed on coins issued by the tribes of ancient Britain and it is possible that the conjunctions of 7 BC may be depicted on coins of one of their kings called Bodouc. Known only by the mention of his name on his coins, he ruled the north of the Dobunnic tribe's territory in the West Midlands for a few years, sometime between 20 BC and AD 5. His name means 'victory' or possibly 'battle crow', and the coins he issued are very rare. One in particular, a gold stater, attracts a special interest, for my interpretation is that it shows astronomical signs which may point to the conjunctions of Saturn and Jupiter.

The coin depicts a stylised galloping horse, representing or symbolising a form of movement, or the effect of gravity, whereby it pulls an imaginary solar wheel (the Sun) across the sky. In this instance the wheel is below the horse's belly and there is a crescent moon above its back, so it is effectively portraying an image of the sky at night. Above the crescent moon we have two annulets, or rings, which may well represent two bright planets, the most likely contenders of which would be Jupiter and Saturn. This is, of course, speculation on my part and it could well represent Venus and Jupiter in conjunction, these being normally the two brightest planets visible, or alternatively two bright stars. However, given the fact that Saturn and Jupiter were so close together in the sky, and for such a prolonged period of time in the years 7 and 6 BC, it is possible that this is what the coin is portraying.

The Eppillus Gold Stater

Around the same time another ancient British king, or chieftain, named Eppillus, of the Atrebates tribe, based in an area of what would now be parts of Kent and north Hampshire, issued a very similar gold stater from his capital in Calleva (modern-day Silchester). This coin shows three rings above the horse and, again, these may well represent astronomical objects. In this instance it could be illustrating the three bright planets, Jupiter, Saturn and Mars in the year AD 6, in other words the planetary massing. Likewise, this is also rather speculative, but it is generally accepted that many Celtic coins of this time-frame do contain astronomical symbols, with spots or pellets indicating stars and well-defined circles representing the planets. Whilst they may also contain hidden meanings within their designs, there is every reason to believe that the bright planets had an important role to play in their celestial imagery.

Conclusion

It should be clear to the reader that the triple conjunctions of Jupiter and Saturn in 7 BC, as well as the other various conjunction theories, are not satisfactory explanations for the star of Bethlehem. Nevertheless they certainly would not have gone unnoticed by Magi of that time, who would also have had access to predictions of the occurrences. However, because they had happened so many times before, sometimes being far superior in appearance, they have to be considered as unlikely contenders for the star. With the benefit of hindsight, the author of Matthew realised that some other celestial sign was necessary in order for the prophecy of an anticipated Messiah to be fulfilled.

7
VENUS & URANUS

In the previous chapter it was noted that Venus and Jupiter conjunctions have, in the past, been put forward as possible contenders for the star of Bethlehem. However, as we have seen, the best conjunction of these two planets took place some time after the death of Herod and therefore cannot be considered as candidates. So perhaps, would Venus on its own be considered a possibility? It is certainly a fabulous object and at its best resembles a bright lantern in the sky. Having a maximum magnitude of -4.6 it is nearly six times as bright as its nearest rival Jupiter and, when at opposition, Mars. Because its orbit lies inside that of the Earth it never strays more than 47 degrees from the Sun. Since it frequently appears high in the dawn sky, it became known as the Morning Star. Likewise it can sometimes be seen in the western sky after sunset as an evening star. As both the Earth and Venus, like the other planets, are travelling in the same anti-clockwise direction around the Sun, an alignment only takes place every 584 days. This means that, in theory, every 292 days Venus appears as a morning star and then as an evening star for a similar period. In practice, however, when the planet is too close to the Sun in the sky, perhaps within about 10 degrees or so, it would not be visible.

The Phases of Venus

As Venus goes around the Sun it shows different phases in the same way that is demonstrated by the Moon as it orbits around the Earth. However, with Venus its apparent size varies considerably according to its distance from the Earth, so that when it is far away on the other side of the Sun, known as superior conjunction, its whole disc will be visible but will appear quite small. Later, as it goes around in its orbit and approaches the Earth, its diameter will become larger and it will show a gibbous phase, followed by a crescent and finally will disappear as it reaches its closest point to the Earth, known as inferior conjunction. The actual apparent size of the illuminated area of Venus is therefore balanced out so that Venus always appears to be very bright, except when it passes close to the Sun in the sky. It is at its brightest whenever its crescent phase is about 256 days before or after superior conjunction. Around this time it is so bright that it can be seen in daylight with the naked eye, provided that you know roughly its position. Whenever it becomes a thin crescent it is actually just about possible to discern its crescent shape, assuming that you have very keen eyesight. With the aid of a telescope, in 1610, Galileo became the first to study the phases of Venus and this provided him with further strong evidence in support of the Copernican heliocentric theory.

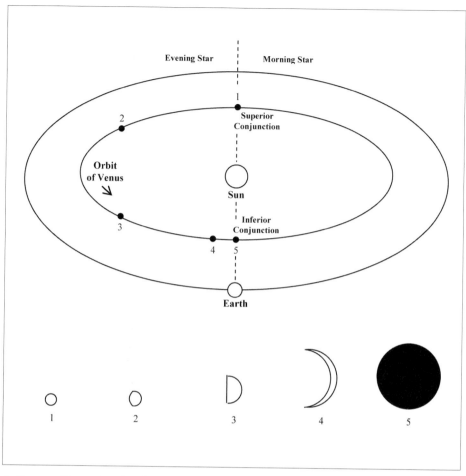

A diagram illustrating the phases of Venus and variations in its size as viewed from Earth. (Prepared and provided courtesy of Richard Archer)

Transits of Venus

Because the orbital plane of Venus is inclined by 3.4 degrees in relation to the Earth, it means that only rarely does it appear to cross in front of the Sun whenever it is at inferior conjunction. This occurs at intervals of either 105 or 122 years and is usually followed by another after eight years, so it could be said that they normally happen in pairs. The last duet of transits took place very recently, in 2004 and 2012, and we will now have to wait until 2117 and 2125 for the next pair.

In 1678 Edmund Halley realised that accurate telescopic measurements of the planet's movement against the face of the Sun, from widely different positions on the Earth, would present the perfect opportunity to determine solar distance. This was based upon the principle of trigonometrical parallax. Consequently at the next transit, in 1761, observations were carried out by teams of recorders, some of whom had been sent out to very remote parts of the world. The results were collated and gave rise to a value for the Sun's distance which was far more accurate than before.

Venus as a God

In ancient times Venus was worshipped for two reasons. Firstly because it was so bright and secondly because it often heralded the dawn and in a sense it could sometimes be used as a substitute for an alarm clock! The planet was worshipped by the Babylonians as *Ishtar* meaning 'mother of gods' and was associated with femininity, and as the third-brightest object in the sky it became accepted as a rival to the Sun and the Moon. It was named Venus by the Romans who regarded it as the goddess of love. One of the earliest astronomical records that has survived shows observations of Venus recorded upon an Assyrian clay tablet which is estimated to date from around 1700 BC. The Venus Tablet, as it has become known, was originally found at Kongunjik and is presently housed in the British Museum. The tablet also contains comments which clearly associate the appearance of Venus with crop fertility.

Telescopic Appearance

Through a telescope, Venus is disappointing. Apart from being able to see its dazzling phase it is virtually impossible to see any features. Occasionally vague greyish patches may be visible, but these do not represent surface details but the thick cloudy atmosphere of carbon dioxide which surrounds the entire planet. One unusual view through a telescope which has been observed on rare occasions is known as the Ashen Light, being a faint glow seen around the unilluminated edge of the planet whenever it is a very thin crescent. Prior to the Space Age, little was known about what lay underneath the clouds and it was commonly thought that the planet supported life, possibly of a sophisticated nature.

Close-Up Images

The first space probe to Venus, *Mariner 2*, successfully made a close fly-past in December 1962 and verified what some radio telescope signals had indicated in the 1950s; that the surface of Venus was very hot, in fact like an inferno. Further probes, both Russian and American, followed. Eventually the Russians managed to soft-land a probe onto the surface of Venus on 21 October 1975. *Venera 9* transmitted for fifty-three minutes before being destroyed by the hostile conditions. The photographs it sent back showed a desolate landscape with what appeared to be flattened stones and dark rocks, indicating chemical erosion. Measurements of the surface temperature recorded nearly 500° Celsius, with the atmospheric pressure at the surface being about ninety times that of the Earth's. It was found that the clouds also contain large amounts of sulphuric acid. The conditions on Venus are the result of a runaway greenhouse effect causing a very high concentration of carbon dioxide in its atmosphere. It now seems that the faint glow called Ashen Light may actually represent the heat of the planet glowing red in the dark.

In the 1990s, Venus was extensively mapped in great detail by NASA's *Magellan*, an orbiting space probe using synthetic aperture radar (SAR). This showed that most of the terrain is covered with volcanic flows. There are also strange mountainous ranges which have been called Ishtar, Aphrodite and Lada Terra. Also discovered were deep valleys, hundreds of impact craters, and volcanic depressions. Another mountainous region, Beta Regio, is host to two large shield volcanoes known as Rhea Mons and Theai Mons, each of which is about 2.5 miles in height. It is quite possible that volcanic activity is still taking place.

Conclusion

Most of the modern theories suggesting Venus as the star of Bethlehem do so because it was a member of a close conjunction with another planet, and it is uncommon to find support for Venus, by itself, as representing the star. However, in the nineteenth century it was considered by some to be a serious contender, one of its advocates being an army colonel, G. Mackinley, who claimed that the Magi saw the planet rise in the east in the spring of 8 BC and travelled to Jerusalem as a consequence. He contended that Christ was born on 20 September of that year and that the Magi visited towards the end of the period in which the planet was visible, in December. One of the reasons he put forward his Venus theory was that he recognised the importance of the planet as a timekeeper for the Babylonians, who it seems were early risers in order to take part in pre-dawn activities such as religious ceremonies. Not everyone in the nineteenth century was fooled by such ideas, however, and the theory that Venus was the star was denounced by many astronomers, including J. E. Gore, who regarded the whole notion as absurd, given the fact that it was such a 'familiar object'.

That would appear to say it all and, in the words of Sir Patrick Moore, if the wise men thought that Venus was the star of Bethlehem, 'they would not have been very wise'! The planet may be dazzling and a glorious sight in the sky but it could not possibly have been mistaken as the star. It had no astrological significance for being so and it can be viewed virtually all the time, except for a few weeks when it is too close to the Sun, so there could have been nothing unusual or special about its appearance.

Uranus

Let us now jump from the brightest to the faintest planet visible to the naked eye, namely Uranus. At opposition Uranus can have a magnitude of +5.3, meaning that it is just visible in clear dark skies. Taking this into consideration it seems strange that it was only 'discovered' in 1781 by William Herschel. Observing from his back garden in Bath, Herschel was using a telescope of high quality that he had made himself when he decided to study stars in the constellation of Gemini. Initially he thought that he had found a comet, but more detailed observations revealed a small bluish green disc, clearly indicating that it was neither a star nor a comet, but a new planet.

However, it is quite possible that Uranus had been detected by Babylonian astronomers as far back as 312 BC, and perhaps even earlier. Unfortunately there are no detailed records to support such identification, but then so few have survived. Did Herschel therefore discover or simply rediscover Uranus?

Another Gas Giant

Uranus is the third-largest planet in the solar system next to Jupiter and Saturn and is another gas giant with a diameter of about 31,000 miles. It is composed mainly of hydrogen and helium but also contains small quantities of methane and ammonia. It has a turquoise appearance due to the methane gas in its atmosphere absorbing sunlight. It is likely that it also contains heavier elements including oxygen, nitrogen, carbon, silicon and iron. Below the gaseous clouds there may be a mantle of highly pressurised heated water which surrounds a rocky core.

The planet is unusual in that its axis of rotation has a tilt of 97.87 degrees to its orbital plane which means that each of its poles points in the direction of the Sun and the Earth. This was probably caused by collisions in its early life with planetesimals or comets. Like Jupiter and Saturn, it has a banded appearance caused by the zonal circulation of clouds, although extensive hazy layers obscure its main weather systems. During its visit by *Voyager 2* in January 1986, clouds of methane were photographed which resembled clouds on Earth.

In 1977, Earth-based observations of a stellar occultation by the planet appeared to show the star flicker close to its disc indicating that it had a faint ring system. *Voyager 2* subsequently discovered two further rings and it now seems that its system contains hundreds of very thin rings circulating around its disc. Over twenty satellites have been discovered, most as a result of the *Voyager 2* mission. The five largest, Titania, Oberon, Umbriel, Ariel and Miranda were all found using large Earth-based telescopes.

A Faint but Discernible Object

Given the fact that Uranus/Jupiter conjunctions occur regularly – every twelve years – and Uranus/Saturn conjunctions every twenty years, it seems feasible that Uranus could have been detected by Babylonian astronomers, although it is extremely doubtful as to whether they ever determined its orbit. During the period 9 to 7 BC, Uranus remained in the constellation of Pisces – as it only appears to drift about 4 degrees in the sky each year. In the year 9 BC, on 5 February it was in conjunction with Saturn, the separation being 1.1 degrees. It seems unlikely that, given the activity of Jupiter and Saturn in 7 BC in Pisces, Uranus did not go unseen. Despite being very faint it would have been discernible.

The Harris Theory

It has been suggested by J. N. Harris that the very faintness of the planet would have meant that the Magi would have been anxious to study it and take measurements of its positions in the sky, possibly necessitating additional observations from different locations around the time of opposition. Such locations may have included Bethlehem, as it was favourably positioned on an elevated site and it was in a westerly direction. Harris suggests that Uranus may have been detected in March of 9 BC, shortly after the first observations of the eastern rising of Saturn would have taken place, and consequently the Babylonians would have reasoned that about six months later it would reach opposition in the same manner as Jupiter and Saturn. This would also have applied to the years 8 and 7 BC, and he deduced that it may be the reason why the Magi embarked on their journey towards Judea. It may have been for astrological reasons as the planet was in Pisces or it could have been purely for astronomical or scientific purposes, as part of a procedure to collect information about the planet and its movements.

Like the opposition of Jupiter and Saturn, Uranus would also have appeared to 'go before' the Magi in their journey from Jerusalem to Bethlehem and 'stand over' Bethlehem as it culminated or reached its highest point in the southern sky. Harris suggests that the Magi may have journeyed to Jerusalem and Bethlehem more than once, in order to observe and measure Uranus in the period 9 to 7 BC. It is possible that Matthew 2:10 refers to them 'being overjoyed' at seeing the planet again because they may have lost track of it on their travels – it was, after all, frequently on the periphery of naked-eye visibility – or because they were now able to collate data on its behaviour.

It has been suggested that Uranus was also possibly observed in the years 312 and 311 BC by the Babylonians, as the planet was occulted on no less than three occasions by Jupiter. The occultation on 23 September 312 BC took place when Uranus was at opposition and at a relatively bright magnitude of 5.4. It would be easy to make the assumption that this was hardly likely to have gone unnoticed. However, when these two planets became so close together the brightness or glare of Jupiter would have drowned or overwhelmed the fainter planet to the extent that it would have been invisible. Their best chance of viewing Uranus was actually when it was an appreciable distance away from Jupiter in the sky.

Earlier Babylonian cuneiform records may also make reference to a moving star-like object in the constellation of Pisces, mentioning that 'if the fish star [in Pisces] approaches the acre star [in the constellation of Pegasus]'. There is also reference to a faint object in an early star list known as the *12 Stars of Etam, Akkad and Amurra*, which tells us:

> When the stars of Enlil have disappeared, the great faint star which bisects the heavens and stands, is *Sag Me Gar*; he [probably the god Jupiter] changes his position and wanders over the heavens.

Harris suggests that this text may refer to 'intermittent sightings of the star' with respect to Jupiter. He concludes by pointing out that given the limited numbers of cuneiform planetary data available, Babylonian astronomy was probably a lot more developed than is generally accepted and that we should not play down their observational abilities.

Conclusion

Could Uranus really have been the star of Bethlehem? Although it is a faint object, it is a more likely candidate than the familiar Venus which is about 10,000 times brighter. Certainly an interpretation of Matthew could indicate a faint object which had appeared and later reappeared and it could also help to explain why Herod and his advisers seem to have not been aware of it. The conjunction of Jupiter and Saturn in 7 BC also involved Uranus in Pisces, which was at opposition on 13 September, and an easy naked eye object in clear conditions, but because the planet remained relatively faint it may well have attracted more attention and possibly been considered of more importance than the other two planets. However, the strong possibility that the Babylonians may already have been aware of Uranus is self-defeating, for then it is in the same category as Venus – it was a familiar object and therefore not exceptional or unusual. Therefore unless Uranus had just been discovered by the Magi in 9 or 7 BC or thereabouts, which seems unlikely, it would seem very improbable that it could ever have been seriously regarded as representing the star of Bethlehem, whether on its own or in conjunction with its much brighter companions Jupiter and Saturn.

8

VARIABLE & EXPLODING STARS

Most stars in the sky appear to shine continuously at the same level of brightness for years on end. However, a high proportion show brightness levels which appear to fluctuate at regular and sometimes irregular intervals, and these are known as variable stars. In fact, our own Sun is a slightly variable star as it has a sunspot cycle every eleven years.

Algol

Perhaps the most famous variable star is Algol, in Perseus, which in the past was referred to as the 'Demon Star'. Every two and a half days, Algol fades quickly over a period of about four hours, from about magnitude +2.2 to +3.4, staying at its minimum for around twenty minutes before proceeding to brighten up again. It is fascinating to watch this happen and the best way to judge its fluctuating brightness is to compare it with two stars close-by whose magnitudes are slightly above and below that of Algol's and which are known not to be variable.

Algol is not actually in itself a variable star. The variations in its brightness are due to another, smaller companion star passing in front of its disc. It is what is known as an eclipsing variable, or eclipsing binary. The two stars must be very close together as it only takes two and a half days for the fainter star to complete an orbit around its primary, and not surprisingly they cannot be seen separately as they are too close together. The diagram overleaf shows a light curve illustrating the variation in the apparent brightness of Algol over time. There is actually a further small blip in the curve as a result of the primary star eclipsing its fainter secondary. Other famous naked-eye eclipsing variables include Beta Lyrae near the bright star Vega, and Epsilon Aurigae, which is close to another bright star, Capella, the latter being variable over a period of twenty-seven years.

Cepheids

A second category of variables are those where the changes in light are as a result of genuine changes in the star's luminosity. One of the best-known types are called Cepheids, named after a star called Delta Cephei whose magnitude varies from about +4.4 to +3.5 over a very regular period of 5.3 days. In fact, all Cepheids' variable intervals of fluctuating brightness are incredibly precise and there is a direct relationship between their period and their luminosity so that the longer the period, the greater the brightness. Knowledge of this relationship has become a very

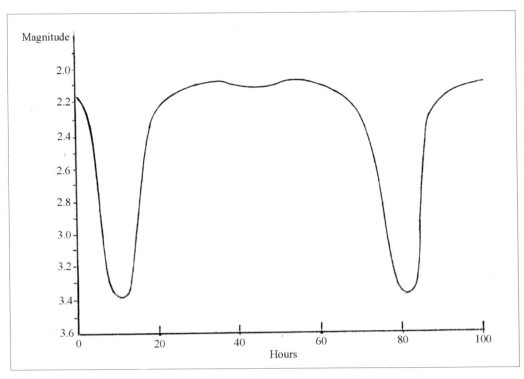

A diagram of Algol's light curve. (Prepared by Richard Archer and David Collins)

useful tool in astronomy in measuring the distance of such stars, not only within our own galaxy but also in other galaxies, since if we know the star's luminosity and its magnitude we can determine its distance. Such stars are giants but they are also very old and actually pulsate, expanding and contracting on a regular basis.

Mira Stars

Another category of variable stars are the long-period variety, known as Mira stars after their namesake Mira or Omicron Ceti in the constellation of Cetus the Whale, which lies below the constellations of Aries and Pisces. Such stars are red giants and their magnitude variations and their periods are much greater than those of Cepheids. However, there is no direct relationship between their period and their luminosity. Mira itself has a magnitude range from about +10 to +2 and has a period of about 332 days, although both its period and magnitude ranges are subject to irregularities and its magnitude has been known to vary between +11.1 to +1.7 and its period from between about 320 to 370 days. Unusually, Mira has a long minimum period of brightness followed by a sharp rise and slow fall.

Mira was one of the first stars to be found to vary periodically, early records indicating that it was David Fabricius, a German theologian, who first noticed the star on 13 August 1596 at about magnitude +3. He realised that it was not included

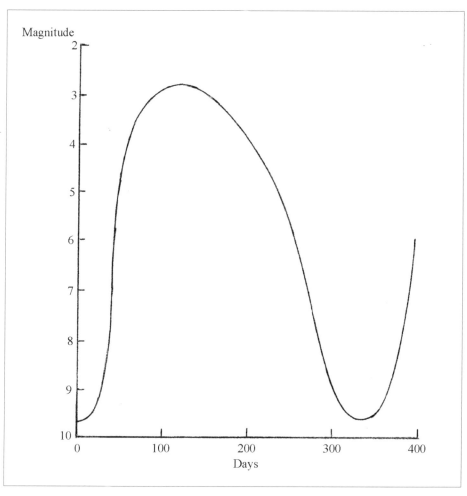

A diagram of Mira Ceti's light curve. (Prepared by Richard Archer and David Collins)

in any star maps or listings and within a few months he found that it had faded to invisibility. On 15 February 1609 he retrieved it, again at about magnitude +3. In 1603 Johann Bayer, a German lawyer and celestial cartographer, named it Omicron and recorded it as being of magnitude +4. It was not until 1667 that Ishmael Boullialdus, an astronomer and mathematician, first established its period at about eleven months. In 1923 Robert G. Aitken, an American astronomer specialising in the observation of double stars, found that Mira has a faint companion which is now called ZV Ceti, or Mira B. The companion itself is variable between magnitudes +9.5 and +12. It orbits Mira about once every 1,800 years and it is possible that it could be a white dwarf with an accretion disc, which means that, due to strong gravitational attraction, it may be pulling material away from the parent star.

Although Mira stars are quite common, only a few are visible to the naked eye at maximum. Another famous example is Chi Cygni in the constellation of Cygnus the Swan, also sometimes referred to as the Northern Cross. Its brightness ranges from about +14 at its faintest to around +3.3 at maximum over a period of 407 days. There are also many irregular variables of which R Coronae is perhaps the best known. However, as its magnitude ranges from around +15 at minimum to about +6 at maximum it becomes barely visible to the naked eye. Another famous example is the star Eta Carina, which was first recorded by Edmund Halley in 1677.

The Richardson Theory

When Mira is easily visible to the naked eye it shows a distinctive red hue and because of this it was suggested by Montague Richardson, in *The Star of Biet Lahm*, that it represented the star of Bethlehem. This was based upon his reasoning that the Magi were Zoroastrians from Persia, and because he thought that they worshipped fire as their primary purpose, they would have applied a very special importance to a star coloured red, especially one which would have seemed to appear suddenly. On this particular occasion the star's maximum brightness would have had to exceed that of its previous appearances, possibly giving the impression that it was a new star, outshining its neighbours so that it stood out in an area devoid of bright stars. Their colour association therefore ruled out all the planets (other than Mars), comets and nova, all of which have a whitish or bluish appearance. Also, because it would have been quite low in the southern sky, it could have given the impression that it was standing low over a specific dwelling in Bethlehem as the Magi approached from Jerusalem. Richardson claimed that the Magi entered Jerusalem around 31 May 6 BC and travelled to Bethlehem early the next morning to witness the bright star from an elevated site and low in the southern sky, appearing to stand over the house where Jesus was.

The problem with Richardson's theory is that even if Mira had brightened significantly above its normal maximum, which is very rare, it would seem that it would still have had little astrological impact, as being in the same category as a nova it would not have been associated with an important event. There is also no real reason why the star had to be red in colour as the Zoroastrians' main religious objective was not in fact the worship of fire, but that of a single god.

Novae

By far the most cataclysmic and interesting variable stars are novae (nova is Latin meaning new). It involves the sudden outburst of a normally inconspicuous star becoming bright for a short period of perhaps a few days or weeks before falling back to its previous magnitude. The most recent bright nova occurred in the constellation of Cygnus in 1975 and reached magnitude +1.8, but within about ten days had ceased to be visible to the naked eye. The star had originally been around magnitude +21, so that at its maximum its brightness had soared by about

40 million times! Novae fall into three broad categories which are based upon the time it takes for a nova to fall in brightness by three magnitudes:

1. Type NA – fast, less than 100 days.

2. Type NB – slow, taking more than 100 days.

3. Type NC – a very slow rise, perhaps over years, followed by a very slow decline.

A combination of large telescopes and sophisticated technology involving the use of CCD cameras has meant that astronomers nowadays can take wide-field images of faint stars, sometimes even revealing a nova's precursor star. Investigations have shown that a nova involves two stars, or in other words a binary system. One star has a low density, whereas its companion is a white dwarf which is a small, exceptionally dense star which has used up its nuclear reserves. The white dwarf has a very high gravitational pull on the primary star and sucks or transfers material away from it to form a ring of material around itself. A nuclear outburst occurs when a lot of material has accumulated and gas is ejected at a very high speed. At the conclusion of the outburst the system stabilises and goes back to its original state known as a post-nova stage. There are also recurrent novae which have been known to outburst on more than one occasion, a good example being T Coronae in the constellation of the Crown which flared in 1866 and again in 1946 followed by two smaller outbursts in 1963 and 1975.

Supernovae

A supernova represents an outburst which is in the region of a thousand times greater than any nova and basically represents an exploding star. There are two broad types of supernovae and these are referred to as simply Type I and Type II. A Type I supernova again involves a binary system with one of its components being a white dwarf, however this time when the outburst happens it is completely destroyed. This causes a gigantic explosion producing a dazzling emission of radiation which can be equal to the combined brightness of hundreds of millions of stars.

A Type II supernova is completely different. All stars are formed from dust and material that condensed out of a nebula, but their mass can vary significantly and it has been calculated that such a supernova can only come about from a star which is more than 1.4 times the mass of our Sun, known as the Chandrasekhar limit after the astronomer who calculated it. Although the star will behave normally for most of its life, when it becomes older its hydrogen fuel becomes exhausted. Its nuclear reactions start to produce heavier elements, and its temperature rises significantly, perhaps to as much as 3 billion Centigrade. A chain reaction takes over where the elements produced become progressively heavier until the core of the star comprises iron. As this element does not react, the nuclear processes cease and there is an implosion followed by a rebounding cataclysmic explosion. Material is scattered into space in all directions and an expanding cloud of gas remains where the star once was. In its centre lies a small, incredibly dense object known as a neutron star because its atomic protons and electrons have been crushed together to form neutrons which have no electrical charge.

Although a neutron star is only a few miles in diameter, its density is so great that a teaspoon of its material or plasma may weigh thousands of tons. Such stars rotate extremely fast, normally many times per second, and emit radio pulses in two opposite directions due to their strong magnetic fields. For this reason they are sometimes called pulsars and they were first detected in 1967 by Jocelyn Bell using a radio telescope array. Initially the pulses could not be explained and they were found to be so regular that it was thought that they were signals from extraterrestrials trying to communicate with us!

Perhaps the most famous supernova to be recorded was that of 1054, which occurred in the constellation of Taurus and is known as the Crab Nebula, as large telescopes reveal its resemblance to such a creature, although in smaller instruments it looks like a faint smudge. In 1987 a supernova appeared in a satellite galaxy of our Milky Way known as the Large Magellanic Cloud at a distance of about 170,000 light years. Unfortunately it was only visible from areas roughly south of the Tropic of Cancer. Both of these supernovae were of the Type II variety and radiate very strong radio wave emissions.

A Shortage of Historical Records

Obviously any bright nova or supernova would have been of great interest to ancient astronomers; however, records of such events seem to be in short supply. One of the reasons for this is that during the Dark Ages in Europe the general belief was that God had created the heavens in a perfect and unchanging image and therefore any phenomenon which suggested otherwise tended to be disregarded and ignored. This was very much as a result of the Christian church accepting into its doctrines the Aristotelian theory of the universe as modified by Claudius Ptolemy.[8] This basically said that the universe was a sphere with the Earth at its centre surrounded by the Sun, Moon, planets and fixed stars, carried around on a series of concentric or crystalline spheres nestled inside one another. At least Aristotle had got one thing right – he reasoned that the Earth itself was a sphere because of the curved nature of the shadow cast on the Moon during a lunar eclipse.

As mentioned earlier it was not until the Copernican or heliocentric model became established that the idea of an Earth-centred universe was finally put to rest. However, it was some time before it became accepted by everyone and it took two separate Type I supernovas in 1572 and 1604 to provide the valuable evidence needed to support it.

Tycho's Star

The supernova of 1572, which appeared in the constellation of Cassiopeia, is known as Tycho's Star for it was the Danish astronomer Tycho Brahe who, although not having discovered it, carried out very detailed observations of it after its first appearance on 11 November of that year. Over its eighteen months of visibility he studied its brightness, estimated to have reached -4, its colour and position, and also collected details of observations from astronomers in other countries such as Thomas Digges in England. Without any telescopic aid he was still able, over time, to determine that as the Earth moved in its orbit around the Sun, the supernova did not shift its position in the sky, appearing fixed, with no parallax effect whatsoever. This meant that the supernova had to be outside the orbit of the Moon and planets and belonged to the fixed stars, providing a body blow to the idea of a perfect and unchanging universe.

Strangely enough, Tycho Brahe was not a Copernican and developed his own Tychonian model whereby the planets revolved around the Sun, and in turn the Sun and the Moon revolved around a static central Earth. This model was very complex and presented numerous problems, but nevertheless it received widespread support, which continued well into the seventeenth century.

Tycho Brahe himself was an interesting character. Having been born into an aristocratic family, he was kidnapped as a baby by his uncle Jorgen Brahe who raised him. Upon his uncle's death he was left a considerable inheritance and he proceeded to go on to Copenhagen University. In 1566 Tycho fought a duel, using swords, with another Danish nobleman, Manderup Parsberg, and ended up with the end of his nose being sliced off! He had it replaced with a gold-and-silver alloy cover which he wore for the rest of his life.

He developed a great interest in astronomy and acquired a large quadrant, at the same time building an observatory at Skane in 1571. This was in order to improve the records of planetary and star positions, having realised earlier that the existing Copernican tables of planetary motion were highly inaccurate. The publication of the results of his observations of the 1572 supernova in his *De Stella Nova* of 1573 made him famous, and in 1576 the Danish King, Frederick II, provided him with the island of Hveen where he built two observatories at Uraniborg and Stjernborg. Using a 78-inch mural quadrant he was able to carry out very precise observations of the stars and planets. In particular, he was able to improve the accuracy of predicted planetary positions thirty-fold. Tycho determined their positions at many different points in their orbits and not just at opposition, which earlier astronomers had concentrated upon. He also took into consideration the effect of atmospheric refraction, to correct the positions of the stars and planets. He wrote two ground-breaking books called *Astronomiae Instauratae Mechanica* (1598), and *Astronomiae Instauratae Progymnasmata* (1602) in which he discussed his work and his instruments.

Later his precise measurements of the Sun's movements across the sky enabled him to calculate the correct length of a year to within one second! This subsequently paved the way for the Julian calendar in 1582 to drop ten days, as he showed that over time it had drifted away from its correct alignment by such a period. He also discovered a change in the rate of the Moon's orbit around the Earth, and a periodic change in its orbital behaviour. Around the same time he also produced a detailed catalogue containing the positions of 777 stars.

Tycho was also an eccentric. For entertainment, his home at Uraniborg contained clockwork statues that moved, and he had a pet dwarf called Jeppe. However, he also possessed a cruel streak; his property contained cells where he would confine tenants who failed to pay their rents, and consequently he became very unpopular and resented by the people of Hveen. Complaints flowed and eventually, having lost friends in the Danish court, he was forced to leave in 1597 and died in voluntary exile in Prague in 1601.

Kepler's Star

Another supernova appeared in 1604, in the constellation of Ophiuchus, and has become known as Kepler's Star. Although Kepler did not actually discover it he certainly was one of the first to view it. Kepler was every bit as meticulous as his predecessor Tycho in measuring its position and varying brightness. This was a Type I supernova but it was not as bright as that of 1572, with an estimated magnitude of -2.5 due to the fact that it was further away, at a distance of about 25,000 light years, and also partially obscured by dust clouds within our galaxy.

Earlier Records of Supernovae

The general shortage of European records of both novae and supernovae prior to Tycho's star of 1572 means that we have to refer to Chinese and Korean archives for reliable records. There were supernovae in 1006, 1054 and 1181 all recorded by the Chinese, with the 1006 event in the constellation of Lupus the Wolf having been described as being much brighter than Venus. That particular supernova was also recorded by observers in Saint Gallen in Southern France.

So were there any supernovae around at the time of Christ's birth? Well, going back further in time we have accounts of such events in AD 393, 386 and 185, with the latter supernova in the constellation of Centaurus apparently having been extremely brilliant. However, it seems clear from the ancient Chinese and Korean chronicles, which are reliable sources, that there was no supernova recorded around the time of Christ's birth. This is based upon the reasoning that during the period from 12 BC to AD 10 no object recorded was seen for more than about three months, whereas if there had been a supernova it would have persisted for a much longer duration, as such objects are usually visible for at least nine months.

Recent Supernova Theories

The research into Chinese and Korean chronicles is a relatively recent development and has been confined mainly to the last fifty years. Consequently, although a supernova can now be dismissed, with reasonable certainty, as representing the star of Bethlehem, in the recent past it was a popular candidate. One of its more recent advocates was Arthur C. Clarke, who proposed that a pulsar in the constellation of Aquila the Eagle, numbered PSR 1913 +16, might represent the collapsed remnant of the star of Bethlehem. This was also the view taken by A. J. Morehouse, who, in an article entitled *The Christmas Star as a Supernova in Aquila*, in 1978, suggested that the same supernova represented the star. He associated it with an object recorded by the Chinese in April, 4 BC and claimed that it was the final sign of three events that led the Magi to Bethlehem. The other two were the triple conjunction of 7 BC and another object recorded by the Chinese in March, 5 BC which he also took to be a nova. Positioned near to the star Gamma Aquila it would have been close to the ecliptic, and therefore easily visible from both Babylon and Judea. In April, 4 BC, over Bethlehem it would have been about 70 degrees above the horizon, so very high up in the sky. It would also have appeared very bright.

Clarke and Morehouse's supernova theory was strengthened by the fact that the pulsar's rotation, or spinning period, at 0.059 seconds is very fast and suggests that it could well have been formed about 2,000 years ago, although it must be pointed out that the rotation period is only a rough guide to ageing a supernova, its actual size being another important factor. This has been determined by studies of the spinning motion of many of the small pulsars that lie at the centre of where supernovae exploded. Because they have strong magnetic fields, the rate of spin gradually slows down over time so that, generally, the faster the observed rotation period the more recent the supernova, hence the pulsar in the Crab Nebula (1054) has a period of 0.033 of a second, which is also considered very fast. To date the fastest recorded is 0.0014, or 716 times a second!

The supernova theory of Clarke and Morehouse seems to falter when they both identify it as an April, 4 BC object, as this is far too late for the star of Bethlehem, for as we have seen earlier Herod would already have been dead by this date and Jesus, as implied by the author of Matthew, would probably have been at least two years old. If instead the same object was to be identified with one as recorded by the Chinese in 5 BC, then this would become more interesting. However, as we shall see later this object was observed for only seventy days or so, which is well short of the normally expected minimum duration of nine months for a supernova.

Ancient Chinese and Korean Records

Like the Babylonians, the Chinese and to a lesser extent the Koreans were also keen observers and recorded details of all types of celestial events. The earliest records indicate that sightings of eclipses of the Sun possibly go back as far as 2165 BC. They developed a great fear of these events and, realising that such occurrences were cyclical, were able to predict future eclipses. Also recorded were naked eye sunspots, which would have been discernible through cloud, fog or smoke, although such visible features are actually quite common. Records of early observations were etched on the bones of large animals or tortoise shells, but as time passed they became written in books or on silk and, with more space being available, greater detail was included, sometimes with the aid of illustrations.

The Chinese also recorded details of aurorae, meteor showers, comets and novae. An ancient Chinese historian, Ssu-ma Ch'ien, who lived around the year 100 BC, compiled a detailed listing of events during the Chou period which covered from about 1100 to 220 BC and the subsequent Han dynasty, known as the *Shih Chi*, meaning 'historical records'. Also of importance was the *Ch'ien-Han Shu*, the 'Official History of the Former Han Dynasty' (206 BC–AD 9), prepared by Pan Piao (AD 3–54), which was subsequently extended by his son Pan Ku and daughter Pan Chao to include astronomical sightings. A further history was later compiled by Ma Tuan-Lin between AD 1240 and 1280 in his *Wen-hsien t'ung-K'ao*, meaning 'Comprehensive Examination of Literature', of which chapters 286 and 294 concern comets and novae.

In 1871, John Williams translated and compiled a list covering 372 comets observed by the Chinese between 611 BC and AD 1640. Each was numbered consecutively and number 51 was Halley's Comet, which appeared on 26 August 12 BC. Number 52 was first registered by Ma Tuan-Lin, who wrote:

In the reign of the Emperor Gae Te, the second year of the epoch *Koen-ping*, the second Moon, a comet appeared in *Keen New* for about seventy days.

Gae Te reigned from 6 to 1 BC, with the epoch of *Keon-ping* lasting from 6 to 3 BC so that the second year is therefore 5 BC. The reference to the second Moon implies a period, or lunar month, commencing around 5 March with *Keen New* representing an area of the sky including the stars Alpha and Beta Capricorn.

The sighting can be corroborated by Ho Pang-Yoke, a Chinese historian, who in 1962 also translated and listed ancient Chinese records of comets and novae. Using as his source the *Han Shu* compiled by Pan Ku and Pan Chao around AD 70, he identified as number 63 in his list the following description of a comet in 5 BC:

Second year of the *Chien-p'ing* reign period, second month [5 BC, 9 March–6 April], a *shu-hsing* appeared at *Ch'ien-niu* [an area of sky including Alpha and Beta Capricorn in the constellation of Capricorn] for over seventy days.

Chien-p'ing and *Ch'ien-niu* are the same as *Keon-ping* and *Keen New*, being simply variations in their spelling. The term *shu-hsing*, traditionally reading as *hui-hsing*, refers to a broad or sweeping star, meaning a star with a tail, or in other words, a tailed comet. It is important to distinguish this from the terms *po-hsing*, meaning a sparkling or bushy star, referring to a comet without a visible tail, and a *ko-hsing*, which means a guest star or nova.

A further interpretation of the *Han Shu* record of the 5 BC event is provided in Hsi Tse-Tsung's 1957 catalogue of ancient novae and comets, the main source of which was the *Wen-hsien t'ung-K'ao* and other ancient historical and astronomical material from China and Japan. Number 11 in his history refers to a *shu-hsing* during the same period as the above, except that this time it is reported as being near to the star Alpha Aquilae, known as Altair, in the constellation of Aquila the Eagle. His source was also the *Han Shu* so it may be that his slightly dissimilar placement in the sky is down to a different interpretation or misidentification of its recorded location.

The above sources would therefore seem to imply that the object of 5 BC was a tailed comet, also indicating that it would have appeared high in the southern sky, being positioned slightly north of the ecliptic.

The Chinese also recorded an object in 4 BC, and this is listed as number 64 by Ho Peng Yoke. The *Han Shu* provides us with the following description: 'In the third year of the *Chien-p'ing* reign period, the third month, *chi yu*, there was a *po-hsing* at *Ho Ku*.' This means that, during a period commencing from 24 April 4 BC, a 'sparkling star' or tailless comet was seen in an area of the sky near the bright star Altair, in the constellation of Aquila the Eagle.

This comet was also noted by Williams as number 53 in his catalogue, using Thung Chien Kang Mu, a twelfth-century historian as his source: 'In the third year of the same epoch, the third Moon, there was a comet in *Ho Koo*.' This also refers to 4 BC, in the month of April, with the term *Ho Koo* implying a similar area within Aquila.

The same object may also have been recorded by the Koreans in their *History of the Three Kingdoms*, the third chapter of the *Chronicle of Silla* mentioning that in the 'fifty-fourth year of *Hyokkose Wong*, second month, *chi-yu*, a *po-hsing* appeared at *Ho-Ku*'. There is a discrepancy here, however, in that the word *chi-yu* refers to a day which does not exist in the second month, but if '*I yu*' is substituted for it, as the two Chinese characters are very similar, in fact almost identical, then the date quoted implies 31 March 4 BC. Some astronomers, such as David Clark, John Parkinson and Richard Stephenson, and more recently Mark Kidger, do believe that the description of the day '*chi-yu*' should have read '*I yu*'.

Although the Korean text appears to refer to the same event of 4 BC as registered by the Chinese, it should be pointed out that as the *Chronicle of Silla* was not compiled until AD 1145, the details of the comet may have been simply copied by the Koreans from the earlier Chinese manuscripts. This may have helped them to correct omissions within their records, as these are considered to be far less reliable than their Chinese counterparts. The difference in the description of the months may simply be put down to an error in translation.

The 4 BC object corresponded very closely to that registered in 5 BC, given that it appeared around a similar time of year and was recorded almost within an identical area of the sky, whilst also indicating no apparent movement. This has led to the belief that they may have been one and the same object, with that of 4 BC being simply misdated.

Nova or Comet?

Surprisingly, despite all the available evidence, Clark, Parkinson and Stephenson and also Kidger considered that the object of 5 BC was a nova rather than a comet. They pointed out the apparent vagueness of the Chinese terms *po-hsing* and *k'o-hsing*, which refer to a tailless comet and a nova/supernova respectively, and the possibility that observations may have been mistaken or misinterpreted between the two. Thus, a description of a nova could have been inadvertently recorded as a comet. Their reasoning is based upon the fact that the object appeared for so long in the sky (seventy days) but contained no note of any movement, which they regarded as an indication that it was probably a nova.

Clark and Stephenson carried out extensive research on a total of seventy-five suspected Nova covering a period of many centuries. They used a rating system between 1 and 5 to indicate the level of confidence that they had in each object studied, with class 1 suggesting a long-lasting stellar event that is either a nova or supernova. The 5 BC object was designated a class 2 rating, which implied that it was a probable nova or even a supernova, although possibly a comet on the grounds that it had been described by the Chinese as a tailed comet.

The fact remains that we have Chinese sources describing the object as a comet with a tail. If there had been any doubt about this then it would seem reasonable to assume that it would have been designated a *po-hsing* rather than a *shu-hsing*. Another argument against the object being a nova is that when we view the constellations of Capricorn and Aquila we are looking towards a relatively remote part of our galaxy. Whilst this area of the sky is close to the main plane of the Milky Way, where the majority of its stars exist, it is nevertheless outside it, and therefore the chances of seeing a nova or supernova are proportionally reduced. Alpha and Beta Capricorn are about 25 degrees south of the galactic plane, although Altair is considerably closer at around 9 degrees south. This view is supported by the fact that only about 13 per cent of the sixty brightest novae and supernovae observed over the last 2,000 years have been found to be outside the galactic equator by more than fifteen degrees, although of these, 75 per cent actually appeared in Aquila, whereas none were recorded in Capricorn. Aquila is also rich in the number of variable stars lying within it in total contrast to Capricorn, the ratio between the two being around twenty-to-one.

One of the earliest to identify the object of 5 BC as a nova was a Jesuit missionary, J. F. Foucquet. In 1729 he translated the reference in the *Han-Shu* as relating to a nova. This was taken up by Sir Hans Sloane, an Irish physician, collector and scientist, who identified it as the star of Bethlehem, and later by Frederick Münter, a German theologian and church historian, who in 1827 published a book on the subject, although he incorrectly thought that it had appeared in 4 BC rather than 5 BC. More recently Knut Lundmark, a Swedish astronomer, in 1953 took up the nova theory and considered that since it lasted for seventy days it would have given the Magi sufficient time to journey to Jerusalem whilst it was visible.

In 1960, Hugh Montefiore, later to become the Bishop of Birmingham, connected the idea of a nova in 5 BC with the triple conjunctions of 7 BC. Bearing in mind a prophecy that the Messiah would be born two years after the appearance of a star, he proposed that the Magi, having witnessed the planetary conjunctions, subsequently commenced their journey to Jerusalem and proceeded to be greeted by the nova. A similar view was taken by Jack Finegan in his *Handbook of Biblical Chronology* (1964) who suggested that the triple conjunction may have attracted the Magi's attention towards Judea and that the subsequent novae or comets of 5 and 4 BC represented the star of Bethlehem. Hughes, in the Christmas edition of *Nature* (December 1976), whilst supporting the conjunction theory, also considered the possibility that the objects of 5 and 4 BC had a significant part to play. However, he subsequently withdrew this option on the grounds that it did not fit in with the description in Matthew, which implies that the Magi observed the same star twice and not two different objects, as he had suggested through a combination of conjunctions and novae or comets.

The Kidger Theory

One of the more recent advocates of the nova theory is Mark Kidger who, in his book *The Star of Bethlehem: An Astronomer's View*, investigated a number of possible candidates in Aquila, and assuming that the nova must be close to the star Theta Aquilae, identified one to its north-west known as DO Aquilae, this being its description in the *General Catalogue of Variable Stars*, which was drawn up by the Russian astronomer B. V. Kukarin. This star is normally very faint, at around magnitude +18, and was only discovered in 1925, when it was around magnitude +9. It is a nova whose brightness is very slow to retreat from its maximum. Its positional coordinates of right ascension 31.7 and declination -11.8 make it lie in between the two constellations of Aquila and Capricorn, and it is quite close to where Clark and Stephenson had suggested. The term right ascension is the celestial sphere's equivalent of longitude, whereas declination corresponds to sky latitude and is expressed as the angular distance north or south of the celestial equator.

Kidger believes that this nova may be a long-period recurrent type and might have experienced a mass eruption sometime in the past. Consequently he suggests that this might have occurred in 5 BC, identifying it as the star of Bethlehem, although he himself admits that it is a 'long shot'. In fact it would have to be a very 'long shot', as to have been readily visible to the naked eye its brightness would have had to increase by about 13 to 14 magnitudes, which would have been exceedingly rare for any recurrent-type nova.

An Ancient British Star

Are there any other indicators of the object of 5 BC, other than those extracted from oriental manuscripts? It has been suggested by R. S. McIvor, writing for the

American Astronomical Variable Star Observers Newsletter, that certain ancient British kings issued coins which depict an object close to the constellation of Aquila. The ancient British King Eppillus issued a coin which shows an eagle and it has been claimed that this could represent the constellation of Aquila. It also has a tiny dot inside a circle to the north of the western wing, which may well represent a bright star – a nova or supernova perhaps? The coin dates to between 10 BC and AD 10.

During the same period King Tincomarus of the Regini tribe, whose capital seems to have been first at Selsey then Chichester in Sussex, also produced a coin with an almost identical image. This design continued under the later kings Epaticus and Caratacus and can be dated to between AD 35 and 43, ceasing when the Roman invasion under Claudius took place.

One of the leading authorities on Celtic coins, Chris Rudd, thinks differently. His opinion is that Eppillus was probably copying an image from Roman coins which frequently showed an eagle, and was using it as a symbol to portray power and domination. This also explains why it continued to be depicted on coins right up to AD 43. Regarding the dot or pellet inside a small circle, known as an annulet, beside one of the wings, Rudd is of the opinion that this simply represents either a decorative 'space filler' or alternatively a solar symbol. Certainly annulets and solar wheels or flowers are very common on Celtic coins of around this period.

Interestingly, Rudd could not rule out completely the possibility that the coin illustrates a bright nova or supernova. In this respect we also have to remember the great importance that was attached to astronomical events by the Druids who, as has been seen, may have had considerable influence over what was to be displayed on coins of this period. They would also have been well aware of the classical image of the constellation of Aquila.

Conclusion

It is difficult to accept that the object of 5 BC was a nova as it was clearly identified as a tailed comet by the Chinese, when they described it as a *shu-hsing*. It has been seen that, statistically, the object was unlikely to have been a nova, as the object appeared just outside the main plane of our galaxy. Also a bright comet is a far more common occurrence than a bright nova, whilst at the same time attracting much more attention. In any case, a nova would have had to flare up twice in order to satisfy the description in Matthew, which clearly suggests that the object at one stage ceased to be visible, before reappearing. There is also a problem concerning its astrological importance, as it would seem that the Babylonian or Persian astrologers would not have applied any special significance to it, being more likely to have been influenced by planetary positions. The nova theory initially may sound plausible, but following our investigation it seems that the balance of evidence is weighted heavily in favour of a comet as having been the object of 5 BC as identified by the Chinese.

9

HALLEY'S COMET & ITS GHOST

The word comet originates from the Greek word *kometes* meaning a long-haired star, although such a description generally would apply to brighter examples displaying a tail. Certainly a bright comet, when it appears, is a marvellous sight, particularly from a dark site, away from the glow of town lights. However, although a comet's tail may look spectacular and may stretch for tens of millions of miles through space, they have a very low mass and weak gravitational attraction, with a solid centre or nucleus which normally measures only a few miles across. This comprises mainly ice and dust and consequently they have been described as 'dirty snowballs'. They shine due to reflected sunlight, although when close to the Sun they may generate a little light of their own, or fluorescence, due to solar radiation.

Comets seem to originate from a theoretical vast cloud of such objects at a distance of about one light year from the Sun. This is known as the Oort Cloud, which is named after a Dutch astronomer, Jan Oort, who developed the theory, although it had also been suggested by Dr Ernst J. Öpik of Armagh Observatory. A comet can be disturbed in the cloud as a result of gravitational pulls of neighbouring stars or molecular clouds as the suburban Sun moves in its orbit around our galaxy. They then accumulate in a flattened disc known as the Edgeworth-Kuiper Belt at a distance of about 100 billion miles from the Sun. Further perturbations may cause the nucleus of a comet to plunge inwards towards the Sun, a journey that may take tens of thousands of years to complete.

When a comet reaches the inner solar system it receives heat from the Sun, causing the ice within its nucleus to sublimate forming an atmospheric coma around it. A tail is produced due to a plasma stream radiating or flowing from the Sun, known as the solar wind, and it is for this reason that the tail of a comet always points in the opposite direction from the Sun, even when it is moving away from it, in which case it travels tail first. Usually two types of tail are produced – a dust tail blown by the solar wind, and a gas or radiation tail which is caused by a build-up of pressure due to the action of sunlight. Dust tails have a tendency to be curved whereas gas or ion tails tend to be straight.

When a comet has completed its long journey into the solar system there are four possible outcomes, summarised as follows:

1. It may travel around the Sun and then be ejected from the inner solar system, making its way back into deep space to rejoin the Edgeworth-Kuiper Belt.

2. It may be pulled into the Sun, also known as cometary suicide.

3. It may be captured by the gravity of a planet, usually Jupiter or Saturn and subsequently crash into it, as witnessed in 1994 with comet Shoemaker-Levy 9.

4. Planetary gravity may force it into an orbit within the inner solar system, perhaps taking only a few years to complete, or into a highly elliptical orbit which may take thousands of years.

Apart from the short-period comets, they tend to be unpredictable and erratic, with very eccentric orbits and a bright comet such as Hale-Bopp (1997) can arrive unexpectedly at any time. They are normally named after the person or persons who discover them, although more recently also after the name of the automated telescopes or spacecraft used to find them, for example Linear or SOHO. Some, however, are also named after the person who first determined their orbit, for example Encke, Crommelin and by far the most famous, Halley.

Edmund Halley

As Halley's Comet is such an important feature within this chapter it is, perhaps, appropriate just to take a brief look into the life of the man who gave it its name.

It was on or around 29 October 1656 that Edmund Halley was born into a wealthy family in Haggerston near Shoreditch, a hamlet outside London. Whilst still young his father took him to live in London, and although some property was subsequently lost during the Great Fire, they managed to survive financially. Halley attended St Paul's School, becoming the school captain at fifteen. In 1673 he went to Oxford University, taking with him his astronomical instruments, for he had by then developed a clear interest in astronomy. He excelled in mathematics and in 1676 he sent a scientific paper, in which he calculated planetary orbits, to the Royal Society, which they subsequently published. Later in the same year, without having finished university, he sailed to St Helena to catalogue the stars of the southern hemisphere.

Upon his return, in 1678, he prepared *A Catalogue of the Southern Stars*, in which he summarised his results, and virtually overnight he became a celebrity. His friend, John Flamsteed, who had accompanied him on his journey, proceeded to describe him as the 'Southern Tycho'. He was awarded a Master of Arts degree from Oxford University on the orders of King Charles II and also elected as a Fellow of the Royal Society, in recognition of his achievement.

Halley continued to make observations and write scientific papers, mainly for the Royal Society. In 1684 he visited Isaac Newton at Cambridge and a strong and lasting friendship began. Tragedy struck in the same year however, as his father, who had always supported his interest in astronomy, was found murdered, and this was followed by litigation between himself and his stepmother. Despite these setbacks, in the following year he helped to finance the publication of Newton's great work *Principia*, a ground-breaking book which formulated the laws of universal gravitation.

In 1696 he accepted the post of Deputy Controller of Chester Mint, under Newton, who had been appointed Warden. However, not liking the work, he returned to London in 1698. He then undertook to chart variations in the Earth's magnetism at sea so that longitude could be determined. This would mean that anyone finding true north by using a compass and studying the chart would, at least in theory, be able to find their longitude. So he set sail from Portsmouth and, surviving a mutiny, eventually returned in September 1700 with his measurements of magnetic variations, which were published in the following year.

In 1705 Halley produced his *Synopsis of Cometry Astronomy*, a book in which he predicted that, in December 1758, a bright comet would reappear, being the same comet that had visited in 1531, 1607 and 1682, the latter appearance having been witnessed by him. Originally it was thought that these appearances represented separate comets, however Halley noticed that these particular comets had very similar orbits and that the intervals between each visitation were about seventy-five and a half years. From his calculations he realised that it was actually the same comet returning each time, as a result of having a regular orbit.

Halley was appointed the second Astronomer Royal upon the death of John Flamsteed at the end of 1719 and set about refitting the Royal Observatory at Greenwich with new instruments. Towards the end of his life he paid particular attention to observing and measuring lunar positions, in order to prepare accurate tables of the Moon's motions in order to further assist seafarers in calculating their longitude. This culminated in the later publication of the *British Mariners' Guide* in 1763, which incorporated a method based upon his results.

Halley died on 25 January 1742 at the age of eighty-five, but before dying, and knowing that he would never survive to see his comet return, he is reputed to have said, 'Wherefore if according to what we have already said it should return again about the year 1758, candid posterity will not refuse to acknowledge that this was first discovered by an Englishman.'

A Christmas Star

On Christmas night in 1758 the comet was spotted, the first sighting being made with the aid of a telescope by Johann Palitzsch, a farmer and amateur astronomer living outside Dresden in Saxony. This was later to be confirmed by a French astronomer, Charles Messier, known as the 'Ferret of Comets', in the following month.

It was not until March 1759 that the comet reached its closest position to the Sun in its orbit, known as perihelion. This meant that the interval between successive returns of the comet was slightly longer than previously estimated and needed to be revised upwards to about seventy-six and a half years. It was realised that its orbit could be affected by the gravitational influences of Jupiter and Saturn, every time it entered the inner solar system. This would therefore cause fluctuations in the time interval between each appearance and it has been calculated that over the past 2,000 years it has varied between about seventy-four and a half to seventy-nine and a half years.

Earlier Recordings

The British Museum holds late Babylonian texts which appear to record probable observations of Halley's Comet at its 164 and 87 BC apparitions. This has led to the belief that Babylonian astronomers may have realised that certain comets moved in fixed orbits in the same manner as planets. So perhaps Edmund Halley was not necessarily the first to determine this fact. Certainly the relatively consistent nature of the comet's orbit, combined with the fact that every appearance was of easy naked-eye visibility, suggests that the Babylonians may well have identified the recurrent nature of the comet's appearance.[9]

Going back in time, Halley's Comet has made some spectacular appearances, many of which coincided with major historical events. Perhaps the most famous reappearance is illustrated on the Bayeux Tapestry, which is said to have been prepared on the order of William the Conqueror's wife, Matilda, a few years after the Battle of Hastings in 1066. As comets at that time were considered to be bad news, it is displayed on the tapestry close to Harold II, sitting on his throne with his frightened attendants pointing to it and with the words *Istimirant Stella* beside it, meaning that they were looking in awe at the star. In that year the comet passed quite close to Earth, to within about 10 million miles, so that it would have appeared very prominent in the night sky.

In 1456 it was very bright and was taken as an omen following the fall of Constantinople three years earlier, with the Turks invading South Eastern Europe. It is said that Pope Calixtus III had the comet excommunicated on the grounds that it was considered evil. In 1222 it was again viewed as a bad omen, preceding the death of the French King Philip Augustus. In 451 it coincided with the defeat of

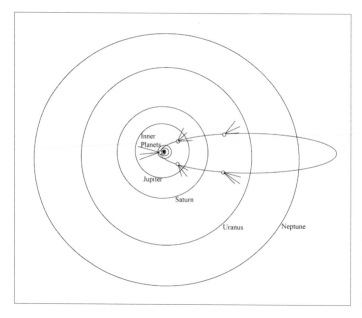

The orbital path of Halley's Comet. (Prepared and provided courtesy of Richard Archer)

Attila the Hun at the Battle of Chalons. It was also probably the comet observed by Josephus in AD 66 over Jerusalem, which was later taken as a sign of its imminent destruction by the Romans. The earliest recorded appearance of the comet goes back to 613 BC, with Chinese annals describing a great comet in that year.

In 1301 the comet was almost certainly witnessed by Giotto di Bondone (*c.* 1267–1337) a Florentine artist who used it in 1303 or 1304 as a symbol for the star of Bethlehem in his fresco the *Adoration of the Magi* on the ceiling of the Arena Chapel in Padua. This was in keeping with the general belief amongst theologians of that time that the star of Bethlehem was a comet. It was probably the first time a true likeness of a comet had been depicted anywhere, as all earlier illustrations were either crude drawings or had shown a great deal of artistic licence.

The 1986 Appearance

At its last return in 1986, five different probes were sent up to visit the comet: two Japanese, two Russian and one European appropriately named *Giotto*, in recognition of his famous fresco. The European Space Agency (ESA), on 2 July 1985, launched what turned out to be a very successful mission to the comet. On 14 March 1986, travelling at 42 miles per second, *Giotto* encountered the comet but in the process was impacted by about 12,000 dust particles, finally ceasing transmissions about fifteen seconds prior to its scheduled closest approach, which brought it to within 370 miles of the nucleus. Contact was subsequently restored half an hour later.

The close-up images that were sent back were the first ever to show the nucleus of a comet, which appeared as black as coal. Measuring only about nine miles long by five miles wide, it showed craters and on its sunlit side bright gases could be seen streaming out. This comprised 80 per cent sublimated water, 10 per cent carbon monoxide, 2.5 per cent carbon dioxide, with small traces of ammonia and methane. Although damaged, *Giotto* was able to continue and encountered another comet, this time Grigg-Skjellerup, on 10 July 1992, using an Earth gravity-assist technique.

The comet's last appearance from Earth in 1986 was disappointing, especially as viewed from the northern hemisphere. From Britain and Ireland it was barely a naked-eye object and even through binoculars it was diffuse and inconspicuous. In fact, it turned out to be the faintest sighting ever recorded. The main problem was that the comet was on the far side of the Sun when it would have been at its brightest. However, there is always 2062!

Halley's Comet – the Star of Bethlehem?

So, could Halley's Comet really have been the star of Bethlehem? The return of the comet in 1758/9, as mentioned earlier, had uplifted its estimated periodic cycle to seventy-six and a half years and some astronomers calculated at the time that if this period were to be multiplied by twenty-three it would imply that there was a visitation in the year o or thereabouts. A link between the comet and the star of Bethlehem was yet again being suggested.

Upon its next appearance in 1835, however, it became clear that its period was in fact even more than seventy-six and a half years, being closer to seventy-seven years. This would indicate that the comet, instead of having appeared in the year o, would have visited around the year 12 BC, and an amateur astronomer, John R. Hind, proposed that a comet seen in 11 BC may have been Halley. However, as no comet was recorded by the Chinese in 11 BC, he may have been referring to the one mentioned in 12 BC in the Chinese *Han Shu*, which is listed as number 61 by Ho Peng Yoke in his catalogue.

Although there remains a shortage of precise dates, the account of this comet is, according to Gary W. Kronk in his *Cometography*, the most detailed produced for any comet up to that time and was not to be matched until the year 568, with the descriptions of its movement referring not only to Chinese constellations but also to individual stars. The *Han Shu* refers to it as a *po-hsing*, a 'sparkling star' without a tail, and it was first detected on 26 August as a morning star, in the east at *Tung-Ching*, a group of stars in Gemini; it was treading on *Wu-Chu-Hon*, another group of stars within the same constellation. As it moved against the starry background it accelerated at one stage to cover more than 6 degrees a day, prior to an observation made on 7 September, when it was seen to traverse *Hsien-Yuan*, which is an area of sky including the constellations of Lynx and Leo. It proceeded to travel through – or close to – Canes Venatici, Bootes, Serpens and Ophiuchus before it went out of sight in *Tshang-Lung*, equating to Scorpio, low in the western sky, shortly after sunset on 20 October, having remained visible for fifty-six days.

It has been estimated that the comet, on this occasion, would not have been excessively bright, with an estimated magnitude ranging from around o to +1, and this may explain why it was described as a tailless comet, as opposed to one displaying a tail. It was also recorded by Dio Cassius in *Roman History*, who wrote that 'a star called comet hung for several days over the city [Rome] and was finally dissolved into flashes resembling torches'.

The same appearance was associated by the Romans with the death of Marcus Agrippa, a famous commander in the army who had become the son-in-law of Augustus, through marriage to his daughter Julia. He had been a long and lasting friend of the emperor and had effectively become his right-hand man. Agrippa had reaped the rewards of a highly successful career, having paved the way for Augustus' rise to power through crucial victories including that at Actium, and it is not surprising that he was later to be made his heir. In Roman society he was a most popular figure and his unexpected death was seen as a complete calamity, being accompanied by varying portents such as owls flying about within the city, strikes of lightning and unexplained fires. As for the comet, however, it was assumed that this object was transporting his soul towards heaven.

It is interesting to note that when the comet first became visible its head was directed towards Leo, and it subsequently proceeded to move into – or close to – that constellation. This could have been interpreted by astrologers as being significant, as Leo was associated, at that time, with the Lion of Judah. It has been suggested by E. Burraus in *The Oracles of Jacob and Balaam* that the constellation of Leo had a very special meaning. It included the bright star Regulus, regarded as the 'Royal Star' of the Jews and given the title 'King' by Ptolemy. This star and the constellation were identified with the conferring of regal powers. So was the prophecy now being satisfied through the apparition of the comet appearing in the area of Leo?

From earlier discussions, it might seem that the year 12 BC is perhaps too early for the date of Christ's birth, although it still remains within the general time-frame. Referring back to Chapter 4, it is found, in one of the models listed in calculating the year of Christ's birth, that the year 13 BC is arrived at. This is based upon the text in John 8:57 in which the Jews say to Jesus, 'You are not yet fifty', and which is taken to imply that Jesus was in his forties when this statement was made. In the model it was estimated that Jesus may have been about forty-six, an arbitrary figure, when crucified around the year AD 33. If instead Jesus was, say, aged forty-

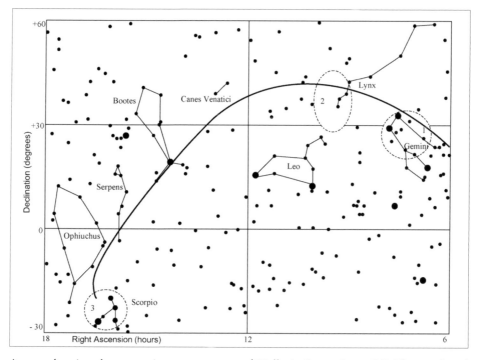

A map showing the approximate movement of Halley's Comet in 12 BC. The numbered circles and ellipse indicate the areas of the sky as identified by the Chinese within the *Han Shu*: 1. *Tung-Ching* (Gemini), 2. *Hsien-Yuan* (Leo and Lynx), 3. *Tshang-Lung* (Scorpio). The map is partially based upon a chart of the comet's movement prepared by Robert Fritzius using coordinates applicable to 12 BC. (Prepared and provided courtesy of Nic Leitch)

five, this would mean that he was born around 12 BC. Now also remember that Josephus recorded that Herod was visited by Magi in 10 BC. Their visit, which included the bearing of gifts, formed part of a celebration following the building of Caesarea Maritima, and it seems that they came to reciprocate for gifts given earlier by Herod to their respective countries, *Antiquities*, 16:5:1, telling us the following:

> The entire building was accomplished: in the tenth year the solemnity of it fell into the twenty-eighth year of Herod's reign and into the hundred and ninety second Olympiad [10 BC].
>   Now when a great multitude was come to that city to see the shows, as well as the ambassadors [a term for Magi] whom other people sent on account of the benefits they had received [from Herod].

Brown also recognises the problem of the time discrepancy between Halley's Comet appearing in 12 BC, and 6 BC, which he accepts as being 'usually assigned for Jesus' birth'. However, he goes on to state the following:

> This argument loses its force if one is arguing, not that Matthew's account is historical, but that it has reinterpreted by association with Jesus an astral phenomenon which occurred in the general time period of his birth. It is possible that the appearance of Halley's Comet in 12 BC and the coming of foreign ambassadors two years later to hail King Herod on the occasion of the completion of Caesarea Maritima have been combined in Matthew's story of the star and the Magi from the East.

Brown also draws attention to the possibility that 'subsequent Christian believers in retrospect may have fastened on to a remembered phenomenon as a sign of Jesus' birth'.

If we want to be historically precise then there is one factor which may contrive against the star of Bethlehem being represented by Halley's Comet in 12 BC. John, written around the year AD 100, is the latest of the four Gospels and therefore is generally considered to be the least reliable when it comes to providing us with factual clues. As seen earlier, the Gospels of Matthew and Luke imply that Jesus was in his thirties rather than his forties when he was crucified, and consequently this would suggest a later year for his birth.

A Comet in 10 BC?

Interestingly, there was another comet recorded by the Chinese in the year 10 BC, corresponding to number 62 in the Ho Peng Yoke catalogue. His source is the twelfth-century *Thung Chien Kang Mu*, which means the 'Epitome of the Comprehensive Mirror'. This tells us that 'during the third year of the Yuan-Yen reign, a *po-hsing* was seen at *She Thi* and *Ta Chio*'. This means that a tailless comet appeared near the bright star Arcturus in the constellation of Boötes.

There have been serious doubts cast about the authenticity of this record and it is not recorded by Williams, but this comet, if it existed, would present us with two separate cometary appearances within the space of about two years. This would therefore have satisfied an important criterion outlined within Matthew's infancy narrative, namely that the star, at some stage, ceased to be visible and then reappeared. This is the reason behind the author having Herod responsible for all male children being murdered under the age of two, presumably calculating the time interval between the star's first and second appearance. There would also seem to be no reason why two comets may not have been regarded as being one and the same object, occurring as they did within a relatively short space of time of one another. And then, of course, we have the visit of Magi to King Herod in that same year.

A Ghost Comet

It seems most unlikely, however, that this comet ever existed. According to Christopher Cullen in *Halley's Comet and the Ghost Event of 10 BC*, the *Thung Chien Kang Mu* was based upon an earlier compilation of history, called the *Tzu Chih T'ung Chien*, meaning 'Comprehensive Mirror for Aid in Government', completed in 1086 and covering a period from 403 BC to AD 959. This in turn incorporated details from within the *Han Shu*. Events were listed in chronological sequence and important occurrences like comets were normally entered first, referred to by a date or head entry. However, the comet of 10 BC was not given such an entry.

In 10 BC there was a calamitous natural event which took place in China, when Mount Min collapsed, creating a catastrophic landslide blocking the Yangtze River in Szechuan. When this happened it seems that the comet of 12 BC was still preying upon the mind of the original compiler of the record, identified as Liu Hsiang (77–6 BC), an influential scholar and writer. The reference to the comet in the *Han Shu* is confined to his discussion of the great landslip and has no separate date entry of its own. It seems that when mentioning the comet, he was simply recalling the object of two years earlier, an afterthought as it were, associating it with the great landslide and reinforcing his conviction that the present Han dynasty needed to act urgently in order to 'set the state to rights'.

Such reasoning is confirmed by the fact that the area of the sky identified for the comet lay in exactly the same track as that of Halley's. In 1847 an attempt had been made by Benjamin Pierce to determine its orbit but, lacking sufficient information, he did not recognise any correlation with that of the path of Halley's. Three years later, however, Hind proceeded to calculate a parabolic orbit, based upon the same observations, and commented that he 'was immediately struck with the similarity of the elements to those of the comet Halley'. All the evidence therefore would seem to confirm that there was actually no comet in 10 BC.

Conclusion

There are no records of any further comets between the years from 10 to 5 BC. This is a contributory factor as to why, in recent years, such an object has not been a popular choice for the star of Bethlehem, as the period hovering from around 8 to 6 BC has frequently been postulated for the birth of Jesus. However, as has been seen, the authors of both Matthew and Luke were not particularly concerned with achieving a high level of historical accuracy in their writings, being far more concerned with the primary message of the resurrection and the spiritual divinity of Christ, and as previously discussed, any time from about 13 BC through to 5 BC would be considered as falling into the relevant time-frame.

10

COMET HOLMES & OTHERS

It has been known for a comet to dim and then unexpectedly flare up, due to an outburst brought about by material breaking away from the nucleus. This may possibly be caused by a collision with another smaller body, perhaps an asteroid or a piece of captured debris which may have been in orbit around it.

A more likely explanation for a cometary outburst, however, is thought to be due to events which arise within the nucleus itself, particularly when its surface, or part of it, is exposed to sunlight. Internal pressures can build up underneath the surface, with amorphous ice releasing energy when it becomes crystalline. If the outer surface is stronger than that of most other comets then this internal energy can build up, giving rise to an explosive release.

An example of such an outburst was Comet Holmes, which was first identified in 1892 following a sudden and spectacular increase in brightness. A further outburst occurred in the following year. The comet subsequently settled down and remained a fairly quiet and inconspicuous object until October 2007 when it flared up again, driving its brightness upwards from around magnitude +17 to about +2.5, an increase of around a million times! It therefore became easily visible to the naked eye, initially resembling a bright star with no tail being visible. Over subsequent weeks its dust and gas emissions expanded outwards, but also diffusely, so that its appearance changed to that of a fuzzy patch; not as bright as before, as its reflected light was less concentrated, now being spread over a much wider area in space. Although no tail was visible to the naked eye, long-exposure photographs did reveal material being dispersed by the solar wind. It has been estimated that only about 1 per cent of the mass of Comet Holmes was released during the explosion in 2007. The particles released were of a fine and fragile nature and pockets of this material continued to break apart over the weeks following the initial outburst.

Interestingly, Comet Holmes also displayed relatively little movement in the sky. This was due to two factors – firstly it was at a considerable distance from the Earth at around 150 million miles, lying between the orbits of Mars and Jupiter; secondly because it was positioned roughly in a line with the Sun and Earth. Although it is a short-period comet, with each orbit around the Sun taking only about seven years to complete, it never comes close to the Earth and as such is normally only detected by large telescopes.

So a distant and invisible comet can, without warning, flare up, becoming very bright, and because it is far from the Earth it is likely to show relatively little movement as it travels in space. Comet Holmes illustrated that a comet can suddenly brighten significantly, dim back and disappear to the naked eye and then experience a further outburst within a relatively short time-frame, as witnessed in 1892 and 1893. Could such an event also explain the apparent appearance, disappearance and then reappearance of the star of Bethlehem as implied within Matthew? Certainly such flaring up is not an uncommon feature amongst comets, although it is more common when they are relatively close to the Sun in their orbit around it.

Even a relatively bright comet such as Halley's has been known to behave in an erratic manner. Brown draws our attention to the experience of the Dominican biblical scholar Père Lagrange who witnessed the comet at its 1910 visitation from Jerusalem. He noted that it came from the east, faded whilst overhead and then 'reappeared' some days later, prior to setting in the west.

The Comet of 5 BC

So what about the comet of 5 BC? This was described by the Chinese as a *shu-hsing* meaning a comet with a tail. This is in contrast to a *po-hsing*, or tailless comet, and a *k'o-hsing*, which refers to a guest star or nova. If there had been any doubt about this object not being a comet then presumably they would have described it either as a *po-hsing* or a *k'o-hsing*. As was seen earlier, some astronomers nevertheless considered that the 5 BC object was more likely to have been a nova, simply due to the fact that the Chinese descriptions indicated little or no movement in the sky.

Implied Movement?

From the Chinese and Korean sources mentioned in Chapter 8, it could be said that the comet of 5 BC was observed in both of the constellations of Capricorn and Aquila. The Chinese *Han Shu*, according to Clark and Stephenson, suggested that it was first seen sometime between 9 March and 6 April 5 BC, close to the stars Alpha and Beta Capricorn. It seems possible that the other object recorded by the Chinese and Koreans in 4 BC was inadvertently registered in that year, instead of 5 BC, and therefore that the two records represented one and the same object; this is a widely held opinion.

Superimposing the two records, we then would have two separate positions for the comet as seen during the month of March 5 BC, initially appearing in Capricorn, and later observed in Aquila close to the bright star Altair, therefore implying a movement and eliminating the possibility that it may have been a nova. Using *Epoch 2000* star positions, which allows for the effect of the wobble of the Earth on its axis every 25,800 years, known as precession, Alpha and Beta Capricorn are about declination -13, right ascension 20 hours 20 minutes, and that of Altair around declination +9, with right ascension 19 hours 50 minutes, so that there was an apparent movement of about 22 degrees or around forty-four diameters of the full Moon. This movement would have continued during April and well into May as we are told that the comet was visible for seventy days.

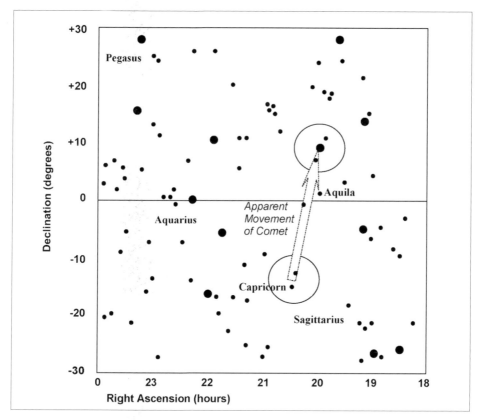

A map showing the possible movement of the comet of 5 BC. (Prepared and provided courtesy of Nic Leitch)

But Was the Same Source Used?

The descriptions within the *Han Shu* of the comet's location may have originated from a single source using the same original information. This therefore implies that any variations in its recorded position can be attributed to different interpretations. Nevertheless there still seems little doubt that the object in question was a comet. Arguments for this conclusion have already been discussed in Chapter 8, but it is also probable that the failure to notify us of its movement over a seventy-day period can be simply put down to the report being merely a summary of the original observations.

The Humphries Theory

Colin Humphries, a professor of experimental physics and supporter of the comet theory, suggested that the Magi's attention would initially have been attracted by the triple conjunction of Jupiter and Saturn in 7 BC and the planetary massing in 6 BC. With their expectations high, they awaited a third sign, namely the comet in Capricorn. He points out that from Persia the comet in that constellation would have been observed first above the eastern horizon in the morning twilight, the helical rising. Since the comet was visible for seventy days, it would have given the Magi ample time to travel the 900 miles or so from their home to Jerusalem. By the time they reached Jerusalem, one to two months later, the comet would have moved from east to south due to the movement of the Earth in its orbit around the Sun, this accounting for 30 degrees each month, and also because of the actual movement of the comet itself against the starry background. When they departed Jerusalem for Bethlehem the comet would, at some stage in the night, have appeared due south and at its highest point in the sky, thus appearing to stand over the town.

The Significance of Capricorn
The fact that the comet appeared in the constellation of Capricorn was also significant as it was associated with great rulers. This was illustrated by the fact that Augustus, in 17 BC, issued a coin – a silver denarius depicting its zodiacal sign – and it subsequently became associated with that emperor. In AD 79, Vespasian copied the design in an attempt to draw a comparison between himself and Augustus. The same zodiacal sign was also used by the ancient British on their coins. In the first decade of the first century AD, King Ammimus of the Conti tribe, who occupied Kent, issued a small silver coin which depicted Capricorn as did Kings Eppillus and Verica, who at that same time were the joint-rulers of other parts of southern Britain.

So how does the comet of 5 BC stand up to the criteria for the star of Bethlehem as outlined at the start of Chapter 6? Well, there are three problems which I have identified and these are summarised and dealt with as follows:

Two Appearances?
The first problem seems to be the question of whether the comet made two appearances, for as we have seen earlier, Matthew implies that the object at some stage ceased to be visible, only to reappear later. Although it is quite possible that the comet did make two appearances, firstly as it approached the Sun, and secondly as it began its outward journey, the Chinese records only seem to reflect the one appearance. It has also been suggested that even if the comet had been seen, both on its inward approach and subsequent outward journey, it may not have been recognised as being one and the same object. However, the second appearance would have occurred within weeks of the first so there is no reason to think that it would not have been accepted as being the same phenomenon. On this point we have to accept the author of Matthew himself as a separate source to confirm an earlier appearance, for it is easy to accept that the biblical text seems to be describing a comet.

Matthew has the earlier first appearance witnessed by the Magi. It could have been a very faint object on its inward approach towards the Sun, perhaps so faint that the Chinese astronomers did not record it. This may have been because the comet was approaching the Sun on its far side as viewed from the Earth. It is possible therefore that the Magi travelled to Jerusalem upon this first faint sighting in the eastern sky before dawn, and that whilst in Jerusalem it reappeared on its outward journey, being brighter than before as this time it may have been on the nearside to the Earth.

A simpler explanation may be that the comet was only visible on either its inward or outward journey, with the brightness of the Moon drowning out its light. Comets tend to be very diffuse objects, always best viewed from dark sites, and the effect of the Moon's brightness always has a severe effect on their appearance. Every twenty nine and a half days, the Moon travels through the constellation of Capricorn, as it is close to the ecliptic, so it is quite possible that it drifted close enough to block out its visible light to the extent that it would have ceased to be a naked-eye object. This would not have occurred at its first close encounter with the comet around mid-March, as it would have still been relatively close to the Sun in the sky, meaning that the phase of the Moon would only have been a thin crescent when in its vicinity, thus having little or no impact on its apparent brightness. At some later stage, however, when the comet would have been higher in the southern sky and further away from the Sun, it would have been more significantly affected by a crescent or possibly a first-quarter Moon, whereby about half of the Moon's surface area as viewed from Earth would have been illuminated, thus drowning out the ghostly apparition. It could also have been affected by the brightness of the full Moon, even though the degree of separation between it and the comet would have been considerable. In any case, even if the comet was bright enough to still remain visible with the Moon close by, or with a full Moon in the sky – which seems improbable – prevailing weather conditions could have meant that the comet was clouded out for a number of days or so, before re-emerging in clear skies.

Another possibility is that the comet of 5 BC simply faded in brightness to the extent that it became invisible to the naked eye. It then suddenly flared up in a similar fashion to Comet Holmes in 1893, before fading away again. As mentioned earlier, sudden flare-ups are not an uncommon feature of comets so this could be another explanation for the star of Bethlehem seeming to vanish and later reappear.

Insufficient Duration?

Whilst the comet of 5 BC may well have reappeared after a certain interval of time, the total period of visibility, between its first and second appearance, is nowhere near to the duration of one to two years implied within the narrative of Matthew for the star. The time intervals between the disappearances and possible reappearances as discussed above, if they ever did happen, would still not be sufficient contributors towards satisfying this important prerequisite.

It has been suggested that Herod's decision to have all the boys of two or younger killed could possibly indicate thirteen months and under, implying that the Magi may have informed him of the earlier triple conjunction and planetary massing. Could it be that the Magi and Herod assumed that Christ's birth coincided with one of the conjunctions, or perhaps the planetary massing which had occurred about a year earlier in February 6 BC? For some this could suggest that this is the month in which Christ was born, with the comet of the following year completing the sequence of events. However, according to the description in Matthew, it is clear that the Magi witnessed the *same* star on both occasions, so that this particular theory can be ruled out.

As was seen earlier, there is, nevertheless, uncertainty as to whether the massacre of the innocents and the consequential flight to Egypt ever took place. The author may be inferring a time interval between the birth of Jesus and the death of Herod, but if this part of Matthew's narrative is to be considered unreliable then this inference to an intervening period of one to two years becomes questionable.

Is the Spring of 5 BC Too Late?

The third and perhaps the most serious problem is that the appearance of the comet, in the spring of 5 BC, is just on the periphery of our calculated time-frame for the star of Bethlehem. Earlier we had determined that the latest possible year for the birth of Jesus was around 4 or 5 BC, being based upon the narrative within Luke. It has been seen that Herod died either in early 4 BC or late 5 BC, but if we were to allow an interval of at least one or two further years for the account in Matthew of the elimination of boys under two and the flight into Egypt, then we run into difficulties. However, there is no certainty as to the actual time intervals involved and, as has been seen, there is considerable doubt as to whether these events ever happened in the first place. Consequently, as there is no evidence of any other comets going further back in time until 12 BC, this one definitely has to edge in as a contender.

Harbingers of Doom?

One of the main reasons why most astronomers dismiss a comet as being the likely star of Bethlehem is that they have assumed that such objects were associated with impending doom and misfortune. In fact, the word 'disaster' is derived from the Greek meaning bad star, and in this context may be taken as referring to a comet. However, around the time of Christ's birth this was not necessarily the case, and it appears that in some instances they were associated with favourable news and the birth of great kings. As pointed out by Humphries, Origen seems to have been one of the earliest to suggest that the star of Bethlehem was a comet. He referred back to an ancient book known as *The Treatise on Comets* by Chaeremon the Stoic, in which were listed comets that appeared when 'good was to happen'. In *Contra Celsum* he writes:

> The star that was seen in the East we consider to be a new star ... Partaking of the nature of these celestial bodies which appear at such times such as comets ... if then at the commencement of new dynasties or on the occasion of other important events there arises a comet ... why should it be a matter of wonder that at the birth of Him who was to introduce a new doctrine ... a star should have arisen?

The Birth and Reign of Mithridates VI

A Roman historian from the second century, Justinus, quoted an ancient source called *The History of the Kings of Timagenes of Alexandria*, which stated that:

> Heavenly phenomena had also predicted the greatness of this man. For both in the year in which he was born and in the year in which he began to reign a comet shone through both periods for seventy days in such a way that the whole sky seemed to be ablaze.

The man he was referring to was a King of Pontus, Mithridates VI. Although this story was regarded as contrived by historians, it was later proved, in 1919, by John Knight Fotherington, a specialist in ancient astronomy and chronology, that comets of 134 and 120 BC related exactly to the years of his birth and the commencement of his reign, and this is now accepted as a matter of fact.

As King of Pontus, an area within present-day Turkey, Mithridates seems to have been content to associate himself with these two separate cometary appearances, and they became symbolic of his rise to power as he led his armies successfully against the Romans, who were attempting to stretch their empire eastwards. Although eventually defeated in 65 BC, his resistance became legendary. He issued bronze coins which illustrated a *hipheus* or horse comet; such comets, according to the Roman historian and naturalist Pliny, resembled the curved mane of a horse displaying curling plumes. In reality, this represented streamers comprising dust in the tail of the comet that appeared to arc around its nucleus as it made its way around the Sun. In fact, similar comets have made recent appearances; for example, Comet McNaught in 2006, and Donati's Comet of 1858, which has been described as the most beautiful comet of all time.

The Chinese Attitude

The Chinese regarded that all celestial activity was, in theory, the responsibility of the present emperor, who was considered to be divine. However, any unusual astronomical occurrences, such as comets, could be indicative of his shortcomings, particularly if it coincided with unfavourable events at home. Also, if a comet appeared, it was sometimes assumed to be under his influence and consequently it could be manipulated to determine the course of future events, so they were often viewed as heralding a change. They sometimes referred to comets as 'broom' or 'brush' stars, being capable of sweeping away old traditions and evil. Frequently they did associate such objects with unwelcome news, and these mixed reactions may be put down to the fact that they compiled such extensive and detailed records covering a huge period in time, so that inevitably, they realised that they occurred during both favourable and unfavourable times.

The Comet of 44 BC

As for the Romans, Octavian proceeded to dedicate a temple to a bright comet that appeared in 44 BC during athletic games which he sponsored shortly after the death of Julius Caesar. A first-century Greek historian, Plutarch, was later to describe the comet as representing a divine manifestation, and it was popularly accepted at the time that the comet was taking the soul of Caesar into heaven.

This particular comet had earlier reached an estimated magnitude of -3 in May and June of that year, but had then proceeded to fade considerably. Like Comet Holmes it then suddenly flared up, its apparent brightness rising about 10,000 times to an estimated magnitude -8, becoming so bright that it was visible in daylight, low in the north-eastern sky. Due to volcanic ash in the Earth's atmosphere at the time, following eruptions on Etna, Sicily, the comet was described as having a reddish hue and being star-like in appearance, with short rays. This exceptional brightness continued for about a week, coinciding with the duration of the games. Octavian himself provides us with a brief description of the event. Writing in his *Commentarii de vita sua*, he tells us the following:

> On the very days of my games a comet was seen for seven days in the northern section of the sky and was bright and visible from all countries. The crowd believed that this constellation signified that the soul of Caesar had been received among the numina of the immortal gods. On this account this emblem was added to the likeness of his head which I presently consecrated in the Forum.

It was not long before the symbol of that comet, known as the *Sidus Iulium* (the Julian star), was also added to all of Caesar's statues within Rome. In 38 BC, this same comet star was placed beside the portrait of Octavian on bronze sesterces.

Further Cometary Symbols
The same comet inspired the issue of a silver denarius, minted in Caesaraugusta (present day Zaragoza), in 19 or 18 BC and showed an eight-rayed star with one of its spikes emitting flames. Shortly afterwards, in 17 BC, an image of the comet star was actually placed above the head of Augustus on similar coins in order to commemorate the *Ludi Saeculares*, secular games celebrated in that year to recognise the start of a 'New Age'.

Following the death of Augustus, Tiberius issued coins which also displayed the late emperor's portrait, again with a small six-pointed star above his head. In all of these instances the representation of a comet was being used to symbolise the emperor's eminence and assumed divinity. Perhaps more important, however, was that the portrayal of a comet had developed into becoming that of a star.

Such cometary symbols were not confined to the Romans, however. Coins of Parthian or Persian kings also show comet-like stars beside their image, with the clear intention of associating themselves with divine selection. Coins of the Armenian kings show them wearing tiaras decorated with a comet star, and these include examples close to the time of Tiridates, who led the precession of Magi to pay homage to Nero in AD 66. Sometimes only the image of the tiara or crown is shown, with the comet star shown separately to the right.

A Celtic Comet

The illustration of a comet on coins from around the date of Christ's birth also applies to those as issued by the Celtic kings of ancient Britain. King Tincomarus of the Regini tribe, which occupied the South Thames area in Sussex, issued a coin which shows a six-rayed star sometime between 15 BC and AD 8. It is accepted by numismatists that it represents the stylised copy of one of the denari of Augustus mentioned above. This comet star also appears on the coins of two other southern Kings of Britain, namely Eppillus and Verica who, like Tincomarus, claimed to be sons of King Commios. Although each of these kings may have been claiming some divinity for their alleged father, or possibly even for themselves when they issued the coins, it seems quite feasible that their depiction of a comet may have been inspired by the actual physical appearance of such an object. Consequently, they could be illustrating either the 12 or 5 BC event.

Within the same time-frame another ancient British king, Tasciovanus of the Catuvellauni tribe, struck a coin which also appears to show a bright star, except that it is of a completely different design with an inner circle and geometric arcs to illustrate its rays. This coin was produced from his mint in Cernulodunan, north of the Thames.

Resemblance to a Star

Another argument put forward against a comet representing the star of Bethlehem is that it is not a star. However certain comets, such as Comet Holmes, can resemble stars in the sky. In any case, it is generally accepted that the star described in Matthew was not an ordinary star within the meaning of the word. Origen, in *Contra Celsum*, concluded that the star of Bethlehem was not a fixed star,

> ... but is to be classified with the comets which occasionally occur, or meteors, or bearded or jar-shaped stars, or any other such name by which the Greeks like to describe the different forms.

Biblical References to Comets

Matthew 2:9 informs us that the star 'stood over' Bethlehem. The terms 'stood over' and 'hung over' appear to be only used in ancient records to describe a comet. As was seen earlier, Dio Cassius described Halley's Comet of 12 BC as having 'stood over' Rome for several days. Also, Josephus in *Jewish War* described the comet of AD 66, almost certainly Halley's, writing that, 'A star resembling a sword stood over the city [Jerusalem].'

Earlier, in Chapter 2, we came across the term 'went before', which is mentioned in Exodus 13:21 in relation to the Israelites in the desert fleeing from the Egyptians. The description is interesting and worthy of being repeated:

And the Lord went before them by day in a pillar of cloud, to lead them the way; and by night in a pillar of fire, to give them light, to go by day and night.

Apart from the obvious possibility of Matthew having borrowed the term *went before*, the above description could be referring to a celestial object that was visible both by day and by night. It is clear that, whatever it was, it became more prominent as darkness fell. It has been suggested that this could be describing the glow of an active volcano hundreds of miles away, or possibly a rare southerly appearance of aurora borealis (the northern lights). However, another explanation is that it is describing a bright comet with the pillar of light representing the tail. Exodus 14:19 goes on:

And the angel of God which went before the camp of Israel removed and went behind them; and the pillar of the cloud went before their face, and stood behind them...

Is this describing the movement of a comet? Perhaps, but this mysterious light may have a much more mundane origin. Some historians are of the opinion that it may simply be referring to a portable beacon, positioned on top of a pole, which was lit by the Israelites and carried about to help guide their people and armies at night. During daylight it emitted smoke to show them the way. The alteration in the position of the light – or smoke – before them may be a reference to a tactical positional movement in order to out-manoeuvre or confuse the Egyptian forces who were in pursuit, with the intention of interception. This preceded the legendary parting of the Red Sea, which may have been a tidal movement, assisting a crossing over a previously watery channel. The shifting of the light and the manoeuvre may have been a ploy in order to take advantage of the sea's tidal forces, so that they could cross just before the waters turned, thus foiling and possibly trapping their pursuing enemies with the incoming tide.

So this may indicate that the Israelites merely changed direction without any form of celestial intervention. Nevertheless we cannot dismiss completely the possibility that there was an object, perhaps a comet, which had moved across the sky and was later viewed from a different perspective, thus giving rise to their unusual movements.

The author of Matthew may also have been aware of another possible Old Testament reference to a comet in First Chronicles 21:16, which states:

And David lifted up his eyes and saw the angel of the Lord stand between the Earth and the heaven, having drawn a sword in his hand stretched out over Jerusalem.

Such a description is very similar to that written by Josephus in relation to the apparition of Halley's Comet over Jerusalem in AD 66, which he described as resembling a sword over the city. This appearance may well have been witnessed by the author of Matthew and it is quite possible that it may have caused him to reflect upon the above verse from Chronicles, and also that of Exodus 13:21. Consequently, such biblical narratives may have made him feel obliged to include a reference to a similar-styled object within his commentary on the birth of Jesus, having first enquired to see if such an object had actually occurred within the approximate time of his birth.

Angels and the Heavenly Host

Although the only specific reference to the star of Bethlehem occurs in Matthew, there are a small minority who consider that there is also a possible hint, or suggestion, of a celestial manifestation within Luke's infancy narrative. This takes place in Luke 2:9 and 2:13 which refer to the shepherds in the fields being visited by an angel, with the glory of the Lord shining around them, followed by a multitude of the heavenly host, praising God.

Could the term 'heavenly host' be construed as referring to celestial objects, perhaps the stars and planets? This is certainly the view taken by Michael Molnar, an astronomer at Rutgers University, in New Jersey, who suggests that 'the term 'heavenly host' used in Luke is a reference to the stars and planets, specifically the 'morning stars'.

It would be easy to assume that Matthew is referring to an imaginary multitude of angels or spirits in the form of a heavenly choir. However, one interpretation is that the angel could actually be a representation of a comet! It has been known for the swirling wispy tails of comets to sometimes resemble strange and ghostly shapes in the sky and it is possible that, under the right conditions, the image of a feathery winged apparition could be displayed. So is the description in Luke describing the appearance of a comet amidst the splendour of the stars and planets?

Brown leaves us in little doubt concerning the real identity of the angel and the heavenly host. It is a reference to 'the spirits who dwell in God's presence in heaven or in the Temple, singing His praise'. He describes this part of Luke's narration as a canticle, echoing passages from the book of Isaiah, with the appearance of the angel and the glory of the Lord shining around them being based upon the verse in that book, which has angels singing 'Holy, holy, holy is the Lord of Hosts, the whole Earth is full of His glory'. It is also in line with Jewish literature of the time, which made use of angels to sing songs of praise to God. Later, Luke (19:38) also uses similar wording when the disciples acclaim Jesus entering Jerusalem, shouting 'Peace in heaven and glory in the highest heaven'. Apparently, Luke's intention behind this is an attempt to explain that whilst the angels from heaven recognised Jesus as the Messiah at his birth, this was only realised much later by the disciples. So it seems clear that there is no hidden or disguised reference to a comet, or other celestial object, within Luke's Gospel.

Atmospheric Apparitions?

During that period, the general belief was that proposed by Aristotle; namely, that comets were objects that moved about freely within the upper atmosphere of the Earth, lying below the heavenly spheres comprising the Sun, Moon, planets and the fixed stars. The belief that comets were atmospheric objects continued right up until 1577 when Tycho Brahe disproved this theory through detailed collated observations. In November of that year a naked-eye comet became visible and was conspicuous for over two months. Tycho's observations, as usual, were extremely accurate and he compared them with those made by other European astronomers. As no parallax effect could be detected against the starry background, this led him to the conclusion that comets were not atmospheric or ephemeral but celestial, representing a phenomenon which lay far beyond the orbit of the Moon. Even though it was not fully appreciated at the time this discovery was effectively the death knell of the ancient theory of the crystalline spheres, as it would have meant that a comet would have to travel directly through a number of these mythical creations.

This suggests that a comet is the only astronomical object which could have been considered low enough in the sky and with apparent freedom to move about to meet the descriptions of Matthew and his contemporaries of a star 'standing over' a particular location for a short space of time. Therefore, when the author of Matthew describes the star as having stood over Bethlehem he is referring to a comet.

Conclusion

Being objective, we have to accept the distinct possibility that the author of Matthew may have had little or no knowledge as to exactly when Jesus was born and may have simply identified either of the comets of 12 and 5 BC as lying within an approximate time-frame of his early infancy. It is all too easy to fall into the trap of speculating on a specific date, or an exact moment in time which presumes a perfect matching of a certain astronomical event with the arrival of Jesus. It is abundantly clear that the authors of both Matthew and Luke were not good historians and did not always go to great lengths to ensure that their narratives were historically precise. Therefore whilst the author is clearly describing a comet within his infancy narrative, it is difficult to specify, with any degree of certainty, which of the above he is referring to.

11

THE MOON & THE SUN

So far there has been no discussion regarding the two most obvious and conspicuous objects in the sky, the Moon and the Sun, which had themselves been worshipped as gods by early civilisations. While neither would seem to qualify for the star of Bethlehem, is it possible that one, or both, could indirectly contribute towards explaining the events leading up to its appearance?

The Moon

It has been suggested that two occultations by the Moon and the planet Jupiter could explain the star of Bethlehem. By occultation we mean that the Moon passes in front of a star or planet as viewed from Earth so that the object disappears behind it, only to reappear shortly afterwards. The occultations of Jupiter occurred on 20 March and 17 April 6 BC, in the constellation of Aries the Ram, and it has been claimed that this zodiacal sign reigned over Judea and its surrounding regions and was of particular significance to the Jews. One of the leading supporters of this theory is Michael Molnar, who was mentioned earlier. He has claimed that the constellation of Aries was considered to be of greater significance at the time of Christ than the adjacent constellation of Pisces which only later became firmly associated with the Christians.

Molnar refers to the Roman historian Suetonius, who had written in the first century AD that Jewish astrologers had studied Nero's horoscope by looking at Aries and concluded that he would be overthrown in Rome, but would recover to rise up in Jerusalem in order to regain his lost throne. Although he was overthrown, the second part of the prediction did not materialise, but it nevertheless caused alarm to both Christians and Jews alike in Judea, and formed a basis for the stories of the rise of the Antichrist or, as some Jews called him, the anti-Messiah.

The Antioch Coins

Molnar is interested in ancient coins and in particular those which contain astronomical symbols. One of the coins he has collected is a small bronze Roman coin, which was first issued between AD 7 and 14 in Antioch in Syria, which had become a province of Rome. It shows a ram, presumably representing the zodiacal sign of Aries, looking back at a bright star. This subsequently gave rise to Molnar taking the view that it was Aries and not Pisces which was the zodiacal sign of the Jews. This followed research by him into the writings of Claudius Ptolemy and his *Tetrabiblos*, or Bible of Astrology, within which this fact was mentioned twice, making reference to it controlling the people of

Judea, Idumea, Samaria, Palestine and Colne Syria. His opinion is that the coin is a depiction of a conjunction of Mercury and Jupiter in the year AD 7 in Aries. A similar coin, issued by Quadratus around AD 55 or 56, which also includes a crescent Moon, is claimed to represent an occultation of Venus by the Moon in the same constellation.

Molnar claims that it should be Aries, rather than Pisces, on which we should be focusing our attention, with the occultations of Jupiter by the Moon in 6 BC being of special interest as Jews regarded that planet as representing the regal star of Zeus and supposed to confer kingships. He has claimed that these occultations would have been interpreted by the Magi as signifying the birth of a king in Judea and therefore corresponded to the star of Bethlehem. Although such views have received considerable support, I have reservations about Molnar's interpretations of the images on the coins and his whole theory. It is not uncommon for zodiacal signs to be displayed on both Roman and provincial coins, and the purpose of the issue of the prototype Antioch coin was to commemorate the Romans of Antioch taking over Judea in AD 6. Whilst the coin does seem to illustrate Aries the Ram, there can be no certainty that the star represents Jupiter. Even if it does, it could be that the coin was designed to symbolise the dominance of Rome over the Jewish people, with Zeus, represented by the planet Jupiter, over the Jewish constellation Aries.

Molnar even suggests that these coins, which were in circulation for a very long period and within the Christian areas of Antioch, may have attracted the attention of the author of Luke who proceeded to erroneously associate them with the year of Christ's birth according to when they were first issued, namely AD 6 or 7. Could the author have identified the appearance of a star on these coins as a Messianic symbol? Does this explain why he has Jesus being born during the census of Quirinius, which took place in AD 6?

Lunar Occultations

The second occultation of Jupiter by the Moon on 17 April 6 BC, happened when Jupiter was 'in the east', a term which is mentioned twice by Matthew regarding the star of Bethlehem. As the Earth continued in its motion around the Sun, later in August Jupiter appeared to become stationary and then proceeded in the opposite direction, which Molnar claims represents the planet satisfying another of the descriptions in Matthew as having 'went before' through Aries. It then became stationary again on 19 December, which he claims represented the planet 'standing over' Bethlehem.

One of the problems about Molnar's theory is that the occultation on 17 April happened around noon, and therefore during daylight. The Moon was almost new, about one day old in fact, so that from Jerusalem it simply would not have been visible. Neither was Jupiter, as it was too close to the Sun. The earlier occultation on 20 March happened just before sunset in Judea and would also have been invisible to the eye, being too low down in the western sky from Jerusalem, and in Babylon it would actually have occurred below the horizon. From Judea the Moon would have been a very thin crescent, about fourteen hours old, and was probably just too thin and faint to be discerned and Jupiter again was too close to the Sun. The Moon set about half an hour after the Sun, and at the time of occultation it would have been a mere 5 degrees above the western horizon. Consequently it seems most likely that neither of the occultations would actually have been witnessed.

Molnar, however, suggests that the Magi could have accurately predicted the two occultations, so that it was not necessary for them to actually see them, with the significance of the events not losing any credence as a result. We have to assume therefore that the Magi were capable of interpreting events that they knew they could not witness. This would also help to explain why the author of Matthew has Herod not being aware of these celestial events. At the same time the dates of the occultations would appear to correspond quite well within the period determined earlier for Christ's birth.

Astrological Significance

It would certainly seem that Aries was an important constellation to the Jews, as well as Pisces. Abrabanel's work, *The Wells of Salvation*, of 1497, included reference to the significance of both constellations in Jewish astrology. As seen earlier, the birth of the Messiah was associated with the Jewish month of Nisan and the feast of the Passover, which celebrated the exodus of the Israelites from Egypt centuries earlier. According to Abrabanel, the month of Nisan was identified with the constellation of Aries, with the preceding month, Adar, being associated with Pisces, representing the month prior to the imminent birth of Christ. Pisces was also a zodiacal sign associated with water and with Moses. Although Abrabanel implied that Pisces hosted the star of Bethlehem by way of the conjunctions of Jupiter and Saturn in 7 BC, he inadvertently seems to have also promoted the importance of Aries in Jewish astrology. So Molnar's view that the star of Bethlehem occurred in that constellation, albeit by way of a double occultation of Jupiter by the Moon, may not seem quite as radical as first thought.

According to Molnar, Jupiter/Moon occultations had a regal significance, and the closer these two objects were to one another in the sky the greater the intensification of their astrological effects. Therefore, such an event in the constellation of Aries could have been interpreted as indicating a royal birth in Judea. To support his reasoning, he quotes from a number of ancient sources which suggest that close conjunctions between the Moon and Jupiter bestowed beneficial rewards. A second-century Greek astrologer, Vettius Valens, in his *Anthology* (1.19), went one stage further and informs us that such aspects manufactured 'notable leaders':

Zeus [Jupiter] and the Moon, then are good, acquisitive, producing masters of ornament and of bodies, and furnishing notable leaders … and those who are deemed worthy of gifts or honours.

Occultations of Jupiter by the Moon are however, not uncommon and apparently the events of 6 BC in Aries repeat themselves approximately every sixty years, so that they are not particularly exceptional or unusual. Earlier individual occultations, of 13 July 17 BC and 4 March 46 BC, were spectacular and yet no special mention or significance was attached to these events. The fact that Magi, or anyone else for that matter, would not have been able to see the occultations of 6 BC also seems to contradict the wording in Matthew that the star had been *seen* in the east. The subsequent movement of Jupiter as it approached and reached opposition in Aries was certainly not a rare event. It recurs about every twelve years and yet this has been used to describe the star 'going before' and 'standing over' the place where the young child was.

The Sun

The constellations of Aries and Pisces were not only astrologically significant; they were also of considerable importance from an astronomical aspect. The path of the apparent movement of the Sun against the starry background, known as the ecliptic, takes it through the twelve constellations of the zodiac. Each year, on or about 21 or 22 March, the Sun reaches the celestial equator, travelling from south to north. It is then said to have reached the First Point of Aries, which is also referred to as the Vernal or Spring Equinox. It is called the First Point of Aries because, in classical times, it lay in the constellation of Aries the Ram and it may be for this reason that such importance was attached to it astrologically. Due to precession, that is the wobble of the Earth's axis, this point drifted backwards very slowly over time out of Aries and into the adjacent constellation of Pisces. It is not possible to put a precise date as to when this happened, as the boundaries between the two constellations are not that clearly defined, but it is generally accepted that it gradually took place during the period around 200 BC to AD 200.

The identification of the effect of precession was first recorded by the Greek Hipparchus, in 134 BC, when he decided to make a star catalogue following the appearance of a nova in that year. However, the precession of the equinoxes would almost certainly have also been known to the Babylonians, whose records of astronomical positions would have gone back millennia, and it would have been impossible for it not to have been detected by them over such long periods of time.

Tails of Two Fish

In ancient Britain the Druids, who had been in existence for centuries, may also have been aware of the precession of the equinoxes, and this could possibly be evidenced by the discovery in 1885 of a secretly buried clay pot containing gold coins in Freckenham, Norfolk. These coins were issued by the Iceni or Eceni tribe, around 45 to 40 BC, with one type of coin in particular being of special interest. On one side it shows back-to-back crescents with a horizontal line below these and a large five-pointed star above with another below the line. There are also a number of pellets shown distributed in groups. The other side of the coin shows a horse with a cabled mane and beneath it is what has been described as a solar flower.

The two opposing crescents and the stylised horse are very common icons on ancient British coins, particularly with those of the Iceni. However, if you look closely at the crescents on this coin you can see that each have attachments at either end. Chris Rudd has come to the conclusion that the crescents have been cleverly developed by the engraver to show two open-mouthed fish complete with tails. Consequently, he is of the opinion that this depicts either the constellation of Pisces and/or its zodiacal sign, which comprises two fish facing opposite one another joined by a horizontal line or bar. It is significant in that it appears to be a rare example of a Celtic coin which may depict a constellation. There seems to be little doubt that the features illustrated were a result of the influence and guidance exerted by the Druids, who, as we have seen, were considered to be a leading authority in the study of astronomy and astrology.

Although Rudd's conclusion may well be correct, it should be pointed out that there is another opinion which considers that the attachments may simply be decorative torcs. Nevertheless, we have to remember that the Druids almost certainly would have been aware of the classical image of Pisces, so it would not be a great surprise if they had decided to have it engraved on a coin. However, the question which then arises is, why did they depict a constellation which appears so obscure and inconspicuous in the sky? It has only three stars, which shine below the fourth magnitude, namely Alpherg, Al Rischa and Gamma Pisces. Why not illustrate a zodiacal constellation which is prominent and clearly defined, with bright stars such as Gemini, Taurus or Leo? We do, of course, have to allow for the fact that, in those days of no light pollution, even stars of around fourth magnitude would have stood out clearly against the background of fainter stars. Nevertheless, the question has to be asked, why did they select Pisces – what was so special about this particular constellation? Well, the answer would seem to lie on the other side of the coin with the solar flower, which is obviously a representation of the Sun, and the horse, which is depicted because it represents the means by which the Sun rode or was pulled across the sky. The Sun effectively took the role of an invisible chariot. It would seem that the Druids may have been aware that this great globe of light was in the process of shifting its position at the spring equinox from Aries to Pisces, considering it to be of such significance that they arranged to have such a coin produced, illustrating that constellation's zodiacal sign.

Obviously, the vernal equinox was of immense importance to all the ancient civilisations, including the Celtic tribes of Britain. To them it signalled the commencement of a new year, representing the beginning of spring, whenever the daily hours of daylight started to exceed those of darkness and the Sun's heat began to make crops and trees, including the sacred oak, grow. Their life and existence evolved around the Sun's cycle. Their religion also included an underlying belief in the immortality of the human soul, and to support this many natural analogies or parallels were presented, one of which was the Sun's daily death and rebirth.

A Christian Emblem

The early Christians also adopted the sign of Pisces as their emblem, initially as a secret symbol designed to protect them from prying Romans. It may be that they too recognised its significance, not only for reasons outlined above but also because they regarded the shifting of the First Point of Aries into Pisces as possibly representing a new beginning, or the birth of a new era. It has even been suggested that the star of Bethlehem may have been an interpretation of the Sun itself, or rather the Sun in its new zodiacal home at the equinox. The author of Matthew, writing some ninety years or so after the birth of Jesus, was in the privileged position of having the option of selecting what may have been considered to be perhaps the most astrologically significant event to have taken place, albeit gradually, over a period of hundreds of years. So, could the Sun in Pisces actually represent the star of Bethlehem?

It is interesting that the early Christian movement used the sign of the two fish as their symbol, so that the Sun in Pisces at the equinox would have fitted in very neatly with such an icon. In other words, that sign could have led to the author of Matthew accepting that Pisces had a special significance to the new religion. The Sun, in the process of entering that particular constellation at the spring equinox, may have exerted a tempting enticement to incorporate it into the story surrounding the birth of Jesus, whilst at the same time only having to make brief and ambiguous references to it. Could this be what the author had in mind when he mentions the star? Although it was of an extremely slow nature, it was nevertheless a significant and gradual celestial occurrence, which may have been interpreted as heralding in the beginning of a new Christian era, associating it with Christ's divinity.

The Sun in Pisces, representing the star of Bethlehem, could actually help to explain why the New Testament constantly seems to make references to Christ being regarded as the new 'light', being associated with the new Piscean age and perhaps taking the place of the Sun as a god to be worshipped. Even in the story of the nativity it is possible to draw a stark contrast between the forces of evil and darkness as represented by Herod, and the forces of good and the light as represented by Christ.

It can, however, be argued that the reference in the New Testament to this sacred light has nothing whatsoever to do with Christ being associated with the Sun, but rather a reference to a new spiritual light or enlightenment. Likewise, the New Testament frequently refers to fish and fishes with Jesus describing himself as a fisher of men, so could this in some way be as a result of the knowledge that the Sun had entered Pisces at the equinox? More likely, the explanation is simply that fishing was an essential and vital industry in many of the areas covered by Jesus during his ministry and it was quite appropriate to draw an analogy with it.

An astronomer, Percy Seymour, in his book titled *The Birth of Christ: Exploding the Myth*, also accepted the significance of the Sun drifting into Pisces at the vernal equinox, realising that the ancient Egyptians would have recognised the effect of precession at least 4,000 years prior to the birth of Jesus, and that the Babylonians would also have been aware of it. He therefore makes the fairly safe assumption that the Magi, as astrologers, would have known that the Sun had, or was in the process of, drifting slowly into that constellation. Thus the combination of a triple conjunction taking place in Pisces, at the start or dawn of the age of Pisces, would have been viewed as being of exceptional significance, heralding not only the coming of a Jewish king but also a great leader for a new era.

Seymour also follows the theory that precession may also explain why the early Christians adopted the symbol of the two fish, pointing out that the letters of the word in Greek for fish are I, Ch, Th, U and S, and were claimed by some to be incorporated into the name Jesus. The symbol may simply have been adopted by the early Christians in recognition of the fact that Jesus, as their Messiah, had been born in the new age of Pisces and was viewed as representing a leader for that age.

Conclusion

The Sun in Aries and then Pisces at the spring equinox undoubtedly does make these two constellations stand out as being of special interest in our quest to identify the star of Bethlehem. Consequently, any unusual celestial activity taking place in either of these two constellations around the time of Christ's birth merits recognition. As such, the triple conjunction of 7 BC, the planetary massing, and the lunar occultations of 6 BC, have been considered by some as contributing towards a growing expectation of the birth of the Messiah.

The Piscean age is starting now to draw to a close. The First Point of Aries will eventually drift out of Pisces and into Aquarius. Modern attempts have been made to define where the boundaries of these ancient constellations begin and end, with the International Astronomical Union in 1929 defining the areas of the eighty-eight official constellations. The edge between Pisces and Aquarius technically locates the beginning of the Aquarian age at around the year 2600, with a computer simulation (*Skymap Pro 11*) suggesting 2597. It takes so long due to the fact that the Sun actually approaches the constellation boundary of Aquarius, at the equinox, at a very oblique angle. That year, however, is disputed by many astrologers due to the varying sizes and overlapping of the zodiacal constellations, with the astrological sign of Aquarius having a different boundary to that of the astronomical constellation. In astrology the signs are based upon 'ecliptic longitude', whereas the astronomical constellations are based upon right ascension and declination. Nevertheless, it appears that the astrologers can't even agree on where the boundaries are! Consequently, there have been reports that the new age of Aquarius will take place sometime between the years 2100 and 2500, but one source has even suggested that it will happen between 2012 and 2150. So be prepared!

12

METEORS, METEORITES & ASTEROIDS

There is an old saying that every time a meteor or shooting star is seen, somewhere on Earth a child is born. So it is, perhaps, not surprising that it has been suggested that a meteor might explain the star of Bethlehem. Certainly anyone who has witnessed a shower of bright meteors on a clear night will have found it to have been a most rewarding and exhilarating experience, worthy of being placed very high on their list of the most spectacular celestial events.

Meteors are caused by interplanetary dust, representing small particles that once formed the tails of comets. As they enter the Earth's upper atmosphere, at speeds of 10–50 miles per second, they collide with molecules of air, producing a high concentration of heat energy, which vaporises the particle by a process known as ablation. Further collisions take place between the vaporised atoms, leading to excitation and ionisation as electrons are detached from atoms and molecules of air. It is this process that produces a streak of light or ionisation which is normally 10–20 miles long but only a few feet in diameter. Maximum brightness usually takes place at a height of about 60 miles. It is estimated that about 100 million visible meteors enter the Earth's atmosphere each day and, over the course of a year, a total of roughly 50,000 tons of material are deposited by way of falling meteoric dust.

Meteor Showers

Meteors fall into two categories – those that belong to a well-defined shower caused by the Earth's orbit passing through streams of short-period cometary dust or debris, and those that are not associated with a shower, known as sporadic. Showers are named after the constellation from which the meteors appear to radiate. It is probable that those categorised as sporadic previously belonged to an ancient shower that had petered out over time. Some of the major present-day meteor showers are summarised as follows:

Stream	Dates of maximum activity	Zenithal hourly rate
Quadrantids	3 & 4 January	100
Lyrids	21 & 22 April	15
Eta Aquarids	5 & 6 May	50
Delta Aquarids	28 & 29 July	20
Alpha Aquarids	2 & 3 August	8

Perseids	11 & 12 August	90
Orionids	21 & 22 October	25
Taurids	4 & 5 November	10
Leonids	17 & 18 November	15
Geminids	13 & 14 December	120
Ursids	21 & 22 December	10

The zenithal hourly rate (ZHR) is a measurement of the anticipated level of meteors to be seen in a perfectly transparent sky, with the radiant of the shower assumed to be exactly overhead. From the table it can be seen that, at present, the best annual shower is the Geminids, with a peak ZHR of about 120. Their radiant, or the part in the sky from which they appear to originate, lies just above the bright star Castor. The Geminids are exceptional in that the particles in space that produce them are not cometary but asteroidal, coming from asteroid number 3200, Phaethon. They are also unusual in that they have slow collision speeds, entering the Earth's atmosphere at about 20 miles per second, and have a higher-than-normal average particle density, probably as a result of their rocky source. This means that they travel relatively slowly across the sky and tend to be brighter than average. The shower is also quite new, having been first identified as recently as 1862 by Robert P. Greg, and it is clear that their activity is on the increase.

Over time cometary material, mainly in the form of dust, becomes spread in a broad band around the orbits of the comet, caused by the effects of interplanetary gravity, particularly from Jupiter which perturbs the dust, causing it to deviate from its original course. Over thousands of years, a stream of cometary debris therefore becomes wider and more diffuse. To produce a shower, however, the comet's orbit must come relatively close to the Earth itself, so that at some point our planet must pass through its stream of material left behind, normally stretching for millions of miles. This is why Halley's Comet, which is estimated to have orbited the Sun about 3,500 times over a period of about 250,000 years, is associated with the Eta-Aquarid and Orionid showers.

Meteor Storms

A much rarer spectacle is a meteor storm, which is really a shower with a short-lived peak of intense activity that may give rise to tens of thousands of meteors every hour. In extreme cases they have been known to come down like rain. One of the most recent meteor storms was that of the Leonids in 1966, visible from the United States, when about as many as 150,000 meteors per hour were witnessed from dark sites. For a storm to occur, the Earth has to pass very close to a recent orbital path of a comet. It therefore encounters a mass of small particles recently emitted by the comet, which appear to radiate out from a specific point in the sky since they will not have had time to disperse and spread out.

A Leonid storm occurs every thirty-three years or so but some are much better than others, with those of 1833 and 1866 being exceptional. That of 1899, however, was relatively unspectacular. This is because the stream of material that can give rise to a storm is very narrow and its orbit subject to perturbations, usually caused by Jupiter's gravitational attraction, so it may be pulled away from the Earth's orbital path. Consequently the nodes of the comet's and Earth's orbits do not come close enough to intersect one another.

Although records of Leonid storms go back as far as AD 902, it does not necessarily mean that there were no earlier similar events. Their source is the comet Temple-Tuttle, which was named after its co-discoverers in 1866, although there are Chinese records of it going back to 1366. It was last visible in 1998 as a rather faint binocular object and produced a minor storm in 1999.

Ancient Reports of Meteor Showers

Some of the above meteor showers were recorded by the Chinese and Babylonians well over 2,000 years ago, and since the tenth century by Arab astronomers. Whilst Chinese and Arabian records show meteor showers which no longer exist, it is clear that they did record the Lyrids going back to around 500 BC, the Perseids since AD 36, the Orionids from AD 288, and the Leonids from AD 902.

Many of the major meteor events, as documented in oriental records going back as far as 2,500 years ago, have been collated by Susumu Imoto and Ichiro Hasegawa within their *Historical Records of Meteor Showers in China, Korea and Japan*, making reference to a total of 118 displays. Number 5 of their listing mentions a display on 27 March 15 BC in the constellation of Lyra, in which stars are reported to have fallen in the form of a shower, and they have identified these as Lyrids. In the same year, during September or October, there was another major event, recorded as number 58, which attracted a similar description, although this time they could not associate it with one of the recognised showers.

For our purpose, however, number 21 in their list is by far the most important as it took place closer to the time of the birth of Jesus. Using the Chinese *T'ien-wen-chih* as their source, they state that this shower happened on the first day of the fourth lunar month, known as *Ting-yu*, in the first year of the era of Yuan Yen, which equates to 23 May 12 BC. It reports that the stars fell like a shower of glittering rain until evening. This is a rather strange description, as it seems to imply that the meteors may have been visible during daylight, so they would have to have been extremely bright, although if they were fireballs they would hardly have fallen like glittering rain! However, a more likely explanation is that the meteors became visible at twilight, or shortly afterwards, and continued until sometime later in the evening. This event was not identified as belonging to any of the known major annual meteor showers, and it is also interesting to note that this preceded the first recorded sighting of Halley's Comet, in that year, by a mere three months.

There must be some doubt as to whether this meteor storm would have been visible further west, namely from Persia and Judea, as by the time darkness had descended in those regions, some hours later, the display may have completely fizzled out. It is a well-known fact that such storms normally persist for a very short period, sometimes as little as one to two hours, and if our reasoning is correct in that it ceased sometime in the later evening, as viewed from China, then it would seem unlikely that it would have been witnessed so much further west. Nevertheless, the Chinese description remains very ambiguous and open to different interpretations, so whilst we cannot be certain if the storm was actually visible from the Middle East, it remains a distinct possibility.

The Moore Theory

It has been suggested by Sir Patrick Moore that two very bright meteors, leaving long trails which remained in the sky for some time, and both travelling in exactly the same direction, one sometime after the other, may explain the star of Bethlehem. The theory is that the first meteor, travelling from east to west, attracted the Magi to the night sky to ponder its meaning. Having witnessed the second meteor, sometime later, their interpretation was that it meant that they should travel to Jerusalem and towards Bethlehem to the place where the young child was. Such a theory does have the advantage of explaining why the Magi and few others, if any, appear to have been aware of the 'star'.

To make this theory seem plausible, we must assume that the two meteors were exceptionally bright in order to make them stand out from other meteors. In other words, they would have to have been fireballs, which are meteors that appear to be brighter than Venus, being visible for perhaps two seconds or so and leaving a trail in the sky that would persist for a number of minutes. With the exception of a meteor storm, to see two such objects within the space of a few weeks or months would be rare, and even more so if both were to be seen to travel in the one direction, but nevertheless it is quite possible.

The Cyrilids

Strangely enough, meteors have been known to appear to travel in exactly the same direction. On 9 February 1913, an unusual meteor shower was observed from north-east America which has become known as the Cyrilid meteor shower, as it appeared on St Cyril's Day. One by one each meteor appeared from precisely the same point in the sky and proceeded to track the same path before disappearing in exactly the same point in the sky. This continued for a period of around three minutes. The most likely explanation is that it represented a small number of particles that somehow had gone into temporary low Earth orbit before being dragged down into the Earth's atmosphere at an extremely shallow angle, so that they all appeared and travelled in the same direction. Although no other records exist of a similar event, it has probably happened on other occasions. If we suppose that the Magi witnessed such an occurrence they may have developed a strong inclination to journey in the direction that the meteors were travelling. They would certainly not have witnessed anything like it before.

Meteorites

Very bright fireballs can actually appear as bright as the Sun and are caused by larger fragments of space debris, which may even survive the dramatic frictional burning by the atmosphere. Such objects which fall to Earth are known as meteorites and are so rare that they are named after the place where they landed. There are presently about 30,000 known meteorites of which the great majority have been found in Antarctica following expeditions designed for the specific purpose of recovering them. Unlike meteors, meteorites generally represent fragments of broken-up asteroids which, over time, have strayed into the orbital path of the Earth. Much rarer types have been known to have originated from the Moon and from Mars. It is estimated that around 20,000 meteorites of more than 100 grams fall annually, but obviously most remain unobserved, falling into oceans, lakes or deserts or simply because many occur during daylight and remain unseen. On average no more than about ten new finds each year are actually recovered.

Recent Falls
One of the most spectacular meteorites to fall in recent years occurred over Britain and Ireland on 25 April 1969. Travelling in a north-westerly direction, its fireball was visible for more than 300 miles over parts of England and Wales, being seen to break up over the north of Ireland. Two fragments were recovered about thirty-five miles apart, the largest being at a farm at Bovedy near Garvagh, County Londonderry, which subsequently gave rise to its name. One of the fragments actually pierced the roof of a police store before landing on a desk! Sonic booms were heard over a wide area shortly after it was seen to break up into three pieces, eye witness reports suggesting that it seemed to pass from one horizon to the other. The main chunk of it probably landed in the Atlantic to the north of Donegal.

The Bovedy meteorite fall is, however, insignificant in comparison to other meteorite falls which have occurred within the recent past, a good example being that which fell on 12 February 1947 in Sikhote Alin in eastern Siberia, when over 23 tons of material showered the area and left over 120 impact holes, fracturing also being caused when the pieces impacted the frozen ground.

In October 2008 a very small asteroid, named 2008 TC3, weighing about 80 tonnes, with a diameter of about 4 metres, was observed by astronomers using the William Herschel Telescope on La Palma whilst it was on a collision course with the Earth. Appearing as an extremely faint object, it represented the first time an asteroid could be studied before impacting the surface of our planet. It was successfully tracked and imaged, enabling its spectral signature to be analysed. Shortly afterwards it exploded in the atmosphere at an altitude of twenty-three miles, scattering small fragments over parts of the Nubian Desert in Sudan.

Different Types

Meteorites can be divided into three broad categories depending upon their composition, namely stony, stony iron and iron. Stony meteorites can be further classified into chondrites and achondrites, and stony iron into mesosiderites and pallasites, although there is not always a clear distinction between them. Around 90–95 per cent of all meteorites which fall are of the stony variety, but these are subject to erosion and more difficult to detect upon the Earth's surface, so the majority of meteorites that are recovered are iron.

The outside appearance of a meteorite is distorted by frictional heating and break-up during its hypersonic flight. Its surface melts away, causing droplets of molten material to fly off into the atmosphere. However, while most of the heat is absorbed by the melted material, the inside of the meteorite remains cold and intact. The melt in the final moments of descent hardens or solidifies on the surface as the meteorite decelerates and this is known as fusion crust. On a stony meteorite it resembles a blackening of its surface, but on an iron meteorite it is less obvious as some of the heat gained during its atmospheric encounter is conducted into its interior. Consequently, the insides of stony meteorites are better preserved and may reveal a history of their life before impacting the Earth, often revealing shock or thermal activity when they were thrown out into space from their parent body. Chondrites, in particular, preserve evidence of what conditions were like in our solar system and of its origin when it was formed some 4.6 billion years ago.

Since its formation, the Earth has been continually bombarded by meteorites, although as time progressed the numbers have decreased dramatically. One meteorite retrieved on Earth is thought to have fallen about 460 million years ago and is a chondrite embedded within a Swedish limestone. Some of the meteorites found in the Antarctic may have fallen up to a million years ago. The famous Meteor Crater in Arizona was caused by a meteorite which exploded before it hit the ground, known as an airburst, around 50,000 BC.

Meteorite Worship

So how would the ancient civilisations have reacted to the rare sight of such an object falling to Earth, and could such an event have been interpreted as the star of Bethlehem? In classical times, a number of ancient religions had been based around cults of fallen meteorites, including that housed in the Temple of Diana in Ephesus, which is mentioned in Acts 19:35. The Romans certainly took the appearance of a falling meteorite very seriously, and recovered fragments were regarded as a sign from the gods, and worshipped.

An example of this may be represented by the behaviour of the Emperor Elagabalus (AD 218–222), who took this to extremes. He was a religious fanatic, worshipping a Sun god called El Gabal, or Baal, the cult of which was represented by a black conical-shaped meteorite which he took to Rome, where it was housed in the Elagaballum, a lavish temple on the Palantine Hill. It became known as the Stone of Emesa, as it originated from Emesa in Syria. However, to the horror of the Romans, Elagabalus attempted to promote his god as the first and foremost to be worshipped. Each year at midsummer the black stone would be shown off in a triumphal parade. Coins were issued about the year AD 219, depicting the stone's annual procession through the streets of Rome, being transported on a chariot with four parasols and drawn by four horses. Apparently the emperor himself would run backwards ahead of the chariot whilst holding the reigns of the horses, demonstrating his commitment to never turn his back on his god.

The actual meteorite was described by an early-third-century historian, Herodium, in *A History of the Roman Empire since the death of Marcus Aurelius*:

> The stone is worshipped as though it was sent from heaven; on it are some projecting pieces and markings that are pointed out, which the people would like to believe are a rough picture of the Sun, because this is how they see them.

Elagabalus soon became unpopular, and like most of the Roman emperors, came to a sorry end. As for the meteorite, it was returned to its true home in the City of Emesa, and later coins dated to AD 253–4 illustrate it housed inside an elaborately styled temple. But it has not survived, and it is thought that it was destroyed by Christians in the fourth century when the temple was converted to a church. However, another sacred stone which was housed in the Temple of Aphrodite on Paphos has survived. It was found not far from the ruins of the Temple and has been proven to be a meteorite. Interestingly, coins from AD 198 to 217 also display this meteorite, showing it housed within a specially constructed tower.

The early Christians frowned upon such objects, viewing them with suspicion, as they attracted such ardent cult worship, with all its traits of paganism. It would therefore seem improbable that a meteorite would even have crossed the mind of the author of Matthew when he makes reference to the star of Bethlehem. His descriptions of the star 'standing over' a specific location obviously could not apply to an actual physical object that had penetrated the atmosphere and fallen to the ground.

A Second Star of Bethlehem?

Another example of the influence exerted on the Romans by a falling meteorite may be that which was witnessed by Constantine I prior to the Battle of the Milvian Bridge in AD 312, against his rival Maxentius. It is thought that a fireball was seen to fall in front of him, the vapour or smoke trail of which was seen to be taken up by the wind in the atmosphere in such a way as to resemble a cross in the sky. The account was taken up by Eusebius, an early Christian church historian, who has obviously exaggerated the event out of all proportion in recounting the life of Constantine:

> Whilst he was thus praying with fervent entreaty, a most marvellous sign appeared to him from heaven, the account of which it might have been hard to believe had it been related by any other person ... about noon when the day was beginning to decline he saw with his own eyes the trophy of a cross of light in the heavens, above the Sun, and bearing the inscription, 'conquer by this' ... at this sight he himself was struck with amazement and his whole army also, which followed him on this expedition and witnessed the miracle.

Upon seeing the event, Constantine took this as a divine sign from God that he and all his followers should convert to Christianity and display the sign of the cross in battle. Proceeding to defeat the forces of Maxentius, he subsequently became the first Christian emperor. In 325 he oversaw the Council of Nicaea, helping to edit the Nicene Creed, which effectively created the Catholic Church and its priesthood out of the early Christian communities in Rome.

Given its enormous consequences, this celestial event, if true, is probably as significant as a second star of Bethlehem, for if Constantine and his army had not been inspired by the occurrence, the battle might have been lost and Christianity would have remained an outlawed religion. Even if he had won the battle but had not witnessed the spectacle of a cross in the sky, he might have remained a pagan and Christianity would not have become firmly established, at least not within his own lifetime. The Catholic Church would not have been formally legalised until much later, if at all, ensuring that paganism would be allowed to flourish in its absence. The significance of the event, if it is true, cannot be underestimated.

The Sirente Craters

While some consider that Constantine's vision may have been the result of a dream or hallucination, or possibly an observation of a comet or a solar halo, the recent discovery in 2003 of an impact crater in a valley called Prati del Sirente in central Italy may lend some credence to the story. A research team led by a Swedish geologist, Jens Ormo, believe that they may have identified the remains of a crater that was formed as a result of Constantine's meteorite. Measuring roughly 120 by 150 yards in diameter, and surrounded by numerous secondary craters, it is estimated that it was formed by an object of approximately 10 yards across. Magnetic abnormalities have been identified under some of the smaller craters, which may be an indication that iron fragments of the meteorite remain under their surface. Radio-carbon-dating, however, suggests that the craters were formed around 1,500 to 1,600 years ago, implying that they were created some time after AD 312.

Such a theory is not without its critics and it has been suggested by a geologist, Fabrizio Speranza, that the crater was man-made by a local tribe in order to provide water for their livestock. Such an idea appears to be in contradiction with the historical knowledge of that tribe's pasture areas and routes. In any case, this explanation could not explain the existence of the smaller secondary craters scattered about close by. Professor Francesco Stoppa of the University Gabriele d'Annunzio of Pescara, on the other hand, suggests that the craters may have been formed naturally through a process of erosion, caused by the flows of mud and water. Another proposal claims that the craters could have been formed by allied aircraft in the Second World War disposing of unwanted ordinance, as iron fragments recovered in the area have been proven to be shrapnel.

A Local Legend

The story of Constantine is supported by a local legend in the area which mentions the subsequent conversion from paganism to Christianity. This is linked closely with the history of the church of Santa Maria della Consolazione at Secinaro, situated in the valley next to the Prati del Sirente. This oral tradition also includes a detailed reference to an event which supposedly created the craters, and its tale was told by the church caretaker to an historian, F. Fabriz, who published it in 1898. In the 1940s an archaeologist, E. Ricci, came across the story and also published it, and later it was taken up and told by Ormo and his colleagues in *Antiquity: A Quarterly Review of World Archaeology* in 2003:

> ... an uproar hit the mountain and quartered the giant oaks announcing the arrival of the goddess. A sudden and intense heat overwhelmed the people and a shout echoed all around, splitting the air with its trail of violence ... All of a sudden, over there, in the distance, in the sky, a new star, never seen before, bigger than the other ones, came nearer and nearer, appeared and disappeared behind the top of the eastern mountains. Peoples' eyes looked at the strange light growing bigger and bigger. Soon the star shone as large as a new Sun. An irresistible, dazzling light pervaded the sky. The oak leaves shuddered, discoloured, and curled up. The forest lost its sap. The Sirente was shaking. In a tremendous rumble the statue sank into a sudden chasm. The satyrs and the Bacchantes fell down senseless. A huge silence fell. It seemed as if time had stopped in the ancient wood near the temple at the foot of the Sirente, and it looked like the mountain had never existed. The entire valley became dumb. Not a breath of wind could be heard, nor a sheep bleating from the numerous herds, nor a rustle from the strong trees, nor a human sound.
>
> After an endless period of time, when the stars shone in the sky without the Moon, a new breeze came to stir the leaves; sheep were heard again and the mountain was dressed in the light of a new dawn. Faint stars disappeared, blue sky slowly came back and the Sirente became a golden mountain in the first rays of the new Sun. It looked like the valley was full of roses. Newly awake, men listened closely to the death rattle of the goddess at the foot of the wood; and then they saw the statue of the Madonna with the Holy Child in her arms who was sitting on a throne of light and was surrounded by light. The mother of God, carried here by the angels through the sky, had come to extirpate sin

... People were absorbed in religion and deep prayers. They abandoned the tragic elation of human passions and sentiments to embrace a new sense of deep peace ... It was the dawn of a new life. Men, after repenting, experienced ineffable feelings, a spiritually derived pleasure, an intimate consolation and they named the Madonna Santa Maria della Consolazione. In her honour, they built the church on the ruin of the ancient [pagan] temple, the statue carried from the east by angels, crossing both the sea and the air, was put on the alter. The prodigious event is presented in the fresco located on the central arch of the church. The painting shows the Madonna with the Holy Child on the scene of the church navigating the sea, with the church tower indicating the ways of heaven.

Obviously this sophisticated account reflects local mythology combined with the accumulation of centuries of supplementary material. However, the rejection of pagan rites and the conversion of the local tribe to Christianity do appear to have coincided with the period during which the meteorite is reputed to have fallen.

The meteorite theory continues to be a plausible explanation and it has been speculated that there was an unusually high rate of meteor and cometary activity between the fourth and sixth centuries AD. In particular, Taurid meteor activity does appear to have been higher in those days, as well as at other times, and it may be that some large fragments had penetrated the atmosphere to create the craters. Nevertheless it seems that the jury remains out as to whether these craters are of meteoric origin and if so, whether there is a possible link with the story of Constantine.

A Fantasy?

Many historians continue to insist that the celestial image was simply a fantasy on the part of Constantine, pointing to the fact that he was almost certainly influenced by his mother, who subsequently became known as Saint Helena (248–328). She had earlier conducted Christian meetings in her palace at Traves, at the same time providing some support and protection for them against persecution, which continued to be rampant. Her palace was later converted into Christian churches prior to Constantine making Christianity legitimate. In 327, aged seventy-nine, she carried out excavations on Mount Calvary in an attempt to retrieve fragments of the cross of Jesus and, according to legend, was successful. As seen earlier, another legend claimed that it was she who discovered the remains of the Magi.

There are some similarities between the story of the Magi and that of Constantine. Both involved a heavenly sign and both could have been regarded as satisfying biblical prophecies. His vision became known as the 'labarum', and the sign of the cross he used, as a symbol of Christianity, actually resembled a star! This was not intentional, of course, and it is thought that the sign was a Christian interpretation of an earlier pagan symbol. It was simply a monogram which employed the first two letters of the Greek word for Christ, which is spelt XPIETOE, so XP was incorporated as the design. It is known as the Chi Rho symbol, after the Greek words for these two letters.

Ironically, it was Constantine who proceeded to abolish the cult of meteorite worship, following his conversion. The Arabians, however, continued to revere such objects, traditionally believing that they had originated from heaven. Some of their shrines continue to exist to this day, perhaps the most famous being the sacred black stone set in the wall of the Kaaba, the ancient building in the centre of the Grand Mosque in Mecca.[10]

Meteoroids and Asteroids

The term meteoroid refers to a small rocky fragment which orbits around the Sun, originating from a broken-up asteroid or comet. There is no clear difference between large meteoroids and small asteroids, therefore a definition distinguishing between the two has to be based upon size; bodies of around 10 metres diameter or less can be regarded as meteoroids, and those over that measurement are asteroids which are also sometimes referred to as minor planets. The term asteroid was first coined by William Herschel and means 'star-like' as through a telescope they appear as points of light. Meteoroids include cometary dust and debris and larger chunks of rock, which produce the meteors and fireballs when they hit the Earth's atmosphere as mentioned earlier. Such objects, when in orbit around the Sun, will be invisible to the naked eye as their size is so insignificant. The larger asteroids, on the other hand, are capable of becoming naked-eye objects if they happen to stray close to the Earth.

Whilst most asteroids orbit the Sun in the Main Belt, which lies between the planets Mars and Jupiter, there are substantial numbers which are to be found elsewhere. These include near-Earth objects, which can make close approaches to our planet and occasionally impact. Within this category are certain classes, known as the Apollo and Aten asteroids, whose orbital paths cross the orbit of the Earth. Other groups, known as the Trojans, track the orbit of Jupiter, whereas two asteroids known as Icarus and Phaethon have paths which take them closer to the Sun than the planet Mercury.

The Planetary Detectives
In the late eighteenth century, the search for a planet beyond Uranus attracted the attention of the 'planetary detectives', a group of European astronomers dedicated to its discovery. Although they failed, they did discover the largest asteroids known within the inner solar system. In 1801 Geovanni Piazzi, a Sicilian, discovered Ceres, which has a diameter of 580 miles. Over the next few years further large asteroids were discovered, namely Pallas, Juno and Vesta. Such asteroids are approximately spherical in shape as their size means that their self-gravity is enough to compress the material from which they are made.

Vesta

Discovered on 27 March 1807 by Heinrich Wilheim Olbers, a German physician and astronomer, Vesta is the fourth-largest asteroid, with a diameter of 334 miles, and is the only one which becomes discernible to the naked eye. It is visible because its orbit lies close to the inner edge of the Main Belt. Hubble Space Telescope images have disclosed that it has ancient lava flows, and a large impact basin so deep that it has exposed its mantle. On 18 July 2011, the first detailed images of Vesta were transmitted by NASA's *Dawn* spacecraft, after it entered into a captured orbit around it. They revealed a complex and shattered surface of craters, depressions, jagged cliffs and one large mountainous feature, reflecting an exposure to meteoroid bombardment and volcanic activity during a turbulent past.

Vesta has a high average density due to it having a metallic core, probably of nickel-iron, and it has been noted that a number of smaller asteroids, known as the Hirayama Family, have the same orbital paths. This has given rise to the theory that certain meteorites, called Eucrites, Howardites and Diogenites, have fallen to Earth as a result of the earlier fragmentation of a related larger body. One recent fall was witnessed by fence workers in Millbillibe in Western Australia who observed a fireball. Ten years later, pieces of the meteorite were found standing out against the soil as they had a shiny black fusion crust. Subsequent examination of their composition points to Vesta as their source as they had the same spectral signature of pyroxene, which is common in lava flows.

An Asteroid as the Star of Bethlehem?

Could Vesta or another asteroid represent the star of Bethlehem? Like the planet Uranus, Vesta is just visible to the naked eye under good sky conditions. It does have one advantage over that planet, in that it would have appeared to move relatively quickly against the starry background. However, common sense would suggest that such a faint object is hardly likely to have been interpreted as representing a sign heralding the birth of a saviour king, even if it were to have a close conjunction with one of the brighter planets.

It is not uncommon for smaller asteroids to make close approaches to the Earth. One such example is Eros. Measuring only about half a mile across, it moves in an eccentric orbit away from the main asteroid belt, so that it can stray quite close to the Earth. In 1937 a small asteroid, Hermes, which is also only about half a mile long, came within about half a million miles of our planet. On 8 March 2002, Asteroid 2001 YB5 passed the Earth by a distance of 288,000 miles and was estimated to be around 1,000 feet across. As it came from the general direction of the Sun, it was not observed telescopically until four days later.

When such small asteroids do come exceptionally close to the Earth it is possible for them to become visible due to reflected sunlight coming off them. Although none in the recent past have been known to come within naked-eye visibility, it is accurately predicted that an object, which has been named Apophis, and measuring about 1,000 feet across, will reach a magnitude of about +3.4 when it makes a very close approach on 13 April 2029. It will come so close that it will actually pass within the orbits of some satellites at roughly 22,600 miles from the Earth and should be visible from Europe, Africa and parts of Asia. The asteroid is scheduled to make another close approach in 2036; after that encounter we are not quite sure as to what will happen to it.

Such an asteroid will appear to move swiftly across the sky. This presents a real problem if a similar type object is to be seriously considered as a contender for the star of Bethlehem. In fact it would fail to satisfy most of the criteria as laid down at the start of Chapter 6. It would not make two separate appearances, as it would simply come and go, and quickly at that. It would hardly have had time to go before the Magi prior to disappearing, as in all probability it would not have remained visible for more than a day or two, depending upon its size and distance from the Earth.

Conclusion

The problem about individual meteors and meteorites is that they all make fleeting appearances, being visible for only a few seconds. In addition, as both astrologers and astronomers, Magi would have been very familiar with meteors and fireballs. In all likelihood they would have already been aware of records or stories telling of stones falling from the sky, so that even if they did witness such a rare event it would seem improbable that it would convey to them any particular message. Likewise, faint star-like asteroids may well have been witnessed before, and therefore it would seem unlikely that they would have been interpreted as conveying any special meaning.

Upon reflection, however, it may be significant that, within the space of only three months in 12 BC, there was what appears to have been a significant meteor storm, with stars falling down like glittering rain, followed shortly afterwards by the impressive spectacle of Halley's Comet. Could this be what the author of Matthew had in mind when he implies that the star of Bethlehem made two separate appearances? Whilst they are not one and the same object, as is implied in the infancy narrative, the combination of these two events would nevertheless have created the most marvellous impression within the minds of those who actually witnessed them, and their reminiscences may have been passed down over the years to reach the ears of the author, almost a century later.

19. Edmund Halley. (Sketch
prepared and provided by Colin
Watson, based upon an original
portrait by Thomas Murray
(1687))

20. Halley's Comet as viewed
from Earth in 1910. (Hutchinson's
Splendour of the Heavens (1923))

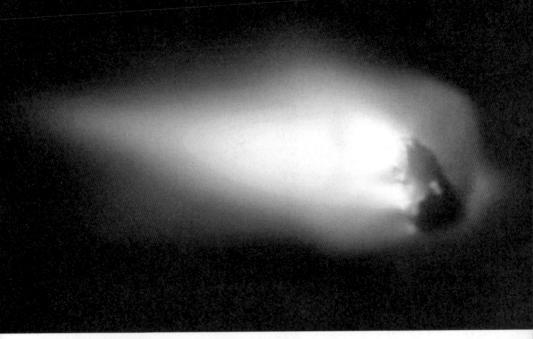

21. A close-up image of Halley's Comet taken from the *Giotto* spacecraft in 1986. (Courtesy of the European Space Agency)

22. Worried attendants belonging to the court of King Harold II point to the comet which appeared in 1066, as illustrated on the Bayeux Tapestry.

23. A telescopic image of Comet Holmes in 2007. (Courtesy of Andy McCrea)

Above left: 24. A denarius of Vespasian showing the zodiacal sign of Capricorn. This coin was issued shortly before the death of the emperor in AD 79. The globe underneath Capricorn represents a symbol of world domination and it is interesting that it appears to display lines of latitude and longitude. (Courtesy of Classical Numismatic Group, Inc.)

Above middle: 25. A denarius of Augustus illustrating the comet of 44 BC. It was thought that the comet was taking the soul of Julius Caesar into heaven. (Courtesy of Classical Numismatic Group, Inc.)

Above right: 26. A gold aureus of Tiberius, with Divus Augustus showing a comet or star displayed above his head. (Courtesy of Classical Numismatic Group Inc.)

Above left: 27. A silver drachm of Orodes II of Parthia (*c.* 45 BC) with a comet or star to the left of his head and another to his right together with a crescent moon. (Photo by Nic Leitch)

Above right: 28. A silver coin of the British King Tincomarus showing a six-rayed comet. (Photo by Andy McCrea)

29. Comet Donati over Paris in 1858. Discovered in early June of that year by an Italian astronomer, Giovanni Donati, it has been described as the most beautiful comet of all time. It was also the first comet to be photographed. (From a contemporary painting)

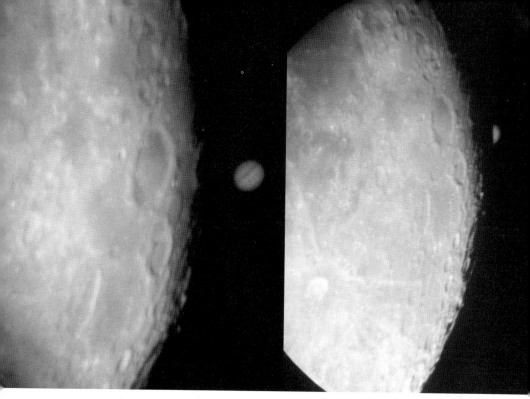

30. An occultation of Jupiter by the Moon, 25 January 2002. (Courtesy of Andy McCrea)

Above left: 31. A coin from Antioch showing a ram, possibly representing the zodiacal sign of Aries, looking back at a star. (Photo by Andy McCrea)

Above right: 32. A Freckenham gold stater, possibly representing the astrological sign of Pisces. (Courtesy of Classical Numismatic Group Inc.)

33. A drawing of a meteor storm on 27 November 1872. (Flammarion and Gore's *Popular Astronomy* (1894))

Above left: 34. A fragment of the Bovedy meteorite of 1969. (Courtesy of the Armagh Planetarium)

Above right: 35. A fragment of the Sikhote Alin meteorite of 1947.

Above left: 36. A silver denarius of Elagabalus illustrating the sacred stone of Emesa (a meteorite). It is shown within a chariot surrounded by four parasols and drawn by four horses. (Courtesy of Classical Numismatic Group, Inc.)

Above right: 37. A coin from Emesa in Syria of the usurper, Uranius Antoninus, AD 253–4. The meteorite is shown housed within a hexastyle temple. (Courtesy of Classical Numismatic Group, Inc.)

Above left: 38. A coin of Constantine II displaying the Chi Rho symbol. (Courtesy of Classical Numismatic Group, Inc.)

Above right: 39. A close-up view of the asteroid Vesta as photographed by NASA's *Dawn* Spacecraft in 2011. (Courtesy of NASA)

Left: 40. The author of Matthew and Halley's Comet in AD 66. (Sketch prepared and provided courtesy of Colin Watson)

Below: 41. King Tiridates of Armenia pays homage to Nero. (Sketch prepared and provided courtesy of Colin Watson)

PART III
SCENARIO &
CONCLUSION

13

A LIKELY SCENARIO

Following the crucifixion of Christ, the disciples and their followers faced fierce opposition from the more orthodox and traditional Jews, who regarded them with suspicion, recognising them as a serious threat to their beliefs. The newly emerged Christian community were persecuted, and eventually forced to flee Jerusalem, with many settling in Syria, particularly within the City of Antioch. It is widely thought that Matthew and Luke were amongst the disciples who gathered there. The church began to flourish in Antioch, and many believe that this is where the books of Matthew and Luke were actually completed. The Apostle Paul also used Antioch as a starting point for his missionary work.

Although the city was Hellenistic, being influenced by both Greek and Roman culture, it comprised a high proportion of both Jews and Gentiles, so whilst Aramaic may have been the local dialect, Greek remained the official language. It is not unreasonable to assume that Matthew, being obviously well educated, was fluent in both of these languages.

Papias, a second-century Bishop of Hierapolis, reported that the Apostle Matthew 'put together the oracles of the Lord in the Hebrew language and that each one interpreted them as best they could'. Papias may have been referring to an early collection of the parables and sayings of Jesus or Old Testament Messianic oracles, which were subsequently compiled by the Apostle. At some further stage this may have been used as source material by the author, who proceeded to translate them into Greek, forming part of an early composition of the Gospel.

The author, whether it was an aged Apostle, or a later Christian, would have realised that a translation into Greek was absolutely essential in order to attract the Gentiles towards Christianity, but he would have also felt under some obligation to make his Gospel appeal to both sides of the community. The later introduction of the infancy narrative may also have been a conscious response to certain other pressures, and these may be summarised as follows:

1. Continued Jewish accusations and criticism against the claims that Jesus was the Messiah. This demanded a response.

2. It had to be made clear that Jesus, as the Messiah, did satisfy Jewish expectations, as reflected in the Old Testament prophecies, including those of Balaam and Micah.

3. There was clearly a 'missing link' between the Old Testament and the commencement of the ministry of Jesus.[11] The author felt an obligation to fill this void by way of an introduction to Jesus, going back to his birth.

But there were other factors at work, represented by actual events that occurred within the author's lifetime and which may have influenced his line of thought before he wrote the infancy narratives:

Halley's Comet, AD 66

This comet could hardly have gone unnoticed, and must have left a memorable impression in most people's minds, including that of the author. It was this appearance that may have provided him with the inspiration to introduce a star into his narrative. Either to reassure himself, or simply out of curiosity, he became aware of records, or passed-down reminiscences, which confirmed to him that two comets had been witnessed some years earlier – in 12 and 5 BC. This would have given himself some reassurance and comfort, in the knowledge that there really had been a similar celestial event, roughly within the generally accepted time-frame for the birth of Jesus.

The Josephus account of the comet, as recorded in *Jewish War*, was written around the year AD 78 and it is possible that the author of Matthew had knowledge of it. For our purpose, the relevant text is as follows:

> There were the miserable people persuaded by these deceivers, and such as belied God himself; while they did not attend nor give credit to the signs that were so evident, and did so plainly foretell their future desolations, but like men infatuated, without eyes to see or minds to consider, did not regard the denunciations that God made to them. Thus there was a star resembling a sword, which stood over the city [Jerusalem], and a comet that continued for a whole year. This also before the Jew's rebellion, and before those commotions which preceded the war, when the people were come in great crowds to the feast of the unleavened bread, on the eighth day of the month of Xanthicus [Nisan], and at the ninth hour of the night, so great a light shone around the altar and the holy house, that it appeared to be bright daytime; which light lasted for half an hour. This light seemed to be a good sign to the unskilful, but was so interpreted by the sacred scribes as to portend those events that followed immediately upon it.

This reference, if taken literally, would seem to imply that there were actually two objects in the sky, but it could be that a misinterpretation has taken place in the translation, as Josephus uses the word *astron* which can either refer to a star or stars. Certainly the description of a star resembling a sword does sound like a comet with a wispy tail, warped or twisted in such a way to give the impression of a sword.

Whilst we are told that one of the apparitions was a comet, it was the other object – the star – that had the tail! It certainly looks like the description has become confused, probably in the course of translation, and what Josephus really said, or meant to say was that there was a comet which resembled a sword in the sky, which continued for a year. The confusion with a star is understandable, as often a comet can resemble a star before it has developed a tail, for example Comet Holmes, which was examined earlier.

Earlier Records

So, what do the contemporary Chinese records have to tell? During the first half of the AD 60s there was a flurry of cometary activity, with reports informing us of no less than four sightings between AD 60 and 64. Number 76 in the catalogue compiled by Ho Peng Yoke, whose source was the *Hon Han Shu*, prepared in AD 445, indicates that there was a further spectacular comet, first observed in the east on the morning of 29 July AD 65. This describes a star with a very long tail, which extended for about 37 degrees. It was first spotted in the constellation of Hydra and proceeded to move close to Leo and into Perseus, with its tail reaching as far as Ursa Major. It eventually faded and disappeared from view after about fifty days. It was also mentioned by the Roman historian Tacitus.

Halley's Comet, in AD 66, is listed as numbers 77 and 78 in the Ho Peng Yoke catalogue, whose source was again the *Hon Han Shu*. This tells us that it was first viewed *in the east* in the morning twilight of 31 January and initially, as no tail could be discerned, it was labelled as a 'guest' star. It was slow-moving and was not referred to again until 20 February when, still as a morning object, it was visible in the constellation of Capricorn. Over the next few weeks it moved into Sagittarius, Scorpio and Virgo, eventually vanishing when it reached the constellation of Crater. The last recorded sighting was around 10 April, so it was of naked-eye visibility for about seventy days.

Interestingly, the original *Hon Han Shu* manuscripts indicate that there were two separate comets, the first being that sighted on 31 January and the second on 20 February. Johann Holetschek, in 1897, was the first investigator to establish a definite link between the two observations, and it now seems almost certain that they were one and the same object. Earlier, in 1850, John Hind had identified that its path was 'in perfect accordance with the track followed by Halley's Comet'.

Duration of a Year?

The comet could not possibly have appeared continuously in the sky for an entire year, as is implied by Josephus, as it would have disappeared into the glare of the Sun in the process of completing its inward approach. Having moved around the Sun, it was seen as it began its long journey outwards, to beyond the orbit of Neptune. As it receded away from the Earth it would fade and subsequently disappear. The period of visibility, commencing from its first sighting to its disappearance, as indicated by the Chinese records, suggests seventy days and not a whole year.

It is possible that Josephus may have simply associated the comet of AD 65 with that of the following year, absorbing their two periods together. If this were the case then we would have a total of 255 days (from 29 July AD 65 to 10 April AD 66), but this is still well short of a year. Now, Josephus was very good at exaggerating and making play of events, and it is probably the case that he has simply 'rounded up' the combined periods to a year.

It is also likely that the reference to a shining great light is an allusion to the comet around the time of the feast of the Passover, the description being clearly another exaggeration. One thing it does tell us, however, is that the comet was seen at the ninth hour of the night, implying that it was seen in the pre-dawn sky, and therefore *in the east*.

The Term 'Stood Over'

The terminology 'stood over', used by Josephus, is a very unusual description and exceptionally rare in ancient writings. As was seen earlier, it was also mentioned by Dio Cassius in *Roman History*, when he described Halley's Comet in 12 BC as having 'stood over' Rome for several days. However he was writing much later – around the year AD 200, and may possibly have been influenced by the description used by Josephus.

It seems unlikely by chance that, within the space of a few years, we are presented with two separate instances where such a description is used, namely that of Josephus and, shortly afterwards, by the author of Matthew, when he refers to the star of Bethlehem. Both of them describe a star standing over a specific area, namely a city or town, with Josephus referring to Jerusalem and the author of Matthew directing us to Bethlehem, literally only a few miles away. A possible explanation for this is that the author of Matthew somehow managed to have access to the account of Josephus not long after AD 78, and has incorporated the reference to the star in his infancy narrative. A more likely explanation, however, is that it was simply the terminology that was in general use at that specific period in time to describe a comet.

The Meaning of the Comet

There is also a similarity in their interpretation of the meaning of the comet. It is clear that Josephus was well aware of the prophecy of Balaam and regarded the comet as a sign that a Messianic figure was about to emerge. Nevertheless, he applied the prophecy to Vespasian, predicting correctly that he would become emperor, whilst also recognising him as the Messiah. This may simply have been a ploy to keep himself on the right side of Vespasian, and there seems little doubt that he ever seriously regarded him as such. He was, after all, not even Jewish; on the contrary, he had been an enemy of Judea of long standing, who had fought against them, and won with great barbarity. He was, like Nero, more likely to have been viewed as the Antichrist. Vespasian, aware that he could never be seriously accepted as a Messianic ruler since he was not descended from the line of David, is reported by Eusebius to have tracked down and eliminated any known surviving members of that House, thus reducing the possibility of such a leader emerging from within the ranks of the Jews.[12] The author of Matthew, however, anticipated at the time that the real Messiah would return; the second coming, so it was thought, was not far away.

Josephus' account tells us that there were contrasting views regarding the significance of the comet's appearance, with the unskilful, or inexperienced, regarding it as a favourable sign, but relying upon 'deceivers'. These were the pro-revolutionaries who enthusiastically predicted a successful campaign against Rome, and the rising of a Davidic Messianic figure.

The description by Josephus of the comet/star is far less ambiguous than that in Matthew, as in all probability he would have actually witnessed the comet for himself. Whether or not he actually saw it from Jerusalem, though, is open to some doubt, as it is known that he was in Rome around the same period in time, leading a delegation attempting to seek the release of Jewish priests who had been arrested by the Roman authorities. However, this is not a critical point, as the comet would also have been clearly visible from Rome.

Being also fully aware of the prophecy of Balaam, the author of Matthew proceeded to include the star within his infancy narrative, identifying and associating it with the one of the apparitions that were seen in 12 or 5 BC. The only problem, however, is that the comet of AD 66 turned out to be a harbinger of doom for the revolutionaries, preceding their failure and the fall of Jerusalem in AD 70. Why then would the author of Matthew associate such an object with the birth of Jesus? It could be that the author had simply picked up on the revolutionaries' initial fervour and enthusiastic predictions, accepting that it *was* a good omen, and this could have been reinforced by the fact that, in its initial stages, the war had gone well for the rebels. Looking at it from a different perspective, however, it was always inevitable that Rome would ultimately have the upper hand, the final say as it were, comet or no comet, so the author may have regarded its meaning as having no conceivable relevance to the final outcome.

The war against Rome was very much a Jewish affair and did not involve Christians. This, together with the fact that there were such strained relations between the Jews and Christians, may have led the author in coming to conclude that the comet's appearance was a clear sign from God, premeditating a punishment to those non believers. Therefore, the author may not have viewed it as being necessarily a good or bad omen.

Subsequent Comets
According to Kronk's *Cometography*, there were further comets seen in the years leading up to the period generally accepted for the finalised version of Matthew, which is around AD 80–85, and these are summarised as follows:

AD 69: Although not recorded by the Chinese, Dio Cassius in *Roman History* informs us that shortly before Vespasian's rebellion against his rival, Vitellius, a 'comet was seen'. He goes on to tell us that 'people saw two suns at once, one in the west and pale, and one in the east, brilliant and powerful'.

AD 71: A 'guest star' was first seen in the Pleiades (the Seven Sisters) on 6 March. An evening object, it faded near to the constellations of Leo and Lynx and lasted for sixty days. It is quite possible that this could have been a nova.

AD 75: A 'brush star' was found in the constellation of Hydra on 14 July. Another evening object, it displayed a short tail and journeyed into the constellations of Coma Berenices, Leo and Virgo.

AD 76: Also described as a 'brush star', it became visible on 7 October, and was another evening object, with a short tail. It appeared in an area of sky covering Hercules, Serpens, Ophiuchus and Aquila, and proceeded to move slowly into Capricorn. It was visible for forty days.

AD 77: A 'broom star' was first observed on the evening of 23 January, close to Aries, with a tail that proceeded to extend for about 8 or 9 degrees. It moved slowly, entering an area of the sky including Draco, Ursa Minor, Cephus and Camelopardalis and lasted for 106 days.

AD 79: This comet was recorded by the Romans and in Korea, with the Korean text telling us that a 'broom star' was first observed in the east sometime between 22 March and 20 April and that it remained visible for twenty days, although Dio Cassius implies that it persisted for a longer period.

It narrowly preceded the death of Vespasian, which took place on 4 June. Knowing that comets were sometimes associated with the death of great men, the emperor had actually ridiculed such beliefs and is reputed to have said that 'this hairy star is an omen for the king of the Persians ... for he has long hair, whereas I am bald'. So much for positive thinking!

AD 84: A 'guest star' appeared on 25 May in the east as a morning object. First seen in Aries displaying a short tail, it moved into the area covering Draco, Ursa Minor, Cepheus and Camelopardalis and lasted for forty days. It was also recorded by the Koreans, although they identified it under AD 85.

Any one, or even all of these comets may also have been witnessed by the author of Matthew, and it is quite feasible that they would have acted upon him as a reminder of past occurrences. Contemplating, he envisaged that a similar celestial manifestation must have been associated with the birth of Jesus. The most influential, however, is likely to have been that of Halley's in AD 66, and possibly the comet that was seen in the previous year, as these appear to have been not only the most spectacular, but also most significant, for as to be seen shortly, they also preceded two other important events.

A Precursor to the Second Coming
It is possible that the author may also have thought that a comet would be a precursor to the second coming of Christ, for in those days many Christians believed that this was imminent. Therefore, he made a connection with an earlier appearance of a comet, nearly 100 years in the past, naturally assuming that this had coincided with the birth of Jesus. A later reference in Matthew 24: 29–30 confirms this expectation of a celestial sign preceding the return of Christ from heaven:

Immediately after the tribulation of those days shall the Sun be darkened, and the Moon shall not give her light, and the stars shall fall from heaven, and the powers of the heavens shall be shaken: And then shall appear the sign of the Son of man in heaven: and then shall all the tribes of the earth mourn, and they shall see the Son of man coming in the clouds of heaven with power and great glory.

Although Jesus did not return, the author, when he included the reference to the star of Bethlehem within his narrative, was still patiently waiting in anticipation of his arrival.

Could his reference to the stars falling from paradise, combined with the heavenly sign of Christ, have been derived from an awareness, or afterthought, of the meteor storm that had occurred in 12 BC, together with the comet that followed shortly afterwards, which he may have associated with the birth of Jesus?

Tiridates and his Magi, AD 66

The spectacle of Magi accompanying King Tiridates of Armenia, himself a Zoroastrian, on his way to pay homage to the emperor, Nero, may also have left a lasting impression. Of course, whether the author actually witnessed the procession for himself is unknown, but he would certainly have become aware of it. Dio Cassius, in *Roman History*, provides us with a vivid and very detailed account of the event:

He presented himself in Rome, bringing with him not only his own sons but also those of Vologaesus, of Pacorus, and of Monobazus. Their progress all the way from the Euphrates was like a triumphal procession. Tiridates himself was at the height of his reputation by reason of his age, beauty, family and intelligence; and his whole retinue of servants together with all his royal paraphernalia accompanied him. Three thousand Parthian horsemen, and numerous Romans besides, followed his train. They were greeted by gaily decorated cities and by peoples who shouted many compliments. Provisions were furnished them free of cost, a daily expenditure of 800,000 sesterces for their support being thus charged to the public treasury. This went on without change for the nine months occupied in their journey...

The entire city had been decorated with lights and garlands, and great crowds of people were to be seen everywhere, the Forum, however, being especially full. The centre was occupied by civilians, arranged according to rank, clad in white and carrying laurel branches; everywhere else were the soldiers, arrayed in shining armour, their weapons and standards flashing like the lightning. The very roof tiles of all the buildings in the vicinity were completely hidden from view by the spectators who had climbed to the roofs.

Tiridates is reported to have approached Nero, and falling down before him, humbly spoke the words, 'Master, I am the descendant of Arsaces, brother of the kings Vologaesus and Paeorus, and thy slave and I have come to thee, my god, to worship thee as I do Mithras.'

Subsequently we are told that, during a banquet, Tiridates was seen to summon a Magus from his retinue, and initiated Nero into the Mithraic religion in the midst of 'magical dinners'. He goes on to tell us that 'the king did not return by the route he had followed in coming – through Illyricum and north of the Ionian Sea, but instead he sailed from Brundisium to Dyrrachium'.

The procession had taken about nine months to complete its journey, the cavalcade having set out initially from the northern Euphrates. It was covered almost entirely by land with the exception of the short passage of the Hellespont, passing through Thrace and Illyricum to the head of the Adriatic, eventually proceeding to Picenum in Italy and then on to Rome. As mentioned earlier, on its way it actually passed through northern Syria, close to the very areas in which early Christianity was starting to take root and where the Gospel of Matthew may have originated. So it is quite possible that these events aroused the attention and interest of the author. It was made all the more poignant by the fact the king, along with his entourage which included *Magi*, who were also Zoroastrians, had come all the way from Armenia, located far away *in the east*, proceeded to *fall down and worship* the ruler, and later departed into his own country *by a different route*.

Recognising the continued high esteem and prestige of Magi, the author has, at some later stage, made a conscious response by including them within his infancy narrative. His willingness to include them may have been reinforced by the possibility that he was also aware that Magi, bearing gifts, had visited King Herod in 10 BC, and that this had been preceded by a comet in the skies about two years earlier.

Nero

Despite a promising start as emperor, Nero soon degenerated into a monster and, like Herod, his mind appears to have become progressively unhinged. Amongst other crimes, he had arranged the murders of his stepbrother, mother, and wife and ordered his former tutor, Seneca, to commit suicide. After the great fire he persecuted the Christians, and became extravagant and a spendthrift, extorting money from the aristocracy to finance his mounting debts. The Senate finally had enough and declared him an enemy of the state. Nero fled, and later attempted suicide, but lacking the courage, had his servant do the job for him.

There are many parallels between Nero and Herod. In their later years both became paranoid about losing their grip on power, taking desperate and violent measures against any suspected opposition, including members of their own family. Both were regarded as great villains, and there seems little doubt that the author would have drawn a comparison between the two. In his narrative, Nero has become Herod, the epitome of evil and the non-believer.

The death of Nero in AD 68 completed a trilogy of events, within the space of just two years, which have found their way into the account of the nativity. Just in the same way that Herod dies not long after the appearance of the star and the visit of the Magi, so does Nero. Is this mere coincidence?

Vespasian

Could the author also have drawn a parallel between Herod and Vespasian? Although Vespasian was not visited by a procession of Magi, with all the pomp and ceremony which that would have entailed, he did allow himself to 'adopt' Josephus initially as a form of a soothsayer, having been fooled by his favourable prediction. Vespasian may have also contrived to eliminate the possibility of the emergence of a Messianic figure from within the Line of David, by using murdering methods, and in the same fashion we find the author having Herod out to eliminate Jesus. Whilst it is clear that members of that House did manage to escape from the clutches of Vespasian, we find the author, in his infancy narrative, having Joseph and his family fleeing into Egypt in order to escape from the clutches of Herod. Then, just as Vespasian dies within a matter of weeks after the visitation of a comet, we find the author having Herod seemingly die shortly after such an apparition.

It is conceivable that these events involving Vespasian, which are relatively close in time to the period generally accepted for the completion of the Gospel of Matthew, have also found their way into the author's infancy narrative.

Symbolism Everywhere

In those days, the appearance of a comet had a special significance in relation to other celestial activity in the night sky. Seneca, writing about the appearance of Halley's comet in AD 66, shortly before his death, noted that comets attracted the interest of people who were blind to other unusual astronomical events, and tells us that they were not sure as to whether to 'admire or fear the celestial newcomer'. Over time this special attention became reflected in artwork, with their illustrations on temples, frescos, mosaics and particularly coins. The engraving of stars or comets on coins was effectively a form of Roman propaganda, with such symbols being specifically designed to connect the divinity of an emperor with a celestial sign.

As was seen earlier, in Chapter 11, some of the coins minted in Antioch displayed the image of a ram looking back at a bright star. This was a point highlighted by Molnar, who considered that the star displayed represented the planet Jupiter, in the constellation of Aries, although my own opinion is that it is a comet, being simply copied from other contemporary Roman coins. He speculated that Luke may have interpreted the image as a sign indicating the birth of the Messiah some years earlier. However, a similar argument could just as easily be put forward regarding the author of Matthew, who may also have handled such coins. Could such images have influenced the author?

It was accepted that the intention of such symbolism was to illustrate the divinity of a great ruler, and in this respect the author would have realised the importance of linking the birth of Christ to the appearance of a star or comet. However, this was no ordinary king. This was the Messiah – the king of all kings, past and present. Some very special, extraordinary celestial sign had to herald *his* arrival. But was there one? Of course not. So he was careful not to indicate in his story what exactly the star was. To specifically mention the appearance of any run-of-the-mill comet, or some other portent, was, in a sense, to compare Jesus with any other earthly king, or emperor. Therefore the comet, although becoming very special, could not be referred to as such, being simply referred to as *the star*.

14
CONCLUSION

The ancient world developed many varied beliefs with regard to comets, meteors and eclipses, but they all had one thing in common – they were all held to be signs from heaven for mankind. Over time such ideas became well established, not only in the Jewish and Roman world, but also in other civilisations that were flourishing around the time of Christ's birth. Meteors and comets were associated with events such as the birth and death of great leaders, kings, and even gods. In India, the births of Krishna and Buddha were identified in sacred books as being anointed with the appearance of heavenly lights in the sky. Likewise, in China, the birth of the founder of the first dynasty, Yu, was associated with a similar celestial event.

As seen earlier, comets were not always regarded with apprehension by ancient civilisations, and this included the Romans during the years leading up to Christ's birth. The Chaldeans also generally regarded comets without fear, comparing them to fishes swimming in the sea. Seneca, and possibly the Pythagoreans, realised that some comets, in particular the one later to be identified as Halley's Comet, did seem to return at regular intervals and ignored the superstitions attached to them.

However, the fears were never far away. Over the next few centuries the idea that comets were to be associated with catastrophes and the destruction of kingdoms grew from strength to strength. Hence we find the Venerable Bede, in the eighth century, writing that comets were responsible for 'revolutions of kingdoms, pestilence, war, winds or heat'. Such writings typified the opinion of church leaders, which stretched into the late medieval period. The association of comets with the death of great leaders also persisted, thus we find Shakespeare having Calphennia say to Caesar that 'when beggars die there are no comets seen; the heavens themselves blaze forth the death of princes'. Such superstitions dwelt heavily upon Charles V of Spain who, in 1556, abdicated in favour of Phillip II in great fear of the comet of that year.

It has been suggested that the reinforcement of these superstitions may have its foundations rooted in the past by way of the Earth experiencing impacts by comets or asteroidal objects. The sudden and unexpected appearance of a comet may have stirred deep primordial fears, originating from a time before civilisation had begun to evolve. The analysis of tree ring data, or dendrochronology as it is known, going back thousands of years, implies that the Earth has experienced dramatic and sudden reductions in temperature, as reflected in relatively weak or non-existent growth patterns. It is assumed that these abnormalities were a result of veils of dust enveloping the Earth's upper atmosphere and persisting for considerable periods of time, therefore reducing the Sun's heat and having dramatic effects upon the climate. The same pattern of these tree ring fingerprints have been identified consistently throughout the world, therefore indicating temperature fluctuations on a global scale. The results were widespread harvest failure, famine and political upheaval. Could some of these relatively recent catastrophes have been caused by cometary impacts? If so, it would not be surprising that, in the event of such misfortunes, comets subsequently became firmly associated with death, doom and disaster. This may help to explain why a comet, as representing the star of Bethlehem, has not been such a popular choice amongst historians, theologians and astronomers as one might have expected.

Strangely enough, few seem to have put forward the case for a comet foretelling the death of Herod, as well as heralding the birth of the Messiah. Does this explain why the author of Matthew has Herod, upon hearing about the star, 'troubled, and all Jerusalem with him'? One can understand Herod's reaction to the news of the star and its implications. However, it seems strange that 'all of Jerusalem' should also share his anxiety. In fact the contrary may have been anticipated, as Herod appears to have been a most unpopular ruler, so the prospect of a new king may have been well received by many. It would seem that only a comet's unwelcome appearance could have inflicted such unsettling and widespread anxiety. Herod's receipt of the news is also very reminiscent of the image on the Bayeux tapestry, completed about a thousand years later, showing worried attendants to King Harold looking at the comet in horror.

It was seen earlier, in Chapter 2, that major aspects of the infancy narrative of Matthew appear to have been written largely by way of a reformulation of certain Old Testament texts and Jewish legend. These include the prophecies of Micah and Balaam; Isaiah and the visit of Magi; the events surrounding the birth of Moses; the patriarch Joseph, who could interpret dreams, and the exodus of the Israelites out of Egypt, who were guided by a column of light. To suggest otherwise – that the key elements of the story are based upon real historical events – presents insurmountable difficulties. Therefore, the only plausible deduction that can be made is that the narrative represents the piecing together of the Old Testament stories. Critics might argue that such an explanation is circumspect, and if we look hard enough at Old Testament texts we are bound to find references that are similar in some form or another. However, all the evidence suggests that these ancient writings have been manipulated and disguised in an attempt to inform us of the divinity of Christ.

It is found that even Bethlehem, as the place of birth, has to be seriously questioned, as it is obvious that the author, as well as Luke, was anxious to satisfy the prophecy of Micah by way of introducing a birth within the ancestral town of David. The clear intention was that this would legitimise and confirm that Jesus was the Messiah.

Such opinion is reinforced by the fact that there is a complete lack of support from any contemporary records. There are no independent witnesses to the birth narratives, other than the mythical nameless shepherds and the Magi, who in any case disappear from the scene, never to be mentioned again in the New Testament. It is clear also that no one who met Jesus later in his life seems to have been aware of any of the remarkable sequence of events peculiar to his birth. It is also difficult to assess as to why Matthew and Luke's birth narratives are so completely at odds with one another.

The fact that there are no other references to the incredible events associated with the extraordinary birth of Jesus in the rest of the New Testament strongly suggests that the infancy narratives were written at some stage after the Gospels had been completed, and were inserted almost by way of an afterthought or preface. It is clear that these narratives reflect an awareness of what was already within the Gospels. The earlier completed Gospels, on the other hand, do not reflect any awareness of the contents within the birth narratives, and so we find the mature Jesus being introduced virtually unnoticed, with those earlier, unforgettable events seemingly forgotten.

It has also been said that Matthew and Luke's birth narratives lacked historical precision, as they were written so long after the actual events that they are supposed to have recorded. However, the fact that these stories were composed so many years after the completion of Jesus' ministry and resurrection may, conversely, lend support to the argument that they must include some underlying truth. Was there any real necessity to invent or create the infancy narratives when Jesus had already been widely accepted as the Messiah? To write texts that were not based upon at least some truth would have provided a target for even further ridicule and opposition from Jewish elements. The author may also have risked tarnishing his reputation and that of the early Christian movement, which by that time was well established and flourishing. But perhaps he was prepared to take that chance, no doubt comforted by the knowledge that the alleged events he was describing had taken place so many years earlier.

The star's actual physical existence remains a distinct and real possibility, but only in the sense that the author may have been aware, from the sources available to him, that there had been some unusual celestial events in the period from 12 to 5 BC. Whilst these occurrences were far from being unique or exceptional, they were nevertheless rare, attracting his attention and possibly directing him to the Old Testament story of the pillar of light or fire that went before or guided the Israelites out of the desert with the star being brought in to act as a guide for the Gentiles to follow. Consequently, the introduction of the star into the infancy narrative may have been based upon historical fact in that the author had in mind one of the comets that appeared in 12 or 5 BC.

Whilst there is no doubt that the author was heavily influenced by Old Testament writings and prophecies, actual events from within his own lifetime have also found their way into the story. These events effectively supplemented the ancient stories and prophecies, so that they all acted in unison, reinforcing his commitment towards producing a memorable introduction to the life of Jesus. They include the sight of two spectacular comets within a short space of time of one another, including Halley's, which according to Josephus, blazed over Jerusalem in AD 66, resembling a sword in the sky. Then there is the visit of King Tiridates with his

Magi to pay homage to Nero, passing Christian areas on their way and returning to their own country by an alternative route. Subsequently, we find Vespasian allegedly giving orders for all those belonging to the lineage of David to be sought out and eradicated so that no future Messianic figure might emerge, and then later dying within weeks after a comet is seen.

It seems likely that these events would have made a lasting impression upon him, playing their part in fashioning his account of the nativity. The author may also have been made aware of another bright comet which had become visible, further back in time, but still within the approximate time-frame of Jesus' birth. So the actual sight of comets in AD 65 and 66 would have had a major role, forming the inspiration for the star of Bethlehem.

The infancy narrative, therefore, seems to reflect a careful blend of both Midrash and events from within the author's own lifetime, with the reference to the star having been based upon his own experiences of actual astral phenomena. The question remains, however – was the author of Matthew even aware of when Jesus was born? Most books or articles on the subject appear to assume that the author knew this precisely, but in all probability he would not have known the actual day and it is quite possible that he did not even know the exact year. In such circumstances the author effectively determined a period, or moment in time for the birth, being ascertained by reference to a celestial occurrence, with his mind and imagination doing the rest.

If all of the obvious Midrashim within the author's narrative regarding the star were to be washed out, relatively little material would remain. There would be blank spaces where verses once stood. In fact, the residue could probably be condensed into a mere three lines, which might resemble something like the following:

In the days of Herod the king, a comet was seen in the east, which proclaimed the birth of Jesus, the Messiah.
And it came to pass that Herod died.
And Jesus was brought up in Nazareth.

Nevertheless, it is probable that the author believed that the Old Testament prophecies predicting Christ's arrival were literally correct, accepting that he was born under the sign of a star, and within the town of Bethlehem. Therefore, his mindset accepted that it really did happen, as if it had to; positive that he was not mistaken, he was prepared, like many other Christians of his time, to make the ultimate sacrifice for his convictions. Of course, to many present-day Christians it is not of paramount importance as to whether the star actually existed or if Jesus was born in Bethlehem. To them Jesus was, and always will be the Messiah, with or without such attached preconditions, relying not upon historical accuracy, but on faith alone.

There can be little doubt that the author had a comet in mind when he makes references to the star, but of the two that have been identified within the general time-frame of the birth of Jesus, namely those of 12 and 5 BC, which one might the author have been making a specific reference to? Whilst this depends upon how well informed he was of such past occurrences, and assumes that he had knowledge of these events in the first place, it would seem that the most likely and appropriate contender has to be the comet of 5 BC, simply due to the fact that it arrived relatively close not only to the time of the birth of Jesus, but also to that of the death of Herod. The author would have associated such an object with the imminent demise of Herod, explaining to us that it caused unease both to the king and to the city. There is no other star-like object in the sky that would have merited the description of such a reaction. For the author, therefore, it effectively served two useful purposes: a warning from God of Herod's impending doom, and an announcement of the birth of the Messiah, initiating a new era.

CHRONOLOGICAL TABLE

37 BC	Herod appointed King of Judea by Mark Antony.
31	Octavian becomes emperor.
31	Herod reaffirmed as king by Octavian.
27	Octavian's name is changed to Augustus.
13/5	Jesus is born.
12	Halley's Comet appears in August, preceded by a meteor storm some three months earlier.
10	Magi visit King Herod as part of celebrations to mark the completion of Caesarea Maritima.
8–6	A census is taken followed by an oath of allegiance to Augustus.
7	A triple conjunction takes place between Jupiter and Saturn.
6	A planetary massing takes place involving Jupiter, Saturn and Mars.
6	Two occultations of Jupiter by the Moon take place in the constellation of Aries.
5	A comet is seen for seventy days.
5/4	King Herod dies. The kingdom is divided between his three sons.
AD 6	A census is taken under Quirinius.
11	Tiberius becomes joint-ruler of Judea with Augustus.
14	Augustus dies. Tiberius becomes sole emperor.
26/29	Jesus is baptised and commences his ministry.
29	A total eclipse of the Sun occurs close to the Sea of Galilee.
27/37	Pontius Pilate becomes governor.
29/33	Jesus is crucified.
37	Tiberius dies.
40/50	'Q' is written.
50/60	'M' is written.
60/70	Mark is written.
62	James, the brother of Jesus, is stoned to death.
64	Fire destroys most of Rome.
65	Persecution of Christians commences in Rome.
65	A comet with a long tail is witnessed.
66	Halley's Comet makes a spectacular appearance.
66	King Tiridates of Armenia leads a procession, including Magi, to pay homage to Nero.
66	The Jewish War begins.
68	Nero dies.
69	Vespasian becomes emperor.
70	Jerusalem falls to the Romans.
70/80	Luke is written.
79	Vespasian dies shortly after a comet is seen.
80	The Shermoneth Esreh, a Jewish prayer, is reformulated to include a curse upon Christians, who are also barred from entering synagogues.
80/85	The final completed version of Matthew is written in Greek.
95/105	John is written.
105/115	The Letter to the Ephesians is written.
135/145	The Protoevangelium of James is written.
312	The emperor Constantine claims to have witnessed a sign in the sky.

NOTES

1. This work, by Raymond E. Brown (1928–98), represents an appraisal of the birth narratives of Matthew and Luke and is frequently referred to in the first part of this book. Brown, an American, was a member of the Sulpician Fathers and his writings invoked considerable debate as he cast doubts upon the historical accuracy of various articles on the Catholic faith. He was one of the earliest Roman Catholic scholars to apply a critical historical approach to the Bible, this being partly in response to the Vatican approving a higher level of such analysis. He was also the first Roman Catholic professor to teach at the Protestant Union Theological Seminary in New York.

2. No one seems to be quite sure as to the special significance attached to the number fourteen. Brown suggests that, in ancient Hebrew spelling, the numerical value of the name David was fourteen and may have been used to indicate that Jesus was a 'son of David'. C. Kaplan, in *Generation*, suggests that the pattern of fourteen may reflect a lunar month of twenty-eight days, split in two to give fourteen waxing and fourteen waning Moons. Abraham commenced the fourteen waxing generations, finishing with David, who represented a full Moon. The following fourteen waning generations led up to a new Moon, perhaps creating an eclipse, represented by the Babylonian Exile. The final fourteen waxing generations then led up to the Messiah, represented by another full Moon.

3. There is actually a second town or village called Bethlehem mentioned in the Old Testament and this lay within the territory of Zebulun (Joshua 19.15 & 16). It may possibly relate to present-day Beit Lahm, located a few miles north-west of Nazareth. This may explain why Matthew clearly refers to Bethlehem *of Judea*, whilst Luke (2.4) also goes to some lengths to identify it as such.

4. Celsus, the Platonist, was an anti-Christian writer from the second century who relied heavily upon Jewish sources. He attacked the origins of Jesus' birth in his work titled *The True Doctrine*, suggesting, amongst other things, that his real father was a soldier known as Panthera. Origen's work, *Contra Celsum*, or 'Against Celsus', was a counter-response to such allegations and was written around the year 250.

   Origen was one of a number of Christians, known as Apologists, who were anxious to convince the Roman authorities that their movement, which represented a small minority, was not seditious in nature and did not pose a dangerous threat to the establishment. They attempted to present the new religion as decent, enlightened and deserving merit and respect from the more intellectual classes of society.

5. The other two references are from the Roman historians Tacitus and Suetonius. Tacitus (AD 56–117), completed five major works, of which two, the *Annals* and the *Histories*, represent the most substantial to have survived, covering a period from Tiberius through to Vespasian. His reference to Christ appears in his *Annals* in book 15, Chapter 44 and is thought to have been written around AD 110. It refers to the aftermath following the great fire which destroyed most of Rome in July AD 64: 'But not all the relief that could come from man, nor all the bounties that the prince could bestow, nor all the atonements which could be presented to the gods, availed to relieve Nero from the infamy of being believed to have ordered the conflagration, the fire of Rome. Hence to suppress the rumour, he falsely charged with the guilt, and punished Christians, who were hated for their abominations. Christus, the founder

of the name, was put to death by Pontius Pilate, procurator of Judea in the reign of Tiberius.'

The most important work by Suetonius (AD 70–135) is *The Twelve Caesars*, written in AD 121. Within the section on Claudius (25.4), we find the following statement: 'As the Jews were making constant disturbances at the instigation of Chrestus, he [Claudius] expelled them from Rome.'

This event occurred in AD 49 and is also mentioned in Acts 18:2, which tells us that 'in Cornith he [Paul] met a Jew called Aquila, a native of Pontus, who had recently come from Italy with Priscilla, because Claudius had ordered all the Jews to leave Rome'.

The name 'Chrestus' is actually Greek and it seems likely that rather than referring to Christ, it related to a post-resurrectional preacher in Rome. Suetonius also makes reference to Nero's persecution of Christians (16.2): 'Punishment by Nero was inflicted on the Christians, a class of men given to a new and mischievous superstition.'

6. This second reference to Christ, supposedly by Josephus, is known as the *Testimonium Flavianum* and is as follows: 'At this time there appeared Jesus, a wise man, if indeed one should call him a man. For he was a doer of startling deeds, a teacher of the people who receive the truth with pleasure. And he gained a following among many Jews and among many of the Greek origin. He was the Messiah. And when Pilate, because of an accusation made by the leading men amongst us, condemned him to the cross, those who had loved him previously did not cease to do so. For he appeared to them on the third day, living again, just as the divine prophets had spoken of these and countless other wondrous things about him. And up until this very day the tribe of Christians, named after him, has not died out.' *Jewish Antiquities*, 18: 63–64.

7. Galileo was one of the first to point a telescope to the night sky, following his receipt of such an instrument from Holland in 1609, although his major discoveries were made using an improved version which he constructed himself. His revelations, however, were not greeted with any great enthusiasm as there was a general reluctance to accept the underlying implications of his findings. As the astronomy historian Colin Rowan explains in *The Astronomers*, 'because so many hate to have their cherished ideas disturbed by even a breath of change, criticisms of Galileo rather than subsiding became more forceful'. Nevertheless, when, in March 1610, he published his observations in a book entitled *Sidereus Nuncius* (The Sidereal Messenger) he received considerable acclaim outside of Rome.

Over the years that followed he attracted further opposition as he fervently insisted that the Copernican system was correct and this culminated in the publication in 1632 of his *Dialogue on the Great World Systems*. This was pounced upon by his enemies and it was not long before it was banned by the Vatican. He was summoned to appear before the Inquisition, being accused of heresy on the grounds that the proposed system was 'false and contrary to the sacred divine scriptures'. Faced with a potential death sentence he was forced to recant, formally declaring that he was wrong, and was consequently absolved but nevertheless had to spend the rest of his life under house arrest. In 1638 another book by him appeared in Holland called *Discourses on Two New Sciences, of Mechanics and Motions*, which outlined the first scientific laws for the Earth's motion, whilst at the same time making no reference to the heliocentric system. Interestingly, the ban on the *Dialogue* continued until 1822 and, incredibly, the Church only formally acknowledged that Galileo was correct in 1992.

8. Claudius Ptolemy, a Roman citizen of Egypt, produced around the year AD 80 the *Almagest*, a manuscript on astronomy, written in Greek. This included tables which could be used to calculate the positions of the five known planets. He also compiled a catalogue comprising forty-eight recognised constellations.

9. It is possible that certain Jewish astronomers in the first century AD may have become aware of the periodic cycle of Halley's. In the Babylonian Talmud there is reference to a reply to a question posed to Rabbi Gamaliel, whilst at sea, who responds by replying that 'a certain star rises once in seventy years and leads the sailors astray'.

10. According to old tradition it was a divine meteorite, pre-dating creation, which had fallen at the feet of Adam, and was later rediscovered by Abraham. It is thought to have been revered for centuries prior to being set into the wall intact by the prophet Muhammad in AD 605, and ever since then it has been viewed as an Islamic relic. Measuring roughly 12 x 10 inches and resembling an oval shape, it was later fractured and repaired. It is presently cemented within a silver frame into the side of the wall. Over time it has been smoothed and polished by the hands and kisses of endless streams of pilgrims.

11. There is one exception, and the reader may be aware of the references in Luke 3:40–52, which covers Jesus, at twelve years old, leaving his parents and entering the Temple in Jerusalem to carry out his father's business.

12. This is based upon an account by Hegesippus, a Christian chronicler from the second century. Although his works have not survived he is quoted by Eusebius, who tells us that he wrote five books or memoirs. Hegesippus had referred to a persecution of the Jews after the destruction of Jerusalem during the early reign of Vespasian. Whilst it is true that men claiming Davidic descent were viewed as a potential political threat, some doubts have been expressed as to whether there is historical accuracy behind Hegesippus' account, as there is no other record of such a response against those descendants and it has been claimed that these references may represent an apologetical myth with the intention of supporting the theme of the Davidic-Messianic Christ. It is obvious, however, that Josephus for one would not have mentioned such unsavoury action, as he was under the wings of Vespasian and Titus.

    Hegesippus went on to claim that the emperors Domitian and Trajan had also attempted to hunt down the remaining Jews of Davidic descent in an attempt to eliminate this royal line, upon which the Jews had pinned their hopes.

SELECTED BIBLIOGRAPHY

Adair, A. M., 'Science Scholarship and Bethlehem's Starry Night', *Sky & Telescope* Vol. 114, No. 6 (December 2007), pp. 26–29.

Baigent, M., *The Jesus Papers* (St Ives: Harper Element, 2006).

Bailey, M., Notes taken from lecture entitled *The Origins of Comets* (Queens University, Belfast: September 2011).

Banville, J., *Dr Copernicus* (London: Mandarin Paperbacks, 1992).

Banville, J., *Kepler* (London: Mandarin Paperbacks, 1991).

Barnes, T. D., 'The Date of Herod's Death', *Journal of Theological Studies* No. 19 (1968), pp. 204–209.

BBC News Update, regarding the craters at Sirente, central Italy (23 June 2003).

BBC Television, *The Mystery of the Three Kings* (2002).

BBC Television, *The Sky at Night*, presented by Patrick Moore, featuring David Hughes and Mark Kidger, entitled 'The Star of Bethlehem' (2001).

Briggs, N. B., 'Reading the images on Iron Age coins: Horses of the day and night', *Chris Rudd*, List 106 (July 2009).

Brown, R. E., *The Birth of the Messiah: A Commentary on the Infancy Narratives in Matthew and Luke* (London: Cassell & Collier, Macmillan Publishers Ltd, 1977).

Coates, R., 'A Linguist's Angle on the Star of Bethlehem', A&G News and Reviews in *Astronomy & Geophysics* Vol. 49, Issue 5 (Blackwell Publishing Ltd, October 2008).

Cullen, C., 'Halley's Comet and the Ghost Event of 10 BC', *Quarterly Journal of the Royal Astronomical Society* Vol. 32 (June 1991), pp. 113–119.

Dio Cassius, *Roman History*, Epitome Book LXIII, 1 to 7, published in Volume III of the Loeb Classical Library edition (1925).

Edwards, O., *A New Chronology of the Gospels* (London: Floris Books, 1972).

Fenton, J. C., *Saint Matthew* (London: Penguin Books, 1991).

Finegan, J., *Handbook of Biblical Chronology* (Princeton University Press, 2001).

Fitzsimmons, A., Notes taken from lecture entitled *Comet Holmes* (Queen's University, Belfast: October 2010).

Goldberg, G. J., *Josephus and the Star of Bethlehem* (December 1999).

Graves, R., *Claudius the God* (Harmondsworth: Penguin Books, 1976).

Harris, J. N., 'The Star of Babylon and Bethlehem', *Time and Tide* website (February 2006).

Harris, S. L., *Understanding the Bible* (Boston/Toronto: McGraw Hill, 2003).

Hetherington, B., *A Chronicle of Pre-Telescopic Astronomy* (Chichester: John Wiley & Sons Ltd, 1996).

Hsi, Tsi-Tsung, 'A New Catalog of Novae Recorded in the Chinese and Japanese Chronicles', *Soviet Astronomy* Vol. 1, p. 163 (1957).

Hughes, D., *The Star of Bethlehem Mystery* (London: J. M. Dent Ltd, 1979).

Humphries, C., 'The Star of Bethlehem', *Science and Christian Belief* Vol. 5 (October 1995), pp. 83–101.

Imoto, S., and I. Hasegawa, 'Historical Records of Meteor Showers in China, Korea and Japan', *Smithsonian Contribution to Astrophysics* Vol. 2 (1958), pp. 131–144.

Josephus, Flavius, *Complete Works*, translated by W. Whiston (London: Pickering & Inglis Ltd, 1963).

Kee, H. C. and F. W. Young, *The Living World of the New Testament* (London: Darton, Longman & Todd, 1966).

Kerner, M., *Keltische Munzen: mit astronmischen Motiven* (Kirchdorf: Switzerland, 2001).

Kidger, M., *The Star of Bethlehem: An Astronomer's View* (Princeton University Press, 1999).

Kronk, G. W., *Cometography: A Catalogue to Comets* Vol. 1 (Cambridge University Press, 1999).

Martin, E. L., *The Star that Astonished the World* (Academy for Scriptural Knowledge, 1996).

Mason, S., *Josephus Flavius: Translation and Commentary* Vol. 1b, Judean War 2.

Matyszak, P., and J. Berry, *Lives of the Romans* (London: Thames & Hudson Ltd, 2008).

Matyszak, P., *The Enemies of Rome* (London: Thames & Hudson Ltd, 2004).

Maunder, E. W., *The Astronomy of the Bible* (London: T. Sealey Clark & Co., 1908).

McCafferty, P., and M. Bailey, *The Celtic Gods: Comets in Irish Mythology* (Stroud: Tempus Publishing Ltd, 2005).

McIvor, R. S., 'The Star of Bethlehem on Roman and Celtic Coins', *American Astronomical Variable Star Observers Newsletter* No. 27 (January 2002).

Midgley, J. B., *The Four Evangelists* (Catholic Truth Society, 2007).

Molnar, M. E., *The Star of Bethlehem: the Legacy of the Magi* (New Jersey: Rutgers University Press, 2000).

Moore, P., *The Star of Bethlehem* (Bath: Canopus Publishing Ltd, 2001).

Moseley, T., Correspondence regarding eclipses and the conjunction of Venus and Jupiter in 1 BC.

Mueller, T., 'King Herod Revealed', *National Geographic* (December 2008).

Nineham, D. E., *Saint Mark: The Pelican Gospel Commentaries* (Harmondsworth: Pelican Books, 1964).

Phillips, J. P., *The New Testament in Modern English* (London and Glasgow: Collins, Fontana Books, 1972).

Powell, M. A., *The Jesus Debate: Modern Histories Investigate the Life of Christ* (Lion Hudson Plc, 2000).

Ronan, C., *The Astronomers* (London: Evans Brothers Ltd, 1964).

Rudd, C., An article on the Freckenham Stater, *Classical Numismatic Group, Inc.*, Catalogue No. 66 (New York: May 2004).

Rudd, C., Correspondence regarding Celtic coins.

Santilli, R., J. Ormo, A. P. Rossi, and G. Komatsu, 'A Catastrophe Remembered: A Meteorite Impact of the Fifth Century AD in the Abruzzo, Central Italy', *Antiquity: A Quarterly Review of World Archaeology* Vol. 77, No. 296 (2003), pp. 313–320.

Schurer, E., *The History of the Jewish People in the age of Jesus Christ* Vol. 1 (Edinburgh: T. & T. Clark Ltd, 2000).

Scott, K., 'The Sidus Iulium and the Apotheosis of Caesar', *Classical Philology* Vol. 36, No. 3 (The University of Chicago Press, July 1941).

Seymour, P., *The Birth of Christ: Exploding the Myth* (Virgin Publishing Ltd, 1999).

Sinnott, R. W., Thoughts on the Star of Bethlehem, *Sky and Telescope* Vol. 36 (1968), pp. 194–197.

Thiede, C. P., and M. D'Ancona, *The Jesus Papyrus* (London: Weidenfield & Nicolson, The Orion Publishing Group Ltd, 1996).

Trexler, R. C., *The Journey of the Magi: Meanings in History of a Christian Story* (Princeton University Press, 1997).

Wansbrough, H., *The Gospel According to Matthew* (Catholic Truth Society, 2002).

Williams, J., *Observations of Comets from 611 BC to AD 1640 extracted from the Chinese Annals* (London: Strangeways & Walden, 1871).

Yeomans, D. K., *Comets: A Chronological History of Observation, Science, Myth, and Folklore* (New York: John Wiley & Sons, Inc., 1991).

INDEX